Congress, the Media, and the Public

From the beginning of the Republic, members of Congress have been in the media spotlight. In recent years, the expansion of media venues has provided both challenges and opportunities to representatives and senators, the public, and even the media themselves. Legacy media such as newspapers and broadcast television each carry with them their own needs and accepted usages affecting the kind and volume of news about Congress delivered to the public. These sources still serve important roles for much of the public and are covered here. This book goes beyond the traditional legacy media to include Congress' portrayal on live television, in political cartoons, in film, as a part of the emerging "infotainment" venues, and through social media such as web pages, Facebook, and Twitter. We increasingly live in a world where the lines between traditional news and other sources of information have been erased.

This is an exciting, if challenging, time for Congress, the media, and the public as each attempts to sort out the new media environment and employ it to its advantage. Using a comprehensive analysis of previous research, dozens of interviews, and the inclusion of empirical data, this book assesses the current status of the relationship between Congress and the media and sorts out the temporary changes from those likely to represent future trends. Whether one is associated with Congress, is an interested citizen, or is part of the media industry, understanding the relationships and developments between and among them is key to understanding how the public behaves in relation to Congress, and vice versa.

Stephen E. Frantzich is Professor of Political Science at the U.S. Naval Academy, where he was selected as outstanding civilian professor in 1990. He is the author of over two dozen books and has served as a consultant to the U.S. Congress, Dirksen Center, C-SPAN, and a variety of foreign parliaments. He was one of the pioneers in the study of the impact of information technology on American politics. In his spare time, he runs Books for International Goodwill (www.big-books.org), which has distributed over 7 million books to underserved populations around the world.

Congress, the Media, and the Public

Who Reveals What, When, and How?

Stephen E. Frantzich

Routledge
Taylor & Francis Group

LONDON AND NEW YORK

First published 2016
by Routledge
711 Third Avenue, New York, NY 10017

and by Routledge
2 Park Square, Milton Park, Abingdon, Oxon, OX14 4RN

Routledge is an imprint of the Taylor & Francis Group, an informa business

Library of Congress Cataloging in Publication Data
Frantzich, Stephen E.
  Congress, the media, and the public : who reveals what, when, and how? / Stephen E. Frantzich.
    pages cm
  Includes bibliographical references and index.
  1. United States. Congress–Reporters and reporting. 2. United States. Congress–Public relations. 3. Press and politics–United States. 4. Mass media–Political aspects–United States. 5. Communication in politics–United States. I. Title.
  JK1128.F73 2016
  070.4'4932873–dc23
  2015030078

ISBN: 978-1-612-05424-7 (hbk)
ISBN: 978-1-612-05425-4 (pbk)

Typeset in Sabon
by Out of House Publishing

MIX
Paper from
responsible sources
FSC FSC® C013056
www.fsc.org

Printed and bound in Great Britain by
TJ International Ltd, Padstow, Cornwall

Contents

Chapter 1

The Media and Representative Government

The Necessary Evil?

This is a book about the media and Congress. Three key rationales stand out for new effort to explain this relationship. First, previous books have limited their attention to relatively narrow media, ignoring the vast array of ways information about Congress enters the public consciousness. Second, both Congress and the media have undergone significant changes in the last few decades, challenging the context of many previous studies. Third, there is little question that Congress is in trouble when it comes to its public relations. Understanding how Congress is portrayed in the media may help Congress more effectively play its intended role in American democracy.

It is important to remember that the word "media" is plural. Individual media formats are transmission tools by which ideas, impressions, images, and feelings flow from a source to a recipient. Much research on Congress and the media focuses on traditional "legacy" media (print, radio, and television news) and emerging media (websites, Facebook, YouTube, and Twitter), but such a list should not imply full coverage of the multiple ways in which the public learns about Congress and its members. To this list we will add editorial cartoons, and gavel-to-gavel coverage on C-SPAN as well as a variety of popular culture entertainment venues. Even with these additions time and resources force us to largely bypass radio, theater, comic books, music, and a variety of other existing and emerging media.

Just as the various media present different content in different ways, the research tools herein will include a variety of approaches. Impressionistic data from interviews, empirical summaries, graphical presentations, and visual examples all will be relied upon. The analysis borrows heavily from the excellent research of others. A number of the research tools highlighted have been or could be used to analyze other political institutions and processes and it is hoped that usage here will encourage an expansion of our thinking and research. What the public knows about Congress and how it affects their behavior is important enough that we should not limit the media we look at or the approaches we use.

The Democratic Conversation

Democratic politics involve a series of conversations between the public and elected officials, facilitated, in part, by the media. Citizens express opinions on what government should be doing and how it should do it, while elected officials communicate back with guidelines for behavior (laws) and reports on their efforts. Useful conversations involve "shared islands of understanding" terminology, and knowledge which allows each partner in the conversation to assume some common understanding and to make the conversation interesting by adding some new information. In the extreme case, two people who have no knowledge of each other's language are reduced to communicating with grunts and visual signals. On the other end of the spectrum, if two people know exactly the same things, there is no need to communicate. A "good" conversation emerges as a building process in which one partner signals a level of common knowledge and adds a relevant tidbit, to which the other partner reacts and adds their own unique contribution. In the congressional realm, a constituent may write, "I read today that Congress is considering a new import tax on shoes. Let me tell you how that will affect my business." The member of Congress might write back,

> Thank you for the insight. That bill has already passed in the House, but you might want to contact Senator Smith, since he is on the tax committee in the Senate and they have yet to take action. Since I hope to be on the conference committee, I would be willing to support the revised Senate version.

In this interchange, both partners have learned something.

The explosion of media sources threatens the development of the necessary islands of shared understanding. As we move from an era of broadcasting to "narrow-casting," the potential for a fragmented citizenry uninformed about major areas of politics, while hyper-informed by information in other realms, could threaten the development of meaningful conversations. In the above example, the citizen unaware of upcoming congressional action, uninformed about the name of his or her representative, or not knowledgeable about how to communicate with them, is unlikely to be a relevant player. It is not so much that contemporary citizens are uninformed, but rather they may remove politics and world affairs from their infosphere altogether.[1]

Members of Congress and journalists both are in the communication game, attempting to deliver their preferred messages to chosen audiences. While the word fails to appear in any dictionary, much of what both members of Congress and journalists do could better be called "munication": communication lacking the "co." Many intended messages fall on fallow ground, having no impact on the intended recipient since they were ignored or misunderstood. "Messages fly back and forth like so many salvos of arrows loosed by hostile tribes, some of which hit their targets while others bury themselves ineffectually in the ground."[2] Both members of Congress and journalists constantly fiddle with the message content (the arrow), and the delivery mechanism (the bow), while attempting to locate and anticipate the nature of the target (the opposing tribe). When one sends the right message, in the right way, to the right people there is potential for an effect. Messages about and from Congress can come in two basic forms, dramatic infusions of new information (the "hypodermic effect") or the slow accumulation of stories leading to similar outcomes (the "stalactite effect") (see Box 1.1).

Box 1.1 Creating the Congressional Story

For the typical citizen, information about Congress, even if acquired, does not reside on one's mental "ready reference shelf," ready to be used immediately or on a regular basis. New information about anything arrives in two ways.

Hypodermic effect: Some congressional events have enough drama to break through everyday concerns and impinge on us like a needle piercing the skin and leaving a residue. When Congress or one of its members acts in an atypical way, the action has the potential to pierce our attention and force a reassessment of our thinking with headlines such as:

"Republican incumbents topped by tea party challengers in primaries"
"Representative Joe Wilson (R-CA) yells out at President Obama, 'You lie'."
"Congress passes Obamacare"
"Bi-partisan congressional delegation sings 'God Bless America' on Capitol steps on 9/11"

Stalactite effect: Is like the slow building up of positive or negative impressions over a long period of time. None of the individual stories stand out as powerful enough to change the publics' minds, but in total they develop a mindset. Each related story helps develop a mindset almost imperious to conflicting evidence. As one congressional staff member put it, the message about Congress "is not something that is delivered overnight. It is the filling in of a mosaic, and has to be assembled over a long period of time."[a] Stories with quotes such as the following repeated enough create conventional wisdom of a partisan, inefficient, and lazy set of lawmakers:

> "In another partisan battle with all Republicans opposing all Democrats…"
> "Just the most current example of kicking the can down the road…"
> "Leaving for vacation break, Congress fails to…"
>
> Source: [a] Robert. W. Stewart, "Lawmakers Perfect Art of One-Minute Zinger," *Los Angeles Times*, October 4, 1992, p. A13.

Congress serves as the source, subject, and creator of informative messages. Information processing is the "core technology" of Congress. Unlike other production processes, the House and Senate do not "make" anything tangible such as cars or refrigerators. Members of Congress receive information from outside the institution, share information within the two chambers, and export information in the form of press releases, speeches, and most importantly legislation. The media play an important role in what information members of Congress hear, what they share with their colleagues, and what they are able to transmit to the public. While members of the public and members of Congress do communicate directly, it is the media that amplify messages from the public and efficiently spreads information from Congress and its members to a wide audience. "Communication is at the core, if not synonymous with, all understandings of politics."[3]

What the Public Needs and Wants to Know About Congress

The idea of an attentive public fed full information by an open Congress through a willing media stands more as the myth of an ideal representative democracy. Few citizens have the time or interest to pay attention to Congress on a regular basis. They have mortgages to pay, jobs to perform, and kids to raise. Congress only enters their consciousness sporadically, if at all. For members of earlier Congresses, invisibility was less of a curse than an opportunity to go about their business with only limited interference. "Congress lived rather happily through generations of comparative anonymity, making scant public relations efforts and feeling little intruded upon by journalists."[4]

Seeking information about Congress is not a driving motivation for most citizens. Few go out on their own to seek unique information and tailor it to their interests. "What citizens know about politics and public affairs is largely determined by what the press *chooses* [emphasis added] to cover."[5] Much classic political theory made the demands on citizens virtually impossible to fulfill. The "police-patrol oversight" model expects active citizen monitoring of congressional behavior reported by the media. The "fire alarm oversight" approach delegates the day-to-day observation to more interested parties (other politicians, interested groups, and the media themselves), expecting them to alert the public through the media when something clearly out of the ordinary reveals something of wide interest and importance about Congress.[6]

The media also support an even lower level of awareness and problem identification. The "public library/archive" analogy points out how print media and increasingly electronic media have developed repositories of past behavior and promises. Testing the veracity of a politician's previous actions and commitments with contemporary behavior may increase accountability by creating a story in which the media may make a politician look good (consistent, farsighted, etc.) or bad (inconsistent, duplicitous, or foolish). By contributing to the permanent public record, the media give members of Congress fewer places to avoid criticism.

It is hard to get a true fix on how much attention citizens pay to politics in general or to Congress and its members in particular. Attentiveness is a socially acceptable behavior and polling responses clearly over-represent the amount of actual interest or absorption of congressional information. While a relatively small percentage of the population actively seeks out congressional stories, the particular medium an individual uses affects the degree to which one's usage pattern leads to inadvertent exposure. Television provides pre-packed sets of stories, making it difficult to pick and choose what one is exposed to. Few people physically or mentally turn off congressional stories if they happen to come along. Print consumers may well have their favorite sections and topics, but receive some inadvertent information as they scan headlines to find the stories in which they are most interested in. Web searchers are much more intentional, aimed at looking for particular content. Once they click on a story, they tend to drill down deeper and more narrowly. Websites, blogs, tweets, YouTube, and Facebook pages allow one to opt in or out with very little effort, presumably focusing one's attention on those stories providing the kind of information preferred. The percentage of citizens who become active congressional "groupies" on these platforms is quite small. Although the size of the constituency may be small, the dedication of some of its members to monitor and spread the word about Congress makes some information venues more important than numbers alone might indicate. If there is a cadre of highly interested "opinion leaders" who act as "watchdogs" the process of enhancing representative government may occur. This only works as intended when "these watchdogs reflect the diversity of interest in a constituency and have easy ways to communicate with citizens when they discover a representative doing disagreeable things."[7]

For constituents, news is a tool by which they can evaluate public officials, but the tool is rather blunt given low levels of information. Surveys from the 1980s and the early 2000s indicate that only about half of the public could name their member of Congress. Incumbents fared better when constituents were asked to identify their name from a list. Senators were generally better known than House members. Even fewer members of the public could identify their member's vote on any key issues.[8] More recent surveys show a decline, if anything, with only about one-third of the public even willing to try to name their member of the House.[9]

In the modern era, information overload is much more of a problem than lack of information, but there is little guarantee that the information gained contributes at all to the understanding of Congress. Individual citizens and decision-makers spend a great deal of time protecting themselves from too much and/or useless information. With everyone trying to get their message through, "the task for members, both through traditional communications techniques and new communications techniques, is to cut through the cacophony of information to reach constituents."[10]

Relieving all citizens from monitoring every congressional action all the time, fails to vitiate the need for some members of the public to pay attention to different portions of congressional activity on a regular basis. While there is an image of well-informed citizens, elected officials committed to transparency, and a facilitating media purportedly combining to undergird representative democracy, there is often an undercurrent of doubt. Citizens have been portrayed as unaware and uninterested, elected officials as committed to secrecy and obfuscation, and the media as disinterested in substance in favor of conflict. Research has shown that the more voters know about an incumbent's voting record, particularly if they agree with it, the more they support that member's reelection. This evidence of informed and rational voters acting in appropriate ways is particularly evident where the media provided extensive and accurate coverage of the positions taken by members of Congress.[11]

Expectations of Congress

In a representative democracy, the public has the right to expect Congress to provide adequate and honest information that allows citizens to identify the issues in which they should take interest and the ability to hold their representatives accountable.

Expecting access to congressional information is like support for public libraries. Most people fail to use the public library on a regular basis, but are appalled if cutbacks in library access are proposed. Although they are not using the library now, they want it available, if and when they should need it. In the same vein, "the majority of citizens, regardless of whether or not they have communicated with their members, want their representatives to keep them informed about what is happening at the federal level."[12]

In their roles as representatives, members of Congress reflect the concerns of the segments of society for which they feel responsible. Crisis events such as school shootings, bombings, droughts, and others push members of Congress into a reaction mode. Congress receives little regular attention from most citizens, but they expect it to "be there and do something" when a crisis strikes.

The initial congressional reaction is often symbolic or rhetorical. The gathering of members of Congress outside the Capitol on the afternoon of September 11th to sing "America the Beautiful" in the wake of the most deadly terrorist attack on American soil was more than a good photo op. It showed social solidarity and reflected Congress willingness to place terrorism higher on the national agenda. By joining with our other expected institutional spokesman for American society – the president – the media and the public could gain some solace that our national leaders "got it" and would marshal their resources to meet the challenge.

Public Expectations of the Media

The public cannot play its role of overseeing and informing Congress without an understanding of what Congress does. It is not enough to simply chronicle congressional actions. Congressional activity must be put into context giving the public reasons for paying attention and projecting consequences as to how congressional actions might affect the ultimate outcome.

There are plenty of reasons why the public fails to understand Congress and why the media find it difficult to explain. In an attempt to make some sense of a complex process, civics classes perpetuate the myth of a simple "a bill becomes a law" process which can be charted with simple graphics. Generations of Americans grew up with the cartoon version of "I'm Just a Bill." While the basic steps in the legislative process establish a benchmark against which alternative routes must be justified, much legislation skips or adds steps seldom outlined in the text. "Unorthodox lawmaking"[13] has become the norm for many important bills. Added to the undue simplification of the bill passage flow chart is the fact that it almost totally ignores the politics of the process, and in the process demeans politics as an unfortunate intrusion. The mechanical flow chart seems to imply that if we just let the legislative machinery run it will rationally produce the best legislation and that gridlock along the way implies a broken "machine." While aspects of politics overemphasizing self-interest do cause problems, the basic nature of politics in which coalitions are created around non-provable preferences provides the best policies when there are not universally accepted "right" answers. The existence of major segments of the public harboring a sour taste in their mouths that "it is all politics," dampens their interest in understanding and participating in the political process.

What Congress Needs from the Media

As much as some members might facetiously assert the alternative, Congress could not operate without the media. As a linkage institution, the media make representative government feasible, as a task no other societal institution is capable of taking on.

Maintaining Legitimacy

The separation of powers concept on which American government is based depends on independent institutions having both the legal power and public legitimacy to carry out their task of checking the power of competing institutions. Reporting on Congress and its powers provides the legitimacy necessary to turn the checks and balances goal into a living reality. If Congress is displayed as an ineffective and/or illegitimate interloper its potential for playing its intended role evaporates. Frustrated with lack of cooperation with Congress in early 2014, President Obama used the State of the Union message to threaten using the "pen and the telephone" to bypass Congress. His comments unleashed a barrage of criticism defending Congress' legitimate role in the policy process to "check and balance" inappropriate use of power.[14]

Personal Promotion

More realistically for Congress, information is a resource harboring the ability to strategically enhance careers and promote policy preferences. On the individual level, members of Congress seek to validate the issues they deem important and desire positive local media coverage to promote their careers. Lacking local media coverage, members lose their name identification advantage among voters and open themselves to charges of ineffectiveness and irrelevancy espoused. Opponents have a right to question an incumbent who fails to use the media to inform voters.

Facilitating the Legislative Agenda

Politics is a competitive process in which players attempt to set the agenda of problems worthy of solution, outline acceptable solutions, and convince a requisite number of other players to go along with a compromise solution. Good politicians recognize there are "no final victories"[15] and no universally accepted solutions. Congress' ability to determine the policy outcome depends on the political environment at any particular point in time. Whichever party controls the White House cedes much of its agenda-setting power to the president with his superior access to the media. Particularly for the minority party in Congress, or the party not holding the White House, "agenda setting [is] the most powerful opportunity for members of Congress to influence the policy process."[16]

Members of Congress and their staffs are bombarded on all sides with information. Numerous groups and individuals hope to tell them what issues to pursue and how to handle them. Information overload is much more important than information underload. Congressional offices are the hub of incoming letters, e-mails, reports, and personal visitors all vying for attention. Many of these fall on deaf ears. Ultimately "the journalists decide which politicians' messages to cover and how frequently to cover them,"[17] but politicians still control much of the raw material from which journalists have to work.

News emanating from Congress can become a dynamic variable in the policy process. Sending out a press release or making a public statement may reverberate in a number of ways. In the first place outgoing messages alert the media as to what members of Congress feel is important. Messages transmitted by the media have the potential for alerting and perhaps convincing the public about the importance of an issue or a preferred stand. Media coverage and public reaction filter back to members of Congress encouraging further public statements. The more media coverage, the more likely an issue is to secure a place on Congress' agenda.

Some members use a "boomerang" strategy, launching a policy idea to the public through the media in the hope that public reaction will permeate Capitol Hill and force action. More than six decades ago, E. E. Schattscheider alerted observers to the strategy of changing policy outcomes by expanding the range of conflict. If an individual or group lacks a majority within the Congress, a viable strategy is to expand the conflict beyond the chamber.[18]

Attempted issue messages falling on fallow ground and receiving little media coverage and insignificant public reaction tend to fall by the wayside.[19] Most members of Congress don't beat their heads against issues lacking a positive reception. At best, they wait for another event that could bring their issue into focus.

Members of Congress with a legislative agenda hope to use the media as a handmaiden to promote their policy goals among their colleagues. Once largely something to react to, the news media have increasingly become a "governing tool."[20] Discussions and debates about the nature of the policy agenda in the back rooms of Capitol Hill have been augmented by, and in some cases replaced with, "going public" using the media. Members of Congress often communicate with each other through the media. As one congressional staffer put it, "We can write reports and papers and then members of Congress don't read it. But if the *Times* or *Post* picks up our report and does a story on it, they do read that and it gets their attention."[21] With members spending more time traveling back to their districts there are

> fewer opportunities to chat with one another in Hill offices and corridors, [and] they take their cases public to telegraph their intentions or stances or to demonstrate their concerns and the depth of their passion to other lawmakers and their aides.[22]

Members of Congress, like most of us, hate to have their preconceptions challenged. Psychologists talk about "cognitive dissonance," a situation where our information presents conflicting cues to guide our behavior or when our behavior fails to match our information. When the Republicans took over the House, they placed the more conservative Fox TV News on the monitors in the gym, improving the chances that when exercising they would not get politically "exercised" over challenging information. Only later was the more liberal CNN added.[23]

Understanding and Mollifying Constituents

Members of Congress are not solely victims of news coverage about them, nor limited to attempts at presenting information they hope the media will pick up and use. Members of Congress are both sources of news stories and consumers of the journalists' efforts. Members attempt to control and anticipate what their constituents are exposed to.

The relationship between members of Congress and the media becomes an iterative process. Members often react to news stories by attempting to correct them and/or explain the behavior in question. In some cases they attempt to anticipate news stories and act in the most politically advantageous way. While some might see such strategizing as the ultimate example of duplicitous politicians acting solely in their own self-interest, a good case could be made that such action portrays the virtue of democratic responsiveness. On many issues, constituent views are not set in stone. Changing conditions and revised information potentially lead to updated preferences. Unless one fully accepts the extreme Burkean (see Box 1.2) outlook of the representative as a "Trustee" who once elected never looks back for guidance, representatives are expected to take into account constituent views.

Box 1.2 Burke: Principles and Pragmatics

Seventeenth century British parliamentarian Edmund Burke casts a long shadow on our study of legislative behavior by laying out a stark set of alternative guidelines as to how a legislator should relate to his constituents. "Delegates" were expected to simply reflect the "wishes" of their constituents, holding their own personal preferences and judgment at bay. "Trustees" on the other hand, drew their legitimacy from broader experience and knowledge, granting them the responsibility to take a broader and longer-term view of constituents' interests and giving legislators the right to use their own judgment on policy decisions. In his famous speech to his electors in Bristol, England, Burke advocated service as a trustee. Often lost in the discussion of Burke's views on representation is the fact that the voters turned him out of office in the next election.

Information about constituent views comes from a variety of sources such as letters, calls, and face-to-face meetings between members and those they are expected to represent. Broader trends in public often come from the media which serve as a "kind of bulletin board."[24] Charged with representing their constituents, members of Congress often find themselves lacking clear data on constituent hopes and desires. Few members have the luxury of regular scientific polls of their constituency. Incoming telephone calls, letters, and e-mails often represent a unique set of constituents with atypical motivations or subject to mobilization by organized interests. Newspaper editorials may well serve as a surrogate measure of public preferences, since editorial writers must take into account community views.[25] Members of Congress monitor both local and national media carefully, and bring their assertions into congressional debates in the hope of influencing their colleagues. House members with their smaller constituencies tend to reference local newspapers, while senators focus more on the national media.[26] References to national media outlets are used most often to justify a political position, with liberals citing liberal sources for back-up, and even more dramatically, conservatives gravitating toward conservative sources. Conservatives are particularly likely to highlight cases where traditionally liberal sources "announce preferences that concur with their [conservative] views."[27]

As rational actors concerned about their support among the public, members of Congress utilize all the tools at their disposal to determine public opinion in their district and, at a minimum, take it into account in their decisions. Due to personal principles or party pressures, they may not be able to satisfy some voters, but at a minimum they want to be aware of potential sticking points to prepare a rationale for their behavior. As the media report on changing opinions, and/or members anticipate future changes, politicians "modify their behavior at the margin ... [and] constantly and immediately process public opinion changes in order to stay ahead of the curve."[28]

In discussing the challenges of satisfying constituents, two members from politically marginal districts pointed out,

> It is impossible for any member of Congress to satisfy all of his or her constituents all of the time. Constituents expect a member to respond to your concerns, but not necessarily vote the way you want ... listening is an important part of leading and shows the kind of respect the public deserves in a representative democracy.

One of the member's extreme willingness to listen forced the media to begin giving her kudos by saying, "she is so in touch with her district that she would come to the opening of an envelope." Another member put it in a slightly different way. "A large part of the congressional job is to be a teacher, explaining issues, analyzing alternatives, and explaining one's vote."[29] The media become a vehicle by which members of Congress can expand the size of the "class" they are attempting to teach.

As the information available about constituents changes, one might expect it to be reflected in their political outlooks. Despite the fact that most members of Congress objectively look as if they are quite politically secure, most of them run scared harboring a series of scenarios by which they might face defeat. As a practical and psychological defense, members keep their political antennae out, seeking evidence of potential trouble ahead.

So What Is News on the Congressional Beat?

Broad sweeping statements about "the media" miss a large variation in delivery mechanisms (print, radio, television, Internet, etc.), target audiences, and individualized goals and structures. While "pack journalism" occurs leading to similar stories and public perceptions, the route to fame and financial success often goes along with journalists taking a risk on a different story or a unique approach to an existing story. Just as members of Congress are constrained by worrying about "what policy positions can I explain to my constituents and still remain in office?" journalists are constrained by their own (and their editors') perceptions as to "what will our readers or listeners accept without canceling their subscription, turning the channel, or ignoring our web presence?" There is no overall foolproof guide on how to make this work. Different assumptions lead to different journalistic output.

What Gets Covered?

As a commodity to be sold or bypassed potential news stories are subject to the law of supply and demand. Traditional media have a usually fixed "news hole" (news pages, television news programs) to fill. During extraordinary periods, the news hole can be expanded with special editions or extended television coverage. Such expansion involves real costs (creation, printing, distribution, and/or loss of advertising revenue) and is only undertaken rarely. Even the new media limit their effectiveness with too much content, since it may overwhelm the website visitor or tweet recipient.

On a typical day each potential news story competes with a myriad of competing events and political actors for coverage. Editors and journalists alike constantly make choices based on assumptions about the relative importance of particular events and actors both in the abstract and for their unique audiences. No absolute measure of a story's importance exists. While political scandal has significant potential to actually make it into the news, competing news stories can even crowd out scandal. When the supply of potential stories is great, the demand to cover any one story falls. In periods of news "congestion" it is more difficult to determine which stories will make it through the gauntlet.[30] Particular individuals or institutions are more likely to receive coverage on slow news days when the overall demand remains constant but the supply is limited. A story about the President or the Supreme Court may crowd out a story about Congress. To a large degree, Congress and its members compete with other political institutions and participants in a zero-sum competition for coverage. From a strategic perspective, political activists try to generate good news on slow news days and hope that behavior that might reflect on them badly emerges in the midst of many other stories. While the supply of negative stories about Congress or members of any other institution varies in an irregular pattern over time, the likelihood that they will be reported on depends on what else is going on in the political universe.

On the aggregate level, Congress has lost out in the competitive process to the presidency (see Chapter 4). A number of reasons stand out:

The president is easier to cover. He is a well-known "news hook" who needs no introduction.

Power shifts in American politics have increased the power and relevance of the president.

Presidents speak with one unified voice and have a staff to manage their public relations.

Congress begins with a task for which universal appreciation is impossible. Congress is the nation's value mediating institution. Values are those preferences about which reasonable people disagree and about which there is no universally acceptable answer undergirded by incontrovertible facts and are easily compromised. When the facts and values line up almost universally on one side, the decision is easy, but such decisions seldom come to Congress. The decision on such things as whether we should add government programs or cut taxes is based on one's view of what the better society would look like. Facts can inform such a decision, but there are often competing facts and and/or competing interpretations. Whatever decision Congress makes, some people will be disappointed. While history may be written by the victors, journalists tend to seek out the potential or actual losers who often trash Congress as an institution and its members as they vent their disappointment with the policy decision.

So What Is News?

There is no cut and dried definition of news. On the most basic level, news is something out of the ordinary. Dog bites man is generally not news, it happens so frequently, fits within the mode of what dogs do, and the target is relatively unimportant and anonymous. At times though, the viciousness of the attack ("Child Killed by Mother's Four Dogs"), the contribution of the attack to a developing story (such as the legislative assault against pit bulls), or the importance of the target ("Presidential Dog Nips Prime Minister") raises a common animal behavior (biting) into a newsworthy event. A "man bites dog" story is more likely to get news because of its rarity. Its chances of reaching news status increases if it was caught on film.

In the political realm, a number of criteria enhance potential newsworthiness:

- Conflict (between individual, political groups, and/or governmental institutions.

    Journalists increasingly look for the "three Cs", controversy, conflict, and confusion.[31] As former Senator Alan Simpson (R-WY) put it, the media

    > gorges itself on conflict, confusion and controversy, then regurgitates this blathering bile each and every day into American homes [where] it lands like a plop on the doorstep in the morning, or, more likely, casts gloomy, silvery shadows from the television set at night.[32]

    From the Democratic side former Representative Tom Allen (D-ME) points out that in focusing on conflict, the media ignore reality, create a false impression, and lead to undesirable behavior.

"Through the media's single-lens view of politics, Democrats and Republicans are arrayed along a one-dimensional spectrum from left to right." Such a view contributes to members who "talk past each other" with members of the media seeing everything as a battle, as "us" versus "them."[33]

- Strategic maneuvering (the "horse-race" coverage of campaigns or the back-room deals on legislation).
- Negative behavior (duplicity of public officials, moral failures).
- Availability of expected content (radio needs sound, television needs pictures, the Internet emphasizes timeliness).
- Known participants. The key news hook (what the story is written about) tends to be the "who" in journalists' "when, what, where, when, and why" set of content prompts taught in journalism school.

Relatively insignificant stories about significant and well-known individuals often trump more important stories about less significant individuals. In ABC's Cokie Roberts' view, "You concentrate on individuals because the rest is so muddy."[34]

News Gathering and Reporting Bias

The question is not so much "Are the media biased?" but rather "in what ways does bias emerge?" The independence of American media enhances the opportunities for bias. Bias is an unrealistic representation of reality. It is not simply saying good or bad things about individuals and organizations. A political actor acting badly deserves bad coverage, just as one acting positively deserves good coverage. Bias occurs when the good or bad behavior of one set of actors is ignored or highlighted in relation to similar good or bad behavior of other actors. The hallmarks of bias involve frequency and tone of coverage. When the media ignore the actions of some members of Congress or issues they fail to provide voters with information on which to judge. In their role as simplifiers and explainers of politics, the choice of adjectives can easily tilt audience reactions. Labeling one set of members of Congress as "far right," "far left," "extreme," or "radical" propels the reader or viewer to a predetermined evaluation. The sin is compounded when groups of Congressmen equally distanced from the mean fail to secure the same extreme label from the media.

The most obvious bias stems from journalistic norms of what makes something newsworthy. These norms have little to do with partisan positions or the issues under considerations. In the battle for readers and viewers, the media assume that people are most interested in news that is timely, out of the ordinary, understandable, and relevant to their lives.

The tedious nature of the legislative process redirects journalists to stories of conflict and scandal. Such stories resonate since they deal with real people, present characters as "good guys" and "bad guys," and cry out for a definitive conclusion where the forces of good overwhelm those of evil. Journalism revolves around storytelling and audiences have a hard time connecting to stories about abstract issues told in a serialized form, and seldom resulting in a clear victory or defeat.

While the media have many choices as to what they cover and how they cover it, an empirical analysis of party promotion of issues and actual media coverage revealed that to a large degree coverage mirrored the media efforts of congressional leaders. If anything the media gave *more* balanced coverage to issues than the raw material provided by media strategies of the parties and their leaders. The analysis also revealed little evidence of a consistent partisan bias in coverage over time and over a series of issues.[35]

Journalists make critical decisions about the knowledge and interests of their audiences. Media such as local newspapers and television stations have a relatively clear picture of "their" audiences and their political preferences. On the other hand, national media Internet sites have little understanding of who uses them and view them as definitive. The journalistic norms of objectivity and balance weaken as media attempt to retain, and in many cases reinforce, the political interests and preferences of their audiences. Journalists in clearly Democratic or Republican districts tend to cover the issues associated with the party in the majority more than the minority party.

Unlike a number of other public personages, there are only limited pieces of hard data on which to make unequivocal evaluations of a representative's performance in office. A baseball pitcher's ERA, a batter's batting average, an entertainer's box office draw, or a business person's financial bottom line, all provide widely accepted criteria for categorizing "heroes" and "zeroes." For members of Congress, things such as attendance records, bills introduced, and roll call votes are easy to measure, but somewhat more difficult to interpret or assign value to. Going back to the district to take care of a problem first-hand might well be more important than a particular vote. Roll call votes are complex, since omnibus legislation combines diverse components, some of which might be evaluated by different constituents as the good, bad, or ugly. From the media, we know very little about the work horses in Congress who create good legislation, build the coalitions necessary to get it passed, and monitor its actual impact through oversight. The temptation for the media lies in reporting the passage of a bill as the end of the story as they rush on to catch the wave of the next controversy. Unfortunately for Congress, many stories lack the media's desire for a clear beginning, middle, and end. Widely experienced government official George Schultz, although speaking about Washington in general, certainly applied his conclusion to Congress that "Nothing ever gets settled in this town. It's not like running a company, or even a university. It's ... it's a seething debating society in which the debate never stops, in which people never give up, including me."[36]

Research on local coverage of members of Congress tends to bear out the penchant for focusing on the unique. Given their limited resources of staff and space, local newspapers evidence a clear strategy in their coverage. Members whose political views are in step with the local voters receive less negative and more positive coverage than members who pursue policy positions less in line with the people they represent. Staying true to the principle that news refers to something "new" and out of the ordinary, members of Congress announcing their intention to vote in an unexpected way get more media attention than their colleagues voting predictably along party, regional, or ideological lines.[37] John Murtha (D-PA), the first Vietnam veteran to serve in Congress and powerful insider in Congress, gained little national attention until he switched from support to opposition to the war in Iraq.[38] The largest bump in coverage for senators comes when they announce a presidential bid.[39]

Far from the common description of local media as "lapdogs" of their member of Congress, local media tend to avoid using their limited resources to report on the minimally newsworthy legislator.[40] Members from the same party as the presidential candidate winning their district tend more to fly under the radar of the local media and serve as less likely targets of investigative journalism efforts. Local media tend to monitor and be more critical of members who seem out of step with other political dynamics of their district.

Needing to fulfill the journalist's obligatory "who" in developing their story-making, much emphasis of the national press falls on members of Congress holding key leadership positions such as party leaders and committee chairs. It is the rare, and atypical, non-leader who breaks through this predilection.

The Institution We Love to Hate

In their role as referees and informers for the public, journalists see pointing out shortcomings as more important than rewarding appropriate action. Personal gaffes, signs of incompetence, and/or illegal behavior become magnets for media coverage. Numerous observers point out that congressional coverage reveals a "nastier edge."[41] It is no surprise that the public seems to see Congress as the institution we love to hate and is even characterized as a "public enemy."[42]

There is no simple answer to why congressional coverage has become so much more critical in recent years. It would be easy to say that Congress is simply drawing more selfish and incompetent individuals, but most observers, even within the media, fail to accept that answer. Still focusing on Congress, certainly some blame goes to its arcane rules and member benefits better suited to an age where efficiency and egalitarianism stood much lower on the scale of public expectations. Members of Congress themselves add to its criticism by making criticism of Congress part of their campaign strategy. Another aggravating factor stems from the fact that many members of Congress have not accommodated to the new environment where more congressional activity is available for public scrutiny via databases or video clips. Opening Congress "doors" to the public – which more often than not means opening it to journalists – provides much more raw material to serve as the basis for criticism.

Journalists themselves must share some of the explanation. Career advancement requires getting one's stories broadcast or printed. Editors impart expectations of the types of stories they feel will draw readers or viewers. A series of "MEGO" stories ("My eyes glaze over") earn little kudos.[43] Editors will accept controversy and disdain over inattention and boredom. The Watergate success of Bob Woodward and Carl Bernstein, two very junior journalists who received the Pulitzer Prize, changed the Washington journalistic landscape. Seeing two colleagues setting themselves up for the fast track to higher success in journalism, whets the appetite of many journalists to follow their lead. Moving from the "old boy network" of cozy relationships between politicians and journalists to the new investigative journalism norm begged for likely targets of behaviors to be exposed. Congress and its members stood ready, if not willing, to provide substance ready to criticize.

News consumers must also be taken into account. If they refused to read or watch negative stories about Congress, editors would give a different set of marching orders to their employees. It is often asserted that the public desires more substantive and fewer conflict-based stories, but when one looks at the ratings and readership for what people actually pay attention to, conflict and scandal rate relatively high.

Scandal introduces a unique situation in terms of supply and demand since another set of actors attempt to influence news content. Not only are journalists and the subject of a potential news story involved, but members of the opposing party and/or policy opponents try to get into the "negotiation of newsworthiness" process.[44] The charges of opponents themselves become a news hook for a story and direct quotes from those sources help legitimize the charges and their importance. Attempting to fulfill the widely touted journalistic norm of objectivity, such stories with their challenger/opponent tit for tat have the trappings of balance. When the purported scandal happens in Washington members of the opposing party are likely to take up the battle cry to make the story news. Back in the district, congressional scandal stories are more likely to make news when there is an election challenger to promote the criticism.[45]

If news deals with the atypical, one might take comfort in the assertion that the media seem fixated on scandal and conflict. Since we lack any actual measure of the number of scandals and the amount of conflict in Congress, it is impossible to determine how much is too much. A detailed content analysis of national television and newspaper news about Congress found the following story content:

Issues	74%
Scandal	14%
Personalities	13%
Political parties	5%
Congress as an institution	5%[46]

Although scandals per se ranked relatively low as the focus for stories, the way in which the issues facing Congress were discussed had the potential to raise public consternation. Close to 70 percent of the stories focused on legislative maneuvering and about 40 percent raised issues of partisan conflict or conflict with the president.[47] To the degree that the public feel uncomfortable with conflict and "just want to get things done," such reporting serves to aggravate the open sores of dissatisfaction with Congress. Many citizens fail to recognize that collective decision-making bodies such as Congress are designed to settle conflicts and disagreements. Lacking disagreement policy decisions would follow cut and dried formulas. Just "doing the right thing" assumes there is virtual universal consensus as to what is right. The messiness of democracy is constantly shoved in the public's face by the nature of media coverage. While there may be too much conflict and too little compromise in Congress it is hard to find in the media situations where the system does work.

The Tone of Congressional Coverage

If there is any consensus on the relationship between Congress and the media it lies in the assertion that "Press coverage of Congress over the years has moved from healthy skepticism to outright cynicism."[48] Skeptics look at a situation and ask "What is wrong and how can we fix it?" Cynics assume the worst and categorize the problems they see as intentional and intractable. Media coverage seems to involve "Journalistic hit-and-run specialists [who] perpetuate a cartoon-like stereotype of Congress as 'a place where good ideas go to die in a maelstrom of bureaucratic hedging and rank favor trading'."[49]

It is a human tendency to assume that the era in which we live is unique and that we are at the pinnacle of success or the depth of disaster. It is important to take a longer view to put the present situation into perspective. In 1992, after a major study of Congress and the media, Thomas Mann and Norman Ornstein argued, "Congress is under siege," with the tone of negative criticism "corrosive."[50] Their words ring true twenty-five years later, and if anything current observers would argue that their implication that Congress had reached rock bottom was optimistic.

Things certainly have not gotten better and Congress today is reflected in the media in an even more negative light. Studies of the media's coverage of Congress over the last four decades reveal an overarching negative set of themes with coverage becoming more and more negative. By the 1970s scholars concluded that congressional stories focused on "conflict, malfeasance and breech of public trust."[51] In the 1980s, another study concluded that two-thirds of the network news coverage of Congress "concerned ... three episodes of turmoil and scandal that had little to do with the constitutionally mandated duties of Congress."[52]

Some Causes

Emboldened by public disrespect for Congress and the successful endeavors of their journalistic colleagues, the media have given the wheel another spin with a spate of stories about corruption, moral failures, and undeserved perks of office. In its 1992 "Man of the Year" issue, *Time Magazine* included an article entitled "Bums of the Year," pointing out a long list of congressional shortcomings.[53] *Washington Post* correspondent Tom Kenworthy characterized many members of Congress as "buffoons, charlatans, blowhards and intellectually dishonest people,"[54] at a time when Congress was controlled by the Democrats, the party the *Post* purportedly favored. Even usually even-handed and moderate correspondent David Broder joined the fray condemning member perks (perquisites) as showing a pattern "of individual self-interest prevailing over collective responsibility."[55] Two decades later, with multiple changes in party control and a wave of subsequent scandals, the level of media righteous indignation at Congress has shown little or no abatement.

The media have turned on Congress more than on other national institutions. While the media have long been skeptical of Congress and its members, the slide into the depths of cynicism where nothing Congress does, nor none of its members deserve even the faintest praise dominate much of the coverage. Journalists taking the balanced view that "it is just as wrong to say that politicians are all crooks as to pretend they are all saints"[56] get drowned out by blanket condemnation of Congress as a "parliament of whores" and the advice "don't vote, it just encourages the bastards."[57]

As a conventional wisdom developed among the media that all members of Congress are lazy, unprincipled, and self-serving, most journalists joined the bandwagon of condemnation. Rather than simply pointing out the errant ways of a few newsworthy uniqueness seemed to focus on the rare member of Congress doing his or her job with skill and selflessness. David Broder, not congressional sycophant, even felt he had to title one of his pieces "Yes There Are Good People in Congress."[58] Congress bashing had become a "national pastime."[59] The penchant for sensationalism and conflict more than content and process gives an unbalanced view of Congress. As one journalist put it, "[If] the media had been around 2,000 years ago, we'd have covered the Crucifixion – and missed Christianity."[60]

Inherent Difficulties of Covering Congress

It is unreasonable to expect that Congress might starve the media and improve their image by avoiding conflict. In its role of taking on those issues about which reasonable people can and should disagree, Congress is required to face up to conflict as a precursor to an acceptable compromise. As public preferences have hardened and congressional districts have been drawn around those divisions, the art of compromise "has somehow gotten a bad name by being escalated in visibility ... In the old days, when a congressmen cut deals that helped different sides, we all thought that was good."[61] Today, the media and especially some of the most active voters see any compromise on policy as a compromise of inviolable principles. It is a recipe for gridlock and another round of media stories of how Congress is not working as intended. As the old joke goes, there are only two things in the middle of the road, yellow stripes and dead possums. The individual member of Congress "who tries to work the middle ... gets carved up by both sides."[62]

Damn the Media, Full Speed Ahead

In many competitions, "the best defense is a good offense." When members of Congress individually or collectively anticipate negative press coverage, their rhetoric will turn to demonizing the media, rather than exploring their own behavior patterns out of which the media stories emerge.[63] Given the critical nature of media coverage of Congress, "the overall tendency of the total rhetoric about the press coming from both parties [in Congress] over time [is] more negative than positive."[64] The competing barbs the media and Congress fling at each other don't simply represent an "inside the beltway" joust. As these two elites fight it out, their rhetoric spills out to the general public, reducing confidence in both institutions (see Box 1.3).

Members of Congress harbor considerable distrust as to the media's mediating role. Few members fully agree with what the media include, what they discard, and how they frame a story. A survey of members of

Congress indicated that over three-quarters of Democrats and 94 percent of Republicans felt they had been "burned" by the media who "wrote or broadcast a bad or false story."[65] Tools for communicating with constituents without relying on the human and strategic judgments of journalists hold great appeal for members of Congress. The popularity of websites, tweets, and Facebook pages lies in the control the member has over their content (see Chapter 11).

As members of Congress and the most politically interested of the public become more distrustful of the media, they may well fall back on less examined partisan or ideological positions, and remain less open to the views of the public which they feel the media has corrupted. The media's distrust of members of Congress (and often of the public) encourages them to see any political action as self-serving and lacking adequate thought. Thus distrust of major political institutions such as Congress and the media contributes to polarization and gridlock. The tendency to "kill the messenger" (see Box 1.3) may put some salve on the media's wounds, but does little to improve the overall position of Congress and its members.

Box 1.3   Killing the Messenger

The idea of harming the bearer of bad news permeates both literature and social conventions. Both Plutarch[a] and Shakespeare[b] point out the tendency to take out one's anger by harming the messenger. To counter this tendency during battle, chivalry required that messengers bringing demands to opposing armies should not be harmed and allowed free passage back to their own troops. Later, when town criers brought news of tax increases or new regulations, they were protected from harm.[c]

Sources:
[a] Plutarch's *Life of Lucullus* (Dryden transl.), paragraph 25; a slightly different account (the messenger was hanged) is in Appian's *Mithradatic Wars*, paragraph 84.
[b] *Henry V, Part 2*, Act I, scene 1, lines 95–103:
   "Thou shakest thy head and hold'st it fear or sin to speak a truth. ... Yet the first bringer of unwelcome news hath but a losing office, and his tongue sounds ever after as a sullen bell, remember'd tolling a departed friend."
[c] http://news.bbc.co.uk/local/bradford/hi/people_and_places/arts_and_culture/newsid_8931000/8931369.stm

---

Self-inflicted Wounds: "We Have Met the Enemy and He Is Us"

The above quote from cartoon character Pogo reveals the often undesirable conclusion that those receiving negative media coverage may well deserve it. The negative image of Congress emerges not solely from media selectivity and the focus on less palatable realities such as conflict and scandal. Individual candidates often run for Congress by running against the institution, arguing that their inclusion would move the mix in a positive direction. Within Congress, House members often point an accusing finger at the Senate, while senators return the "favor" when its counterpart chambers fails to act in the way they desire. Within each chamber, the minority party members show little hesitancy to reveal the shortcomings of the majority and how poorly the organization is faring under their stewardship. The media become a megaphone for washing this "dirty linen" in public.

There is no question that the media should cover legal and ethical breaches in Congress. We, the citizens, would be ill-served by a media that failed to inform us of breaches or downplayed their importance. That said, we are equally ill-served when minor infractions are turned into major scandals and all members are dragged into the swamp of disrepute. The problem is exacerbated by the tendency of the media to focus on charges and give short shrift to the outcomes of serious investigations which find the person not guilty. Former Secretary of Labor, Ray Donovan, charged, forced to resign, and then acquitted made the plaintiff plea a number of members of Congress would like to echo, "Which office do I go to get my reputation back?"[66] (see Box 1.4).

Box 1.4 The Fox in the Chicken House?

The spread of the avowedly conservative Fox News during the 1990s provided an interesting natural experiment to test the strategic behavior of members based on news content. As local cable outlets seemingly randomly included Fox News in their lineup, it was possible to compare the voting behavior of members before and after Fox's arrival. True to expectations, the arrival of Fox News in a news market was reflected by reduced support for President Clinton's policies, but such reduced support did not occur in similar constituencies where voters lacked access to Fox. Members of Congress seemed to preempt the possible shifts in district opinion due to the introduction of Fox by altering their policy positions.

Source: Joshua D. Clinton and Ted Enamorado, "The National News Media's Effect on Congress: How Fox News Affected Elites in Congress," working paper available at: ttp://papers.ssrn.com/sol3/papers.cfm?abstract_id=2050570.

Congress is filled with fallible individuals, subject to the same temptations, if not more, than others. As one staff member put it, "members of Congress have a hard time keeping their pants zipped and their billfolds closed." Misbehavior in terms of sex and money (bribes and illegal campaign contributions) make headlines. The litany of members who have transgressed moral codes, legal restrictions, and the ethics provisions of their chamber is long. The big difference for members of Congress is that their indiscretions often go public and the media promote the public's right to know. Each time a new transgression appears the individual's shortcoming diminishes the image of all members. Some have been punished by their chambers, others by the voters. The chance of getting away with misbehavior is significantly lower for a member of Congress than for most other professions. Both the media and his or her political adversaries are watching for the fatal misstep. There is no evidence that members of Congress are more corrupt or morally bereft than other well-off and powerful people in society, but the transgressions of businessmen, priests, and entertainers tend to be seen more as exceptions than standard operating behaviors reflecting poorly on the entire institution.

Some criticism of Congress looks more serious on the surface than in reality. "Perk" is a dirty word for the media. They point out in-house credit unions, member dining rooms, gyms as undeserved benefits of office. At the same time members of the media and many critics in the public reveal little hesitancy to use similar benefits provided by their employers in order to increase efficiency and reduce the stress of a busy work schedule. The question is not whether members of Congress have perks, but rather whether those benefits of office facilitate the legislative process.

Who Cares About Negative Coverage?

While egos of members of Congress might well be soothed by positive coverage of their individual actions and those of the institution, it is important to ask whether media portrayals of Congress make any fundamental difference. If Congress and the media were simply two independent institutions trading barbs and granting each other minimal respect, the importance would be minimal. That assertion misses the key point that in a representative democracy, the media serve as a key transmitter of information and perspectives citizens need to play their role. "The impression most people get of Congress and its members comes through the prism of press coverage."[67] To the degree that the media bypasses Congress and its members for other news, the public is hampered in its potential for evaluation. If those stories that get written leave an unrealistic negative feeling, public cynicism develops. Ignorance relegates Congress to irrelevance, while cynicism undermines its legitimacy and is more likely to discourage legitimate citizen entreaties to its members than to foment effective engagement.

"A Congress discredited and disdained by the American people will lack the legitimacy and credibility to address the public challenges that confront the country."[68]

Who Gets Covered?

As will be discussed in more detail in Chapter 4, only a few members of Congress have the perceived clout and importance to call a press conference on their own and expect a reasonable crowd. Most members must either work through the media back home, or join together with a team of colleagues to create enough pressure to overcome the inertia of media interest in just a few well-known "stars" with news hook capability. On the one hand, the modern Congress is the most permeable of our national institutions.[69] Five hundred and thirty-five primary actors and thousands of support staff are privy to interesting information they have a motivation to share. The closed meetings in the White House or the private conferences of the Supreme Court are hard to cover. The increasing openness of Congress can be seen in the rules adopted by various committees over the years. Fifty years ago, most committees operated with rules requiring an affirmative vote by the committee to *open* meetings to the press and public. In the current age of government in "sunshine," it takes an affirmative vote of a committee to *close* a committee when dealing with national security or personnel issues.[70]

One of the few congressional advantages of belonging to the party failing to control the presidency lies in the potential for an individual member to gain media attention. Journalistic norms of objectivity often define that concept as giving equal time to each side of an issue, no matter the validity of the position or the cogency of the argument. For simplicity, most issues are defined as having only two sides. When the president takes a stand, the media needs to go somewhere to find a dissenting voice. Since members of the president's party counter his position to their own disadvantage, leaders and even outspoken followers of the opposition party emerge as the legitimate place to go.[71]

Despite the opportunities for exposure, most individual members of Congress fail to satisfy the key attribute of a good news hook – instant recognition. By the time a journalist explains who a member is, why he or she is important, and why the information recipient should care, there is little time for the rest of the story.

The Contemporary Congressional and Media Environment

Both Congress and the media have changed in recent years. When one partner in a relationship experiences an altered reality, the other entity feels the effect.

The "New" Congress

A former member of Congress from even fifty years ago, or even less, would probably find the current Congress a strange place. The more closed "baronial" Congress which "valued collegiality more than compromise" has morphed into "a variegated, competitive, and more partisan breaking-news environment, [where] speed and drama increase the chances that any one political actor's voice will be heard amidst all the others clamoring for attention."[72] Former Senator Russell Long (D-LA) who literally grew up on Capitol Hill while his father was a senator and who then served twenty years himself (until 1989), described each session of Congress as like "going off to summer camp, leaving behind friends and family and spending the duration with one's new colleagues."[73] Constituents and the media reporting them remained pretty far from the average member's daily concern. Former Speaker Sam Rayburn who served in the House from 1913 to 1961 reflected the more hierarchical chamber when he advised junior members that in order to "get along, one must go along."[74] A few decades later House Speaker Thomas P. (Tip) O'Neill (in Congress 1953–1987) handed out the political advice that "all politics is local," challenging his colleagues, at least on the Democratic side, to find ways to use the media to solidify their local political base.

By the 1970s the hierarchal structure of Congress had weakened, with challenges to the seniority system, reductions in the power of committee chairs, and government in sunshine rules that opened congressional committee proceedings giving the media direct access. More members of Congress could be called on to legitimately comment on more things. The rise of candidate-centered congressional campaigns drew more "entrepreneurial" candidates familiar with the value and use of media.[75] Presidential success in using the media to their benefit by the likes of Kennedy and Reagan spurred the congressional reaction to fight fire with fire.[76]

The motivation for change often involves running faster just to stay in place. As long as members of Congress reached their personal and political goals of promoting preferred policies and assuring job security, the good old ways were good enough. Getting elected and going to Washington once meant virtually disappearing until the next election cycle. As presidents began using new media approaches to their benefit, members of Congress turned to radio and then television to assure their role in the policy process. James Wilson, a political scientist, argued that "organizations come to resemble the organizations they are in conflict with."[77] The late Senator Daniel Patrick Moynihan (D-NY) referred to this as the "Iron Law of Emulation" asserting that "Whenever any branch of government acquires a new technique which enhances its power in relation to the other branches, that technique will soon be adopted by the other branches as well."[78] As the White House became more media savvy, hiring press secretaries, facilitating television coverage, and embarking on social media initiatives, members of Congress followed along for fear of being left behind. If imitation is the sincerest form of flattery, Congress attempts to outdo other news sources makes the White House and interest groups look good. The old stigma of being a "show horse," rather than a "work horse"[79] on Capitol Hill has largely disappeared as members realized that in order to get the work done they had to engage the power of the media.

The growing partisanship in Congress, the media, and the public is well documented and it has become a popular parlor and academic game to attribute blame, often in simplistic ways. Each player tends to eschew their role to quickly point fingers at the others. While the media serve as good whipping boys stirring up partisan feelings with the emergence of clearly ideological slants on cable (Fox News, MSNBC), broader studies tend to show that most media outlets are more centrist than the members of Congress they cover.[80] Pointing one's finger directly at the ideological histrionics of cable programs misses the point that the increase in partisanship began in the 1970s when cable penetration was low and ideological programming had yet to be produced.[81]

It is true that well-informed voters have become more partisan. These news junkies tend to gravitate to sources, especially on cable TV, with a clear ideological slant. Such ideological selectivity is less common on the Internet.[82] Recognizing an activist and ideological cohort of constituents may lead congressional candidates to cater to the interests of constituents more likely to follow congressional actions, contribute money, and vote. Although blaming the people seems premature. For one thing, polarization does not seem to have increased among the mass of voters. Second, voters seem to be reacting to the more partisan ways the parties have sorted themselves out and thus are able to offer voters a more coherent package of policies.[83] The realignment of the South almost erased the anomaly of many Democratic voters and office holders expressing more conservative views than comparable Republicans. The increased precision in redistricting through the use of computers and the court dictates to require population equality to trump traditional geographic boundaries freed politicians to draw district lines for partisan purposes.

Media reports of increased partisanship in Congress seem more to reflect the reality of congressional behavior than stories trumped up by the media. While the media do gravitate toward conflict, they need legitimate raw material with which to work. Media coverage may give the wheel another spin, but cannot legitimately be blamed for causing the entire cycle.

A key component of representative government lies in the relationship between the represented and the representative. Uninformed constituents lack the tools to communicate their interests and hold their representative accountable. Until relatively recently the cost and effort required to provide information relevant to groups of constituents with particular policy interests was relatively limited. Today "e-mail, the Internet, databases and other technologies make it faster, easier and less expensive to develop interactive, but manageable, relationships with constituents."[84]

Not only have the means of congressional communications changed, but also the format. Members of Congress once relied on slogans, graphics, and broadly structured rhetoric. Today it is feasible to focus more on "substance, cross-channel [multi-media platform], information on-demand and viral campaign [energized by constituents] ....to get a message delivered"[85] (see Chapter 11).

The Changing Media Messengers

Capitol Hill observers living through the last half century point out a significant change in media norms, strategies, and operations. After World War II, the Washington press corps was described as "rather sleepy" and "content to report from handouts and routine press briefings" provided by their "pals" in public office.[86] The "overprotective"[87] reporter has given way to a harder, tougher, and more cynical set of political actors.[88] Watching from the sidelines, many traditional journalists saw others advance their careers through hard-hitting investigative journalism. The upcoming generation of journalists accepted that role model more than that of a transmitter of press releases and protector of the powerful.

Congress is but one of the many government institutions the media are charged with monitoring. General trends in media coverage are quite likely to apply to Congress also. Through the use of content-analysis, Fink and Schnudson discovered five trends when comparing the 1950s to the 2000s:

- news stories have become more critical of established power;
- journalists have come to present themselves publicly as more aggressively challenging political leaders;
- news stories have grown longer;
- news stories now focus more on politics than on official actions of government, looking at the power plays and potential electoral consequences of various strategies; and
- news has grown more contextual, seeking out explanations of the longer- term causes and consequences of political behavior.[89]

The most dramatic change they found was the decline of "conventional stories" which report on the short-term official actions of government or government officials as one-time events ("The Minimum Wage Bill

Passed," "Senator Smith Retires," "The Tax Filibuster Was Broken").[90] Once the staple of political reporting, such descriptive stories are now matched (at about 45 percent of coverage each) by "contextual stories" which focus on the big picture, historical, patterns and/or trends ("Use of the Filibuster has Increased," "Federal Minimum Wage in Conflict with State Laws," "Vote in Congress Likely to Draw Presidential Veto"). In such reporting, congressional stories are linked to the actions of other political institutions and participants.

Increasingly observers of American media recognize that the era of "mass media" is past. The insistence on recognizing the term "media" as plural reflects the more basic truth that with the decline of the dominance of the major television networks and reduced reliance on newspapers, homogeneity of news created, transmitted, and received no longer represents reality.[91] The arrival of new media such as web pages, Facebook, YouTube, and Twitter (see Chapter 11) facilitated increased "narrowcasting" standing alongside traditional broadcasting as viable news and economic models.

Members of Congress contributed significantly to the new media environment and may well have been party to their own demise with their focus on the local media. During the heyday of true "mass" media coverage of politics (roughly the 1950s–1970s), a number of factors came together to encourage more extensive coverage of local members of Congress. First, the limited number of channels gave viewers few choices as to what to watch and local stations were widely watched, often as a prelude to the national news.[92] The impact of local news was enhanced by the technology requiring everyone choosing to watch the news to consume it at the same time, since the era of video recorders and on-demand viewing was more than a quarter century away. Government policy also played an important role. Laws passed by Congress and enforced by the Federal Communications Commission (FCC) required significant public service programming to maintain a station's license. Coverage of members of Congress produced by the station, or even produced directly by the member of Congress "could offer exactly what local stations wanted: cheap, professionally produced public affairs coverage with a local angle."[93] Many members simply went down to the House or Senate recording studios, provided at public expense, and created "Congressman X Speaks" or "Report to the District" segments that looked like news and simply found their way onto the air without journalistic comment or editing. By 1964, almost two-thirds of the members were taking advantage of the studios provided at taxpayer expense to develop regular programming to be sent via mail, or later beamed by satellite, back to their districts.

Two key characteristics of television are its limited demands on the viewer and the potential for unintentional reception of messages. Research shows that local television was a particularly important source of political news among the less educated segments of the population, decreasing "the gap between well and poorly informed news viewers by presenting political information in a form easily processed by those less educated and less interested."[94] Viewing local television news significantly increased knowledge and electoral support for incumbents, but not challengers.[95] The nature of coverage also affected member behavior, with more conservative media associated with members leaning in that direction in their votes.

The arrival of the Reagan administration, with its commitment to deregulation, dramatically limited the FCC's enforcement of the requirement of public affairs programming. While deregulation was a philosophical commitment, a strategic factor also crept into the calculation. Reagan's ascent to power coincided with the development of talk radio and the emergence of widespread adoption of cable television. With scarcity no longer serving as the universally accepted rationale for government monitoring, and conservatives' early domination of talk radio, Reagan's backers saw little danger in allowing a free market to reign in the distribution of news. In the process local stations no longer lived under the requirement of required coverage of their member of Congress.

Economic pressures as we approached the 2000s shifted significant attention away from local coverage of individual members of Congress. With increasing financial challenges, the cost of locating a local reporter in Washington factored more prominently in newspaper budgets. At the same time, more and more newspapers became part of national chains and economies of scale suggested that the Washington reporter for a chain should focus on general stories about Congress and not tie them to the local members their paper media market encompassed.

Both Congress and the media have changed in recent years and with it the public conversation about Congress and its members. Upcoming chapters will discuss both the changes and the current situation both in general and associated with various players both in the media and Congress.

Notes

1 Markus Prior, *Post-Broadcast Democracy*, New York, NY: Cambridge University Press, 2007.
2 Ross Baker, "Congress – Boom Box and Black Box," *Media Studies Journal*, vol. 10, no. 1, 1996, p. 7.
3 Timothy E. Cook, "The News Media as a Political Institution: Looking Backward and Looking Forward," *Political Communication*, vol. 23, no. 2, 2006, p. 161.
4 Ronald Elving, "Brighter Lights, Wider Windows: Presenting Congress in the 1990's," in Thomas E. Mann and Norman J. Ornstein (eds.), *Congress, the Press, and the Public*, Washington, D.C.: American Enterprise Institute and The Brookings Institution, 1994, p. 173.

5 R. Douglas Arnold, *Congress, the Press, and Political Accountability*, New York, NY: Princeton University Press, 2004, p. 7.

6 See Matthew McCubbins and Thomas Schwartz, "Congressional Oversight Overlooked, Police Patrols Versus Fire Alarms," *American Journal of Political Science*, vol. 28, 1984, pp. 165–179.

7 Arnold, p. 252.

8 Gary C. Jacobson, *The Politics of Congressional Elections*, New York, NY: Parson/Longman, 2009, pp. 123–124. See also Matthew Wilson and Paul Gronke, "Concordance and Projection in Citizen Perception of Congressional Roll-Call Voting," *Legislative Studies Quarterly*, vol. 25, 2000, p. 445.

9 Ibid., p. 123.

10 Mark J. Rozell and Richard J. Semiatin, "Congress and the News Media," in Mark J. Rozell and Jeremy Mayer (eds.), *Media Power and Politics*, Lanham, MD: Rowman and Littlefield Publishers, 2008, p. 58.

11 Jason Barabas, William Pollock, and Joseph Wachtel, "Informed Consent, Roll-Call Knowledge, Mass Media, and Political Representation," paper presented at the 2011 Annual Meeting of the American Political Science Association, p. 31.

12 Kathy Goldschmidt and Leslie Ochreiter, *Communicating with Congress: How the Internet Has Changed Citizen Engagement*, Washington, D.C.: Congressional Management Foundation, 2008, p. 44.

13 See Barbara Sinclair, *Unorthodox Lawmaking*, Washington, D.C.: Congressional Quarterly Press, 2000.

14 See www.nationalreview.com/article/369560/governing-pen-and-phone-victor-davis-hanson and http://online.wsj.com/news/articles/SB10001424052 702303553204579349203326044972

15 Larry O'Brien, *No Final Victories*, New York, NY: Ballantine Books, 1975.

16 Karen M. Kedrowski, *Media Entrepreneurs and the Media Enterprise in the Congress*, Creskill, NJ: Hampton Press, 1996, p. 103.

17 Patrick Sellers, *Cycles of Spin: Strategic Communication in the United States Congress*, New York, NY: Cambridge University Press, 2010, p. 4.

18 E. E. Schattschneider, *The Semisovereign People*, New York, NY: Holt Rinehart and Winston, 1960.

19 See Sellers, p. 154.

20 Gary Lee Malecha and Daniel J. Reagan, *The Public Congress*, New York, NY: Routledge, 2012, p, 10.

21 John Kingdon, *Agendas, Alternatives, and Public Policies*, New York, NY: Longman Press, 2003, p. 60.

22 Malecha and Reagan, p. 15.

23 Author's interview with a member of Congress.

24 James A. Stimson, Michael B. Makuen, and Robert S. Erickson, "Dynamic Representation," *The American Political Science Review*, vol. 89, no. 3, 1995, p. 545.

25 Philip Habel, "Whose Opinions Matter? An Analysis of References to Editorial and Opinion Columns in Congress," paper presented at the 2009 annual meeting of the Midwest Political Science Association, p. 5.

26 Ibid., p. 15.

27 Ibid., p. 12.

28 Stimson et al., pp. 545 and 560.

29 Author's interviews.

30 Brendan Nyhan, "Scandal Potential: How Political Context and News Congestion Affect the President's Vulnerability to Media Scandal," *British*

Journal of Political Science, forthcoming, available at: www.dartmouth. edu/~nyhan/scandal-potential.pdf

31 Elaine Povich, *Partners and Adversaries*, Arlington, VA: The Freedom Forum, 1996, p. xii.

32 Quoted in ibid., p. 6.

33 Tom Allen, *Dangerous Convictions*, New York, NY: Oxford University Press, 2013, p. 197.

34 Povich, p. 55.

35 Sellers, p. 207.

36 "Quotation of the Day," *New York Times*, December 9, 1986, p. A13.

37 Peverill Squire, "Who Gets National News Coverage in the U.S. Senate," *American Politics Research*, vol. 16, no. 139, 1988, p. 150.

38 www.nytimes.com/2010/02/09/us/politics/09murtha.html? pagewanted=all&_r=0

39 Squire, p. 151.

40 Brian Fogarty, "The Strategy of the Story: Media Monitoring and Legislative Activity," *Legislative Studies Quarterly*, vol. 33, no. 3, 2008, pp. 448 and 451.

41 Larry Sabato, *Feeding Frenzy: How Attack Journalism Has Transformed American Politics*, New York, NY: Free Press, 1991.

42 John R. Hibbing and Elizabeth Thiess-Morse, *Congress as Public Enemy: Public Attitudes Toward American Political Institutions*, Cambridge: Cambridge University Press, 1995.

43 See William Saffire, "The MEGO News Era," *Washington Star*, September 6, 1973, p. A15.

44 Nyhan, p. 5.

45 Robert M. Entman, *Projections of Power: Framing News, Public Opinion and U.S. Foreign Policy*, Chicago, IL: University of Chicago Press, 2004, pp. 292–293 and Brian J. Fogarty, "Scandals, News Coverage, and the 2006 Congressional Elections," *Political Communication*, 2013, available at: www. tandfonline.com/doi/abs/10.1080/10584609.2012.737431#.Utw2TBAo7IU

46 Jonathan S. Morris and Rosalee A. Clawson, "Media Coverage of Congress in the 1990s: Scandals, Personalities, and the Prevalence of Policy and Process," *Political Communication*, vol. 22, no. 3, pp. 297–313.

47 Ibid., p. 307.

48 Rozell and Semiatin, p. 46.

49 Roger H. Davidson et al., *Congress and Its Members*, Washington, D.C.: Congressional Quarterly Press, 2014, p. 12.

50 Thomas E. Mann and Norman J. Ornstein, *Congress, the Press, and the Public*, Washington, D.C.: American Enterprise Institute, 1992, p.1.

51 Robert E. Gilbert, "President Versus Congress: The Struggle for Public Attention," *Congress and the Presidency*, vol. 16 (Autumn) 1989, p. 99.

52 Norman Ornstein, "What TV News Doesn't Report About Congress and Should," *TV Guide*, October 21, 1989, p. 11.

53 Stanley Cloud, "Bums of the Year," *Time*, January 6, 1992, p. 48.

54 Tom Kenworthy, "Keep the Bums In," *Washington Post*, April 26, 1992, p. C5.

55 David Broder, "House at Play," *Washington Post*, March 17, 1992, p. A17.

56 David Broder, "Yes There Are Good People in Congress," *Washington Post*, November 6, 1991, p. 25.

57 Both books by P. J. O'Rourke, *Parliament of Whores*, New York, NY: Grove/ Atlantic Monthly Press, 2003, and *Don't Vote It Just Encourages the Bastards*, New York, NY: Grove/Atlantic Monthly Press, 2010.

58 Broder, 1991, p. A16.

59 Mark J. Rozell, "Press Coverage of Congress, 1946–92," in Thomas E. Mann and Norman J. Ornstein (eds.), *Congress, the Press, and the Public*, Washington, D.C.: American Enterprise Institute and The Brookings Institution, 1994, pp. 59 and 102.
60 Carl Session quoted in Povich, p. 60.
61 Journalist Carl Leubsdorf quoted in Povich, p. 23.
62 Povich, p. 23.
63 Jonathan Ladd, "Attitudes Toward the News Media and Political Competition in America," doctoral dissertation, Princeton University, 2006, p. 211.
64 Ibid., p. 211.
65 Povich, p. 49.
66 www.mrmediatraining.com/tag/ray-donovan/
67 Mann and Ornstein, p. 3.
68 Herb Asher and Mike Barr, "Popular Support for Congress and Its Members," in Thomas E. Mann and Norman J. Ornstein, *Congress, the Press, and the Public*, Washington, D.C.: American Enterprise Institute, 1992, p. 36.
69 David Paletz, *The Media in American Politics*, New York, NY: Longman Publishers, 2002, p. 244.
70 Brian F. Schaffner and Patrick J. Sellers, "The Structure and Determinants of Local Congressional News Coverage," *Political Communication*, vol. 20, no. 1, 2003, p. 42.
71 Ibid., p. 42.
72 Malecha and Reagan, pp. 144–145.
73 Author's interview.
74 www.nytimes.com/learning/general/onthisday/bday/0106.html
75 Malecha and Reagan, p. 39.
76 Malecha and Reagan, p. 41.
77 Doris Grader (ed.), *Media Power and Politics*, Washington, D.C.: Congressional Quarterly Press, 2007, p. 263.
78 Daniel Patrick Moynihan, *Counting Our Blessings: Reflections on the Future of America*, Boston: Little Brown, 1980, pp. 117–118.
79 See John R. Hibbing and Sue Thomas, "The Modern United States Senate: What Is Accorded Respect," *Journal of Politics*, vol. 52, 1990.
80 Markus Prior, "Media and Political Polarization," *Annual Review of Political Science*, February, 2013, p. 103.
81 Ibid., p. 107.
82 Ibid., p. 122.
83 Ibid., p. 107.
84 Brad Fitch and Kathy Goldschmidt, "Communicating with Congress: How Capitol Hill Is Coping with the Surge of Citizen Advocacy," Washington, D.C.: Congressional Management Foundation, 2005, p. 45.
85 Ibid., p. 45.
86 Larry Sabato, *Feeding Frenzy: How Attack Journalism Has Transformed American Politics*, New York, NY: Free Press, 1991, p. 31.
87 D. R. Matthews, *U.S. Senators and Their World*, New York, NY: Vantage Books, 1960, p. 207.
88 M. J. Robinson, "Three Faces of Congressional Media," in Thomas E. Mann and Norman J. Ornstein (eds.), *The New Congress*, Washington, D.C.: American Enterprise Institute, 1981, p. 55.
89 Katherine Fink and Michael Schudson, "The Rise of Contextual Journalism, 1950s–2000s," *Journalism*, 2013, pp. 3–6.
90 See ibid., pp. 8 and 11.

91 See Cook, p. 164.
92 Markus Prior, "The Incumbent in the Living Room: The Rise of Television and the Incumbency Advantage in U.S. House Elections," *The Journal of Politics*, vol. 68, no. 3, 2006, p. 658.
93 Ibid., p. 658.
94 Ibid., p. 659.
95 Ibid., pp. 662 and 664.

Chapter 2

The Love/Hate Relationship

The Media Approach Congress

> Whenever the people are well-informed, they can be trusted with their own government.
>
> Thomas Jefferson

> Knowledge will forever govern ignorance; and a people who mean to be their own governors must arm themselves with the power which knowledge gives.
>
> James Madison

Although hard to imagine from our current vantage point, "the Constitution included no presumption that legislative activities should be open to the press."[1] Members of the Constitutional Convention recognized the difficulty of making decisions under watchful eyes and closed their doors to the public and the press. James Madison did take notes, but refused to publish them until after the death of all participants.[2] Since early newspapers were largely partisan organs, the fear of inflaming public opinion was legitimate.

Despite the Founders' call for a well-informed populace, the ability to monitor the congressional branch exhibited a rocky start. After keeping the public out of the Constitutional Convention, Representative Aedanus Burke of South Carolina introduced a resolution banning reporters from covering House procedures only one day after the House had passed the First Amendment guaranteeing freedom of the press. Although the resolution failed, its intention caught the fancy of the Senate which forbade reporters until 1795.[3] Whereas the House accepted the principle of meetings with journalists in attendance from the beginning.

When the Capitol was built, special seats in the House and Senate chambers were created for legitimate members of the press. Sitting above and behind the presiding officer, they had an unrestricted view of the members speaking and were granted by the rules of the chamber, the right to take notes during debate, a privilege denied to the general public sitting in the other galleries. From early on, the House and Senate press galleries served as locations for members of Congress and the press to interact. The galleries now host press conferences and members (or their staffs) drop off press releases.[4] The growth of the Washington press corps required increased regulation of access.

Who Gets Seats in the Gallery?

The first formal "Reporter's Gallery" emerged in the Senate in 1841 in the hopes that certified reporters would present a more responsible image of the Senate. Congress turned over the control of the galleries to members of the press themselves resulting in rules for both chambers forbidding the media from lobbying (or serving as "claims agents" as they were once called)[5] and granting the Executive Committee of the Periodical Correspondents' Association (made up of journalists elected by their peers) the right to control access to the galleries. A journalist applying for admission must be a "bona fide resident correspondent of reputable standing ....employed by a regularly published periodical ... owned and operated independently of any government, industry, institution, association or lobbying organization ... [and] published for profit."[6] Although each chamber reserves the right to refuse the recommendations of the Executive Committee, they have never done so.

Membership in the gallery provides a number of benefits such as a seat in the press gallery, support facilities (telephones, typewriters, computers, etc.), staff support, access to the House Speaker's Lobby and Senate President's Room in which to seek and conduct interviews, and access to press conferences by House and Senate leaders.[7]

Once one has reached a certain status in life, it is common to "pull up the drawbridge behind them." Well-established immigrant groups often become some of the harshest critics of granting opportunities to the next wave of immigrants. Academics promoted to higher ranks often attempt to impose stricter standards than they could meet on those following them. The same is true of the media. Until the 1930s, the print journalists who dominated the Committee of Correspondents refused to accept their colleagues in radio.[8] Relations between electronic and print journalists reflected competition for sources and seats in the various hearing rooms. Old-time print reporters "fought grimly to defend the little plots of table on which they scribbled,"[9] (notice the negative connotation of "scribble" versus "wrote" or "analyzed") and begrudged the space taken up by television cameras. In an "if you can't join them, fight them mode," Congress created a Radio Gallery in each house in 1939, later repurposed as the Radio-TV galleries. Congress also established a Periodical Press Gallery for magazine and newsletter writers, and a Senate Press Photographers' Gallery. Non-profit news organizations were excluded until 1979.

NUMBER

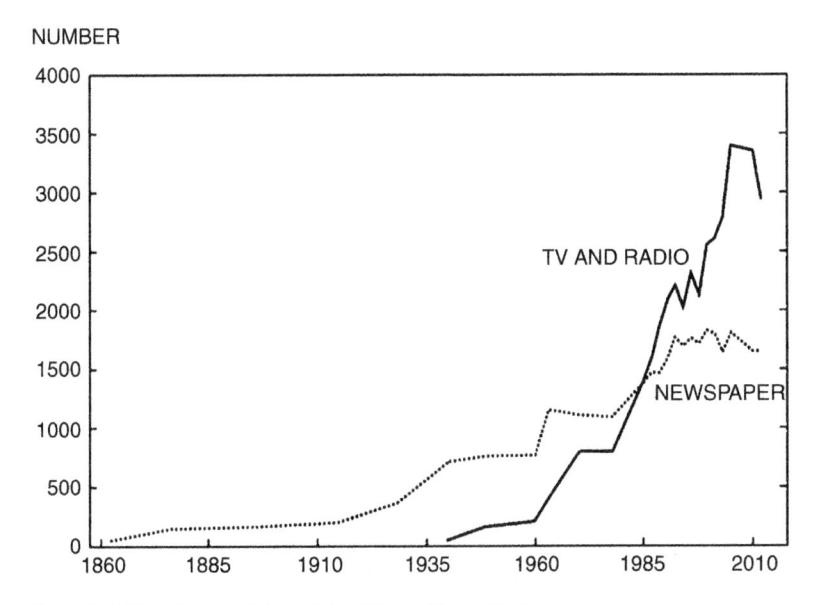

Figure 2.1 The Composition of the House Press Gallery

Interest in Congress by various media reflected changing media dominance. As television became the medium of choice for most Americans by the 1970s the composition of the congressional press gallery shifted. By the 1980s the congressional radio and television press gallery membership tripled, matching parity with the newspaper gallery (see Figure 2.1).[10]

Other restrictions have been used to thin the ranks of those not perceived as professional journalists. The "old boys club" nature of Capitol Hill as a whole emerges dramatically when one realizes that women and minorities were not allowed full membership in the galleries until the 1940s. Gallery members knew they had a good thing going and did not want to share it. As rejected applicants went to the courts for redress, their cases were largely ruled "non-judiciable," meaning the policy involves a political policy issue, not a constitutional right.[11] In 1999, the press chief of the American Baptist Convention was denied a place in the gallery, with the committee arguing that it was not an independent news service.[12] In order to be validated, the committee requires that reporters be paid and work full time for a commercial media enterprise.[13]

Changing technology continues to redefine "journalists" and to challenge access to the press galleries. After some controversy, full-time bloggers gained admission to the House and Senate galleries in the 1990s. Control by the print and legacy electronic media continues. Of the over five hundred members of the Periodical Press Gallery today, only a handful represent purely online news outlets.[14] In order to qualify, an online reporter must make their living primarily from journalism and not be associated with a lobbying organization, as well as fulfilling all the other requirements. Since many online journalists are part time or work for non-profits, they simply do not apply for membership. The committee seldom turns anyone down, but the rules and 6–8 month time for applications to be approved have a chilling effect on online reporters.[15] Online and other representatives of new media outlets face a number of difficulties in gaining accreditation. Often they are not making a profit at the beginning and can be excluded for that reason.[16]

The Challenges of the Congressional Storyline

Don Hewitt, legendary CBS producer, titled his memoir, *Tell Me a Story*,[17] and revealed the basic goal of a journalist. "Good stories" have a number of important characteristics. They have a clear beginning (the context), a middle (a relevant conflict between individuals, institutions, or ideas that need to be handled), and an end (the outcome and its consequences). Interesting stories have clear heroes and villains working their way through a significant conflict. Many congressional stories are just too complex for the average consumer – and actually for many journalists. Congress appears like a "black box, in which invisible wheels, cogs, gears and semiconductors whir away unseen and uncomprehended."[18] Stories emanating from Congress often involve "too many players, too many stages, and no single hero."[19] When journalists try to simplify the story, they often get it wrong (see Box 2.1).

Box 2.1 When the Media Got it Wrong: House "Bank Scandal" Versus the Savings and Loan Scandal

It wasn't a bank and nobody lost any money, but that is not how the story was told.

Like many Americans members of Congress are eligible to deposit their funds into a credit union at their place of work. Most credit unions provide overdraft protection, allowing members to write checks for more than the amount in their account with the amount of the overdraft turning into a loan requiring repayment with interest. When news emerged that a number of members of Congress had overdrawn their accounts in this way, a furor erupted about special treatment and the assertion that "How can those responsible for the economic well-being of the national budget not handle their own finances more effectively?" A tug-of-war with the media over releasing the names dominated the headlines. Members with large numbers of overdrafts were pilloried in the press. Even though all the overdrafts were eventually paid with interest, many of those "outed" lost in the next election. For the average constituent familiar with checks and overdrafts it was a simple story of personal incompetence and perhaps moral failure. The "bank" story greatly overshadowed the savings and loan scandal occurring about the same time and having much more real impact on the public. The stakes in the savings and loan scandal were high and the cost to the American taxpayer enormous, but the story almost never got told, and when it did, the most important factors were left by the wayside.

When Congress deregulated the savings and loan industry in the 1980s the new rules and regulations were so complex that most journalists backed away from doing stories on them.[a] Even though improper actions by savings and loan officials cost taxpayers billions of dollars, the media took little interest until it became clear that some members of the Senate had received significant campaign contributions from savings and loan officials. Now there was a storyline with the American public (the good guys) being cheated by the senators and bank officials (the bad guys). Investigation of the big recipients (the "Keating Five") resulted in a mixed result with two senators exonerated (Glenn [D-OH] and McCain [R-AZ]), two members criticized for acting improperly (Riegle [D-MI] and DeConcini [D-AZ]), and one reprimanded (Cranston [D-CA]). Without a "slam dunk" conclusion, the story became muddied. Little was done to analyze the policy involved.

[a] See Julian Zelizer, *On Capitol Hill: The Struggle to Reform Congress and its Consequences, 1948–2000*, New York, NY: Cambridge University Press, 2004, p. 223.

News stories are usually told through a series of events, but as former Congressman Bill Frenzel (R-MN) lamented, "The press thinks it can only report events. Congress is not an event, it is a process."[20] A veteran Capitol Hill reporter chimed in that her editor says, "Tell me when Congress is going to do something." The editor wants "final action. And that isn't what Congress is about. Congress is about process."[21] To make things worse, Congress is composed of hundreds of processes occurring simultaneously.

Journalists confront the decision of which processes to cover and when to cut into the stream of actions. On Capitol Hill, the process begins with the introduction of bills, most of which face the prospect of no significant action. To give full coverage of the process one would have to trace the filing of a bill back to the constituent letter, interest group request, campaign promise, or appeal from another politician to pursue that policy initiative. With numerous bills competing for action, betting on the wrong bill for one's process analysis leads to numerous dead ends. Waiting for some action before covering a piece of legislation requires determining the threshold for significance. Is passage in the sub-committee of one house enough? Should one wait for full committee action, or even a vote on the floor? Once committed to covering the processing of a bill, the journalist must decide how much background and context are necessary for the reader to understand what is going on. Ideally interested voters need "heads up" information so they might have a chance to affect the outcome. If the coverage of the bill comes too late it makes citizen involvement in the legislative process a moot point. Presenting Congress actions as a series of done deals can do little to motivate those intended to be represented to make their voice heard.

Too Many Bit Players

The Congress beat is a tough one. While there are many people ready to talk relatively few are relevant to specific reporters, and many reporters are not relevant to specific members of Congress. Both congressional districts and most media markets are geographically defined, but the boundaries of districts and media markets often fail to coincide. The people a member wants to talk to may be spread across a number of media markets, or he or she may be in competition with a number of other members of Congress whose constituents live in the same media market. It is the rare member of Congress with enough power, expertise, or notoriety to capture the attention of the national media or a wide variety of markets outside of his or her district.

As will be discussed more in Chapter 4, a spate of studies point out the tendency of reporters to focus on formal chamber leaders[22] although some find that in the age of senators as "policy entrepreneurs" that tendency has declined, at least for the Senate.[23] The pattern of focusing on formal leaders crosses the boundaries of various media and formats (network news, interview programs, and newspapers) and remains true across all time periods studied.[24]

The Difficulty of Seeing the Big Picture

A reasonable case could be made that journalists tend both to overgeneralize and undergeneralize. On the one hand they want to reveal a coordinated entity with abiding characteristics (such as partisanship, parochialism, etc.) while most insiders recognize that there is no such thing as "The U.S. Congress" taking action. It is tempting but anthropomorphic to portray Congress as a unified entity able to do anything on its own. Congress is a collection of 535 individuals who join together in shifting coalitions to pass, delay, or block legislation. Each time a journalist expresses a comment that "today Congress ..." they are looking at a different entity. While it is possible to make generalizations about the House and Senate as political actors (partisanship, personal motivations, etc.) there are usually a number of exceptions to the rule. Since news is often defined as exceptions, journalists often gravitate to the exceptions; who failed to vote with their party, whose dramatic floor speech seemed to sway votes, whose behavior seemed inappropriate.

On the other hand, after each election, the demographics stories tend to focus on women, gays, Muslims, and other minorities in Congress. When Senator Frank Lautenberg (D-NJ) died, many of the stories focused on the fact that he was the last World War II veteran in the Congress. While such stories indirectly tell us something about the individual members of Congress, they tend to divert attention and understanding of the full institution.

What You Don't See, You Don't Tell

> Sometimes the most important thing about Congress is what they're *not* doing.[25]

Non-decisions, or the inability to get an item on the policy agenda, significantly affect society, but often fly under the radar. Additionally perfect coverage would give the public a clear idea of the actual consequences of proposed legislation. In the legislative process, though, much of the controversy surrounds not only what the government should be doing, but also alternative guesses as to the consequences of various means. Even if members of Congress agree on an end goal – a rare phenomenon – projecting consequences remains the realm of presumptions and beliefs, not universally accepted formulas. Journalists who jump into the quagmire of making projections open themselves to being seen as favoring one side and/or losing legitimacy when the intended outcome falls short of the projections.

Media in America have become increasingly more visual with the ability to transmit photographs to the printed media, the arrival of television, and now the availability of aggregating sites such as YouTube. Congress suffers in comparison to the executive branch since much of its important behavior remains difficult to capture visually. Congress is a multi-ring "circus" with a series of processes playing out simultaneously, filled with long periods of boring sequences. Actions, such as considering a budget, are long-term processes filled with confusing language and numbers.[26] Presidents, on the other hand, offer discrete events, such as bill signing ceremonies whose content can be understood in a static photograph or brief video clip.

The Remaining Allure

Despite the challenges and frustrations, many journalists like the Capitol Hill beat, "where appointments were unnecessary and where reporters could see the most important members every day." *Wall*

Street Journal's Al Hunt described it as "the greatest beat in town," although some of his access came from the prominence of the paper he represented.[27]

Journalists are from Mars and Members of Congress are from Venus: The Role of the Journalist

To some degree, members of Congress and the journalists who cover them come from different worlds in terms of career paths, perceived roles, and professional demands. To add complexity, journalistic norms and practices have changed over time and across media outlets. There is little consensus either within the journalism community or among members of Congress as to how journalists should go about their jobs. Each reporting approach has its strong advocates and practitioners.

The Partisan Mouthpiece

In the early days of the Republic, newspapers were closely aligned with specific political parties and reinforced the party message. The need to expand audiences and not offend potential consumers of the products of their advertisers, who increasingly funded their operations, led to attempts at objectivity from the later nineteenth until the end of the twentieth century.

The twenty-first century emerged with a resurgence of islands of more partisan media as a number of media outlets saw a market for covering politics with a point of view. Eschewing the "myth" of objectivity and seeing an economic market for allegedly "fair and balanced" news to counteract perceived biases in the rest of the media, some media outlets unabashedly provide "news coverage [that] factors one side in a debate, regardless of underlying events, issue details, or promotional efforts."[28] Building on public perception of the media as liberally biased, Fox News created an economically effective conservative alternative with wide appeal to conservative voters. At the same time, MSNBC more clearly staked out its place among liberal views. Similar ideological and partisan preferences emerged on talk radio, websites, and blogs. Studies of the reality of a consistently liberal bias represented in actual reporting "suggest that the news media do not consistently give one party more extensive or favorable coverage."[29] Even if that is true, Fox News and other more partisan sources have found a lucrative niche market to counter an ideological ogre which may or may not exist.

The Mirroring of Events

In the attempt to avoid bias, some journalists limit their efforts by simply reporting the facts. Serving largely as a stenographer, this approach tasks the journalist with the role of faithfully reporting what politicians say. Providing the audience with honest and objective facts about an event is important. Although more constrained than other approaches, the journalists still retain the power to choose which events to cover, who to interview, and which official sources to highlight.[30] Mirrored stories are not necessarily politically balanced. Those members of Congress who work harder to get their message out have the potential for dominating the dialogue since they show up at more events and speak with multiple voices.

In the early Congresses, the ideal of "faithful reporting" was seen as both possible and amenable to legislative control. In 1814, there was an unsuccessful campaign to require reporters to take an accuracy oath. An 1820 effort proposed that reporters swear to report debates "without addition, diminution or alteration."[31]

While the Joe Friday's "just the facts Ma'am" approach on the 1960s television drama "Dragnet"[32] seems like a guiding principle for objective journalism, it fails to take into account personal biases and the desire to infuse interest into a potentially dull story. "Framing" involves selecting particular aspects of a story on which to focus, classifying a story into a particular category, and/or summarizing the basic ideas of a story through the choice of words. Looking at the budget battle by focusing on statements by members of Congress and the president (leaving out many other players), looking at it as an example of conflict, and using the term "gridlock" each leave a different impression than would emerge from a different set of frames.

The Balancing Game

Playing more the role of a referee, another media approach involves journalists independently framing their stories "to give equal attention to competing messages, regardless of the frequency of promotion."[33] Journalists taking this approach retain the ability to determine what balanced coverage would look like and spend considerable time ferreting out competing viewpoints in hopes that all perspectives enter the public dialogue.

The pro-con form of reporting takes on a Hegelian "thesis/antithesis" view of the world assumption that all issues have two sides and that each position is equally valid.[34] Many issues facing Congress have more than two sides. Even when it comes down to a pro/con vote, the basis for support or opposition can vary significantly. Votes on omnibus legislation including a variety of non-related topics can't be explained by simply asserting that one "package" received total agreement and one was rejected. On omnibus bills, members must take an "on balance" approach arguing that one bill includes more positives than negatives.

In a similar vein, politics often makes strange bedfellows. When President Obama sought congressional support for intervention in Syria, his opposition came from liberal Democrats who felt he was going too far and conservative Republicans who felt he was not going far enough. They were joined by isolationists who wanted America to focus more on its internal problems and those who felt U.S. restraint would make us a better moral example for peace and strengthen our international position. Support came from an equally diverse group. Choosing which side to present gave the media significant power and a real challenge.

Civic Journalism

A more recent role adopted by some media outlets suggests that the media are part of American society, not simply observers viewing its successes and failures from the outside. In this view, the media have a responsibility to improve the political process by encouraging citizen participation, inserting new issues into the public dialogue, and moving the policy process along. Journalists committed to civic journalism convene policy summits, facilitate voter registration, carry out polls about policy preferences, and chide citizens to get involved. Journalists opposing such strategies express the fear that by becoming part of the story, journalists give up their more important roles as honest information brokers and potentially undermine their status as objective observers.

The drive toward civic journalism is based, at least partially, on the fact that journalists get into the profession believing that they can make a difference. Americans are socialized into the "can do" perspective implying that all problems are solvable. That is what Americans do; we solve problems. The media often reinforce this view. In reality there may well be some insolvable problems, or "solutions" that grossly offend some members of the polity. In participating and then criticizing the policy process, the media may well reinforce the pipe dream of easily solvable problems when they publicize the solutions, and then wait on the sidelines for alternative solutions to be shot down.[35] The media seem to increase the amplitude of raised expectations and dashed hopes, leaving the public feeling like it is riding a roller coaster. Some proposed "solutions" ought to be left on the editor's desk or filed in the circular file and taken out with the garbage.

Charges of Media Bias?

The concept of media bias presents a difficult definitional and operational challenge. From a definitional perspective bias is not simply saying something positive or negative about a person, idea, or institution. Bias involves transmitting an unrealistic representation of reality. If a member of Congress does five things right and one thing wrong, only reporting the right things is just as biased as just reporting the wrong thing. The problem for the journalist arises from the common definition of news as something out of the ordinary. If the media only report on what is out of the ordinary, they by definition fail to objectively represent reality. The "ordinariness" of reporting the ordinary makes it a poor target for news. The greatest problem for a polity is when undesirable activity increases to the point of challenging the dominance of ordinary good behavior, or when good behavior becomes out of the ordinary.

Perhaps the best we can hope for is that reporting of the atypical is fairly applied to all participants. Bias is more obvious when some members get coverage while others in similar situations are bypassed. If only the missteps of Republicans are reported while Democrats performing similar actions are bypassed, bias has occurred. If only liberals get descriptors like "ultra" before their names, while conservatives just as far out of the mainstream of their party lack such labels, bias is in play.

Much research on journalists reveals the degree to which their personal political preferences identify them as very different from the public as a whole. It is very easy to slip to the conclusion that their personal preferences lead them to report in a biased manner. That may be the case, but other factors may come into play. Professional norms of objectivity could well overwhelm personal preferences. Screening by editors often tempers bias.

Two kinds of bias stand out. "Structural bias" arises from the unintentional aspects of the situation at hand. The smaller membership of the Senate makes it likely that more of its members will be known by the public, thus making them viable "news hooks" on which to hang a story. The rules of Congress giving the majority party more public tasks (convening committee meetings, presenting legislation on the floor, presiding over the chamber) attract more media attention to their actions. Leaders of the president's party often find themselves called on to "carry water" for the president by introducing his preferred legislation and shepherding it through the legislative process, gaining visibility as the president's surrogates.

"Intentional bias" stems from the deliberate attempt to tell a story in a particular way. A journalist may want to help or hurt a particular politician or cause, selecting facts or making assumptions to accomplish that end. To the degree that such stories fail to reflect reality, the public is cheated out of a fair reflection of the person or issue. Not all intentional bias is unwarranted. Reporters for local newspapers or televisions stations focus their stories on the member from that district, knowing that is what their editor and audiences want and expect. If "a national reporter sees a plane crash into the Washington Monuments [he] asks, 'How many died?' A regional reporter asks, 'Was there anybody on the plane from

Ohio?' "[36] A reporter assigned to cover the economic implications of congressional action will focus his or her efforts on particular committees and bills, while ignoring many other important things going on.

The Decline of the "Buddy" System

We often forget that Congress is a human institution in which friendships and personal favors mean a lot. Finding a way to help a journalist may buy a member of Congress positive coverage on an issue about which they are concerned. As emerges in many parts of life, what goes around comes around. Reciprocity remains the default position in most human relationships. Reporters admit giving members who cooperate with them better coverage. As one reporter who moved from a local to national position put it, "The ones who were nice to me when I was a regional reporter tend to be quoted more often now that I have an opportunity to pick the ones I want to talk to."[37]

Despite the goals of objective reporting, journalists and members of Congress are human beings who develop personal relationships. As one Washington bureau journalist argued, members of the media and of Congress developed positive relationships "in direct ratio to their intimacy."[38] Journalists and editors practicing "cozy coverage of Congress"[39] often gave their local member a pass on criticism because they knew them, while journalists and editors viewing Congress as a whole from a distance took the institution and its other members to task in a case where "unfamiliarity breeds contempt."[40]

For much of our history, journalists and politicians enjoyed a much cozier relationship. In the early years of the union, the partisan press boosted the political fortunes of the politicians of their favored party and denigrated those from the opposition. Even when economic considerations and accompanying professional journalistic norms encouraged objectivity, journalists tended to grant politicians a wide zone of personal privacy when observing misbehavior was not deemed important to the legislative process. To a large degree, journalists erred on the side of not reporting embarrassing activity. Until the 1970s virtually every journalist kept a list of who drank too much, who was sleeping with whom, and who gained personal benefit from specific legislation. There was an "unwritten rule in Washington reporting in those days that if he is a drunk and it doesn't affect his duty on the floor of the House or sitting on a congressional committee, it's nobody's business but his own."[41] A similar rule applied to sexual dalliances, gender definitions, and other "improprieties." A key manifestation of the coziness between journalists and their congressional subjects is a highly sought after invitation to the elite Gridiron Club dinner, a social event open to Washington's top journalists. An invitation indicates one has "arrived" (see Box 2.2).

Box 2.2 Out of the Frying Pan

No event better represents the clubbiness of the denizens of Capitol Hill – reporters and members of Congress alike – than the annual Gridiron Club dinner. This closed event allows invited politicians and journalists alike to blow off some steam with silly songs and skits. Media outlets favor particular politicians with seats at "their" table, seating them between top reporters and celebrities.

The vestiges of segregation and sexism hung on at the dinner well after the issues moved toward settlements in the rest of society, yet neither politicians nor journalists were quick to blow the whistle. Until 1972 women were not even allowed to attend as guests. The first black reporter, Carl Rowan, gained admittance in 1973. It was not until 1975 that the "old boys club" admitted women reporters into the fold as full-fledged members. Despite entreaties from some in the media, the dinner remains an off-the-record display of satire and funny costumes, although many of the one-liners by presidents, members of Congress, and the media eventually find their way into the news. For example:

Reading a mock telegram from his father in 1958, Senator John Kennedy reported his father saying, "Dear Jack. Don't buy a single vote more than is necessary. I'm damned if I'm going to pay for a landslide."[a]
In 2006, then Senator Barack Obama sang "If I Only Had McCain" to the tune of "If I Only Had a Brain" from the *Wizard of Oz*.[a]
At the 2011 dinner a group of "fake" Republican congressional leaders sang the following, to the tune of "Rock Around the Clock":
We're gonna move Obama to the right
We're gonna mock mock mock his election fight
We're gonna talk, gonna talk, and then we might indict![b]

While no one expects the congressional and journalistic denizens of Capitol Hill to live parallel or disconnected existences, the image of the two sharing insider jokes at a closed session begs the question of whether either or both are negatively "known by the company they keep."

Sources:
[a] John Hayden, "The List: The Funniest Moments from the Gridiron Club Dinner," *Washington Times*, March 5, 2011.
[b] Elspeth Reeve, *National Journal*, www.nationaljournal.com/dailyfray/jokes-from-the-gridiron-club-39-s-annual-dinner-20110314

Beginning in the 1970s, an increasingly larger portion of the media entered an era of professional introspection, perhaps recognizing that their decline in public respect along with declining audiences and readers may well have developed from the view that the media were part of the problem in American politics and not part of the solution. Fellow journalist Ben Bagdikian's description of congressional reporters as "partners in propaganda,"[42] added to the litany of complaints of journalists described as "propaganda arms," "conspirators," "mouthpieces," or unfettered "bulletin boards"[43] for legislators whose goals and interests diverge from the goal of presenting the unvarnished truth.

Although not the beginning of investigative journalism, the Watergate scandal presented a significant challenge to traditional journalists. In front of their eyes, two very junior reporters (Bob Woodward and Carl Bernstein) took on the President of the United States, helped build the case that brought him down, garnered a Pulitzer prize and dramatically improved their career opportunities in the process. A generation of reporters now had a set of heroes to emulate and many traditional reporters retooled their reporting approaches. Issues and approaches once considered off limits became widely accepted. Journalists began to ask tougher questions, scour public records for personal improprieties, stake out politicians in once private venues, and readily accept tips from enemies and disaffected former supporters.

The Snipers from Within

Members of Congress are not totally innocent in the negative image portrayed by the media. Many members campaign for Congress by campaigning against the institution, giving the media the raw meat to facilitate the attack. In a strange and seemingly illogical dance, candidates portray Congress as a collective barrel of rotten apples that will only be saved by electing them as the paragon of virtue. The analogy breaks down when one understands that in the natural world, the good apple thrown into the barrel with the rotten ones is less likely to transform the others in a positive direction than to become rotten itself.

While it would seem logical that members of Congress would incessantly worry about disrepute meted out to the institution of which they are a part and would eagerly seek to improve Congress' public image, such is seldom the case. Members of Congress often provide the ammunition for the media as they "run for Congress by running against it." Polls consistently show that voters have much higher respect for their own member than they do for Congress as a whole. Hiding behind this natural protection offers very little motivation to take on the media and public disdain for Congress.

The Terrain of Battle: Emerging Areas of Attack

There are numerous things to criticize about Congress and its members. The litany of shortcomings has increased in recent years.

Discomfort with the Legislative Role

As indicated in Chapter 1, the very fact that Congress makes decisions between non-provable values places it in the crosshairs of individuals whose preferences were not chosen. In a discussion as to whether members of Congress should emphasize compromise over maintaining "principles," former congressman Connie Morella (R-MD) rightfully objected by saying that the choice is between securing compromises or maintaining one's "opinions." As another member of Congress described it, "The business of Congress is working out deals. Effective members of Congress make a commitment to getting something positive done, a goal that trumps blindly following one's opinions and crowning them with the legitimacy of 'principles'." The media on the other hand often set up members for failure by defining them as one-dimensional promoters of intractable principles and then criticizing inconsistencies when a compromise is floated.

The public seems to want it both ways, seeking for themselves members who stand firm on principles, while expecting other members of Congress to compromise in order to accomplish the constituent's particular goals. A "good" compromise seems to be when we get our way with ease. Content analysis of newspaper and television coverage indicates a greater focus on the partisan conflict over policy choices. The penchant for such stories harms Congress in the public eye since the "conflict, haggling, extensive debate and deliberation, competing interest groups, and procedural inefficiency ... are the political characteristics the American public finds particularly unappealing."[44]

On the level of the individual member, congressmen who look out for their constituents often earn the degrading description of "parochial." Members who look beyond their constituency may find themselves used as examples of those who fail to represent the public to whom they are supposed to be responsible. A member's political base tends to reflect a much narrower set of principles than his or her constituents in general. This makes it even more difficult to compromise and gives the media another target to shoot at.

The Processing of Legislation

On a broader scale, much of the criticism of Congress revolves around the false yardstick of efficiency. The Founders did not create Congress to be efficient, if so they would not have created a bicameral legislature and members of Congress would not have adopted rules requiring successful legislation to pass through numerous decision-making stages involving different groups of members. While one can argue as to the degree of gridlock desirable, the redundancy of congressional decision-making was designed to require careful consideration and a thorough airing of viewpoints.

The Nature of the Membership

At the beginning of each new Congress, a spate of stories appears about the demographic make-up of each chamber. The implied question is whether Congress has "enough" women, minorities, veterans, etc. While different life experiences bring with them differing outlooks and skills, it is questionable to completely assume that one must be like someone to understand their interests and to promote them. Representation is a process by which one person re-presents (presents a second time) the wishes and/or interests of another. While it might help to be like the person represented, it is not required.

Perks of Office

Most jobs come with some "perquisites of office," benefits to make employees more effective in their job and/or more satisfied in their rewards. The waitress receiving a free meal, the secretary using the office fax machine to send personal medical records, or the employee having access to an in-house cafeteria all seem reasonable to most people – unless *they* are denied access. The question is not whether members of Congress have perks, but rather whether those perks serve a useful purpose and whether they grant unreasonable privilege. The House and Senate barbershops seem like a better use of members' time than having to dash out to get a haircut, as long as they are not getting a better deal than the average American would get. Free parking, in-house gymnasiums, and restaurants could well be justified for members of Congress trying to manage a very busy schedule. While reporters on the Hill are granted many of these same privileges, they seldom acknowledge the fact. Sensitive to public reaction, Congress has limited press coverage of locations of these perks.[45] Members of Congress realize that the typical story about perks would emphasize that members fail to live in the real world by having their basic needs provided, and by extension it limits their ability to understand what life for the average individual is like.

The media's simplistic listing of perks more honestly should take into account the rationale behind them and the fairness in which they are provided. Providing free or below market cost benefits to members of Congress who are well paid compared to most voters gives the media the "raw meat" to engender disgust among the public.

Moral and Legal Failures

As will be discussed in more detail in Chapter 5, there are personal and legal standards that apply to everyone, and especially those in public life. Falling short of those standards draws media attention.

Running with the Pack

Journalism is not a solitary endeavor affording the luxury of extended contemplation and independent thinking. Journalists compete with each other constrained by tight deadlines and overseen by both editors and news consumers. Going with a story that has one standing out in the crowd often leads to more vulnerability than votes of confidence. Seeking safety in numbers, journalists often retreat to "pack journalism" in which common sources, quotes, and storylines develop similar conventional wisdom, some of which may be based on misinformation.

News coverage is not solely for the general public. News gathering and reporting in Washington is an incestuous relationship. Reporters and editors read and listen to their competitors standing ready to beg, borrow, or steal stories. Reporters on the Hill also interact formally at hearings or story filing areas asking, "What are *you* working on?" It is a small step from independent reporting to pack journalism where the stories and their content begin to look very similar. Each day reporters have dozens of committee sessions from which to choose. A reporter arriving at a hearing and seeing his or her usual competitors can assume "this is where the action will be." Being the only reporter at a hearing may give the journalist pause, unless he or she has some insight that important material will be coming out and an "exclusive" might be in the works.

As one congressional reporter put it,

> I always hated those 11 p.m. calls from Ben Bradley [editor of the *Washington Post*] who after seeing the first edition of the *New York Times* would ask me, "Why don't we have that story?" I would then have to begin calling my sources, often interrupting their sleep, and putting together a story for the later editions.[46]

While all journalists would like exclusives, at a minimum they don't want to miss out on a story. Journalists are not above looking over the shoulders of their colleagues. listening in on telephone calls, or following tweets.

"Bravery" is taking a risk resulting in a positive outcome. Risks that fail most often get labeled as "foolhardy." Traditionally most reporters approached a story like children coming into a kitchen to find a tray of hot cookies aside the piles of cool ones. The careful approach was to grab one of the cool ones and fight over the crumbs as those cookies began to disappear. Although the hot cookies had an appealing aroma, the fear of burning one' fingers and receiving an approach from the cook dissuaded most attempts to secure one. It only took a brave (or perhaps foolish) child's extraordinary temptation to break the pattern. Experiencing the pleasure of the hot cookie created jealousy in the less daring children, not primed to take their time and exhibit safety. If the reaction of others is "Oh what a brave person you are," the norm of waiting for the cookies breaks down. Once a journalist breaks out of the pack with a well-received story, others are sure to follow.

The image of a "pack" might seem like a random group of participants alternatively playing the role of leader and follower. In reality, there are some "big dogs" in the media pack whose choice of stories and methods of presentation set the pace for others. The very appearance of a story on the front page of the *New York Times* or the *Washington Post* grants it legitimacy and leads other media to scurry for their own take on the same story. The leadership is "now so institutionalized that the Associated Press alerts its members each day to the agenda of stories scheduled for the next morning's front page of the *Times*."[47] In order to avoid unpleasant surprises and obvious gaps in coverage, the *Washington Post* and *New York Times* share front pages prior to publication; that decision led the *Post* to initially place its index on an inside page during a redesign process in order not to allow the *Times* full access to all its storylines. There is no doubt that the major papers risk missing important stories, but members of Congress recognize that stories in the major papers will be repeated again in state and local news outlets.

New technology has increased the potential for "pack journalism." The virtually costless storage capacity for content and the efficiency of online database searching make it easy for journalists to "borrow" from each other. The demands of the 24/7 news cycle reward getting the story out there first, more than getting the story right. One factual error can propagate into dozens of erroneous follow-up stories.

The Mutual Disapproval Society

Both journalists and members of Congress see the other, at best, as necessary evils. As one member put it, "If my mother were a reporter, I would still love her, but I wouldn't trust her." Another, when asked how he felt about the coverage of Congress, retorted with a wry smile, "Does the media really cover Congress?"[48] Congressional staff members are even more frank asserting that the media "seldom have any idea of what they are doing," while members of the media write that members of Congress are simply "very adept at manipulating the media."[49] In a reversal of the American principle of being presumed innocent until proven guilty, a litany of government bad behavior, lying, and undesirable outcomes – only some of which should have legitimately fallen on Congress' doorstep – created a new environment in the post-Watergate and post-Vietnam period. "The old healthy skepticism that all good reporters held toward politicians turned into suspicion. Today, no Congressman, no Senator, no tier elected official is presumed honest."[50]

The criticism goes beyond singular stabs. If journalists display cynicism toward Congress, it is returned collectively in spades by congressional staffers. Ninety-five percent of staffers in a 2012 survey perceived media bias that influences congressional decision-making.

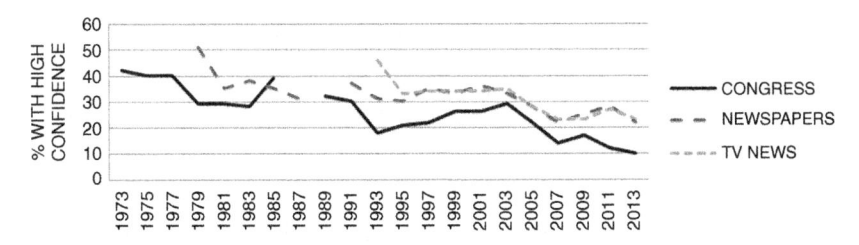

Figure 2.2 Confidence in Congress, Newspapers, and TV News
Source: Gallup poll of national adults indicating "a great deal" or "quite a lot" of confidence in the institution in question, available at: www.gallup.com/poll/1597/confidence-institutions.aspx

More Republicans (75 percent) than Democrats (53 percent) identified the bias as "a lot."[51]

If misery loves company Congress and the media stand out as likely commiserates since both emerge as "bottom dwellers" in polls measuring confidence in American political institutions (see Figure 2.2). There has never been a public love affair with Congress, but its contemporary position is far below earlier levels of acceptance. Over time, the media have seen a greater drop in public repute. Different groups of partisans display varying levels of confidence, with Republicans most likely to reflect dissatisfaction with the media. Confidence in Congress tends to depend on whether one's party holds the majority in the chamber. Satisfaction with the Congress is greater when one's party controls the levers of power.

It is a mistake to view journalists as a monolithic group. Life experience, self-selection, and job demands affect different types of journalists in different ways. Surveys show that journalists who specialize in covering Congress generally hold the institution in higher regard than those journalists who move in and out of the congressional environs.[52] Cynics might see this as selfish protection on one's home turf and/or the desire not to cut off one's sources. Psychologists talk about the "Stockholm syndrome" in which captives tend to start sympathizing with their captors.[53] Research on journalists embedded with troops indicates their tendency to write more positive stories.[54] The old Washington dictum that "where one stands depends on where one sits" applies to journalists as well as to those they cover.

Catch Me If You Can: The (More) Open Congress

Public and media access to congressional activities has been more like a slowly opening door than a dramatic tearing down the walls. While the public and press galleries existed almost from the beginning, those "windows" on the congressional process included severe limitations.

Until 1929 debates on treaties and nominations in the Senate were closed to the press and the public. As a last gasp of defending secrecy Senator Thomas Heflin (D-AL) unsuccessfully proposed closing the press galleries completely.[55] Television crews face severe limitations as to where they may tape segments in and around the Capitol building. Even today, visitors in the public galleries are prohibited from taking notes on the proceedings.

Over the last century the doors of Congress have slowly swung open giving the media and the public a full, if more complicated, view of Congress in action. Committee procedures have shifted from affirmative votes required to *open* a meeting, to affirmative votes required to *close* a meeting. The burden is now on those who wish to work behind closed doors.

In 1977 the open meeting initiative spread beyond standing committees to the conference committees in which the differences between House and Senate versions of bills are ironed out. Open conference meetings not only provided more information to the media, but also granted interest groups access. An unanticipated consequence of open conferences is that "under the watchful eye of lobbyists, conferees fight harder for provision they might have dropped quietly" when few people would know about it.[56]

The arrival of C-SPAN (see Chapter 10) provided a window on the political process for both journalists and the public, allowing both to monitor Congress in a more efficient manner. Online versions of the *Congressional Record* and the development of the Thomas.gov databases provide more people the opportunity to monitor the content and progress of legislation. Commercial databases and search engines (Lexis-Nexis, YouTube, Google, Legistorm.com, etc.) allow the most interested to analyze issues independently and/or to create dossiers on members of Congress discovering their past promises and/or discovering seeming duplicity. Only a small portion of the journalistic community or the public use such resources to their full advantage, but bits and pieces are regularly interjected into news coverage and enter the public mind.

An early study of the relationship between political institutions, the public, and the media argued that in a democracy:

- public officials are responsible to popular control;
- effective control requires an informed populace;
- citizens have a "right to know"; and
- citizens have the right to freely avail themselves of information about governmental activities.[57]

Congress itself took up the issue of the public's right to know in 1955 through a series of hearings by a special committee of the House

Committee on Government Operations. Unlike the common line-up of interests today, members of the media came to Congress for help in breaking through the "paper curtain" of secrecy erected by the bureaucracy.[58]

Testimony before the committee asserted that reporters act as "a representative of 'the people's business,'" and that newsmen help the citizen to find out "what he cannot discover directly for himself."[59] The committee's findings emphasized shortcoming in public access to executive branch information and the concern eventually led to the Freedom of Information Act passed in 1966. With some meaningful recourse to access to executive branch information, the media turned its attention to Congress, recognizing it would be hard for members of Congress to grant themselves the secrecy they and the media found faulty in the bureaucracy. The "government in sunshine" initiatives affected Congress, encouraging committees to open most committee meetings to the press and the public, the introduction of television coverage (see Chapter 10), and eventually providing a wide variety of congressional information online.

The openness of Congress has allowed some of the public debates that in the past only occurred in the halls of Congress to spill over into the public sphere. Sunday television talks shows, the Op-ed page of newspapers, discussions on blogs all have the potential to feed back into the consciousness of members of Congress who are in the position to give the policy advocacy wheel another spin. The opening of Congress through the use of fewer closed committee meetings and televising both committee and chamber sessions has pushed much congressional debate from behind closed doors into the public arena. It is more difficult to cut deals and make compromises when the media and public stakeholders can see what is going on. Increasingly, policy-making has become linked with news-making and policy promoters ignore public relations strategies at their peril.[60]

Veteran CBS news anchor Bob Schieffer agrees with many of his colleagues that the openness and number of players on Capitol Hill make it the "best news beat in Washington."[61] Since members owe their electoral security and rise in institutional power through seniority to their constituents, they have little motivation to focus on making the institution look good. In fact polishing their personal reputation by tarnishing the institution may pay more dividends back home where the votes are counted. Today, Congress as an institution "is being attacked from the inside out, whereas once it was only pundits and outsiders who focused on congressional failings."[62] Far from institutional control of Congress' message, Congress tends "to leak from every office door and window."[63] Whispered or shouted messages to the media tend to fall in the self-serving, rather institution-supporting category. In despoiling their own "nest," few members think about the long-term consequences.

Congressional openness is a mixed blessing. While gaining some kudos from those who prefer, in Woodrow Wilson's terminology, "open covenants openly arrived at," the messiness of coalition-building in Congress gives the institution and its members a bad name. The observation attributed to German Chancellor Otto Von Bismarck that "Laws are like sausages. It's better not to see them being made," invites journalistic revelations about the unpalatable content and the messy aftermath of a legislative decision. There is a great temptation for journalists to report what is wrong or missing from a bill and to chronicle the bruised egos and lasting animosities emanating from the legislative battle. A common storyline follows the ritual of revealing the deep flaws in legislation and playing the blame game of who stood in the way of good legislation. Much of this is possible since most congressional work is done in public hearings and floor debates. Even when the decision-making forums are not public, Congress leaks like a sieve. It is often possible to find participants in closed-door sessions or private discussions who readily spill the beans.

Over the last few decades, Congress has become more open, reducing the number of closed committee meetings dramatically, and expanding the press gallery membership. Many of the changes were at least partially justified on the expectation that "to know us is to love us." Members were proud of their efforts and felt they deserved public exposure and expected such exposure would lead to public acclaim. In reality, the result seemed to be more of "familiarity breeds contempt." The more Congress went public the lower its aggregate evaluation went. Among the public, those most exposed to the media reduced their admiration of Congress the most.[64] It is impossible for Congress to "un-ring the bell." Any attempt to reduce public access would lead to the negative conclusion that "they must be hiding something." At the same time, the media have changed both the volume and nature of their coverage of Congress. Both sets of movements interact to provide the public with a different, and generally less attractive, image of our first branch of government.

Notes

1 Timothy Cook, *Making Laws and Making News*, Washington, D.C.: Brookings Institution, 1989, p. 13.
2 www.virginiamemory.com/online_classroom/shaping_the_constitution/doc/madisons_notes
3 Elaine Povich, *Partners and Adversaries*, Arlington, VA: The Freedom Forum, 1996, p. 8.
4 Rick Willis, "The Collection of Media by U.S. Senators: A Preliminary Study," MA Thesis, University of Nebraska, 2013, p. 5.
5 http://tumblr.thefjp.org/post/2644040062/new-journalism-orgs-struggle-to-cover-capitol-hill

6 Ryan Witte, "It's My House Too! Online Journalism and Discriminatory Access of the Congressional Press Gallery," http://ssrn.com/abstract=1426190, pp. 7–10.
7 Ibid., p.10.
8 http://history.house.gov/Exhibitions-and-Publications/Electronic-Technology/Radio/
9 Donald Ritchie, *Press Gallery: Congress and the Washington Correspondents*, Cambridge, MA: Harvard University Press, 1991, p. 225.
10 Ibid.
11 Witte, p. 222.
12 www.bpnews.net/printerfriendly.asp?ID=103\
13 www.mcclatchydc.com/2013/08/01/198338/senators-spar-over-definition.html#.Ujs9y4ZJPaM
14 Witte, pp. 27–31.
15 See "Citizen Journalism Access," www.theopenhouseproject.com/the-open-house-project-report/8-citizen-journalism-access/
16 Witte, pp. 229–230.
17 Don Hewitt, *Tell Me a Story: Fifty Years and 60 Minutes in Television*, New York, NY: Public Affairs, 2001.
18 Ross K. Baker, "Congress – Boom Box and Black Box," in Everette E. Dennis and Robert W. Snyder (eds.), *Covering Congress*, New Brunswick, NJ: Transaction Press, 1998, p. 7.
19 Journalist Jim Cannon quoted in Povich, p. 70.
20 Quoted in Stephen Bates (ed.), *The Media and the Congress*, Columbus, OH: Publishing Horizons, 1987, p. 23.
21 Quoted in ibid., p. 43.
22 James H. Kuklinski and Lee Siegelman, "When Objectivity Is Not Objective: Network News Coverage of U.S. Senators and the 'Paradox of Objectivity'," *Journal of Politics*, vol. 54, no. 3, 1992, p. 821; Peverill Squire, "Who Gets National News Coverage in the U.S. Senate," *American Politics Research*, vol. 16, no. 139, 1988.
23 Kuklinski and Siegelman, p. 821.
24 Squire, p. 146.
25 Povich, p. 136.
26 See Neil Postman and Steve Powers, *How to Watch TV News*, New York, NY: Penguin Books, 1992, p. 111.
27 Ritchie, p. 225.
28 Patrick Sellers, "Winning Media Coverage in the U.S. Congress," in Bruce I. Oppenheimer (ed.), *U.S. Senate Exceptionalism*, Columbus, OH: Ohio University Press, 2002, p. 149.
29 Ibid., p. 152.
30 Ibid., p. 144.
31 Povich, p. 8.
32 See http://tvtropes.org/pmwiki/pmwiki.php/Franchise/Dragnet?from=Main.Dragnet
33 Sellers, p. 148.
34 Kuklinski and Siegelman, p. 815.
35 See John R. Hibbing and Elizabeth Thiess-Morse, *Congress as Public Enemy: Public Attitudes Toward American Political Institutions*, Cambridge: Cambridge University Press, 1995, p. 55.
36 Povich, p. 91.
37 Povich, p. 97.
38 Quoted in Ritchie, p. 220.

39 Ritchie, p. 225.
40 Ritchie, p. 220.
41 Povich, p. 14.
42 Ben Bagdikian, "Congress and the Media: Partners in Propaganda," *Columbia Journalism Review*, (Jan–Feb) 1971.
43 Daniell C. Vinson, *Local Media Coverage of Congress and Its Members: Through Local Eyes*, Cresskill, NJ: Hampton Press, 2002, p. 172.
44 Jonathan S. Morris and Rosalee A. Clawson, "Media Coverage of Congress in the 1990s: Scandals, Personalities and the Prevalence of Policy and Process," *Political Communication*, vol. 22, no. 3, 2005, p. 300.
45 David Paletz, *The Media in American Politics*, New York, NY: Longman Publishers, 2002, p. 245.
46 Author's interview.
47 Maxwell McCombs, *Setting the Agenda: The Mass Media and Public Opinion*, Malden, MA: Blackwell, 2004, p. 113.
48 Author's interview.
49 Vinson, p. 172.
50 Journalist Jim Cannon, quoted in Povich, p. 69.
51 http://mediarelations.gwu.edu/gw-survey-reveals-money-and-power-lobbying-orgs-are-less-influential-gaining-access-members-congress
52 Kimberly Coursen Parker, "How the Press Views Congress," in Thomas E. Mann and Norman J. Ornstein (eds.), *Congress, the Press, and the Public*, Washington, D.C.: American Enterprise Institute and The Brookings Institution, 1994, p. 167.
53 http://medical-dictionary.thefreedictionary.com/Stockholm+syndrome
54 www.academia.edu/948065/How_We_Performed_Embedded_Journalists_Attitudes_and_Perceptions_Towards_Covering_The_Iraq_War
55 Ronald Elving, "Brighter Lights, Wider Windows: Presenting Congress in the 1990s," in Thomas E. Mann and Norman J. Ornstein (eds.), *Congress, the Press, and the Public*, Washington, D.C.: American Enterprise Institute and The Brookings Institution, 1994, p. 199.
56 Roger Davidson et al., *Congress and Its Members*, Washington, D.C.: Brookings Institution, 2014, p. 242.
57 Dan D. Nimmo, *Newsgathering in Washington*, New York, NY: Atherton Press, 1964.
58 Ibid, p. 174.
59 Ibid.
60 See Cook.
61 Bob Schieffer, *Just In*, New York, NY: G.P. Putnam's Sons, 2003.
62 Povich, p. 1.
63 Povich, p. 45.
64 Mark J. Rozell, *In Contempt of Congress*, Westport, CT: Praeger, 1996, p. 4.

Chapter 3

The Congressional P.R. Machine
Selling a Single Product

Members of Congress and their staffs expend considerable effort seeking recognition and coverage by the media. In this cynical age, one might see members of Congress' gravitation toward the media as little more than an ego trip. It has often been said in jest about some members of Congress that the most dangerous place to be is between them and a camera. A more fair reading is that media coverage is "more than merely a means of ego gratification or a way to project a diffuse image to the constituency; it may be a way to enhance the salience of an issue and to become a key player in Congress."[1] Members of Congress need the media to advance both their careers and their policy preferences. Prior to key decisions, key members of Congress hold press conferences in an attempt to sway the outcome. During hearings, the media are accorded premier seating and access to testimony handouts. After important hearings, members of the media "stake out" the hallways in an attempt to get interviews and members eagerly gravitate toward them. Congressional offices grind out press releases, schedule media events, and use social media to sell their most relevant "product" – the member they work for.

Media coverage plays a key role in representative government. Media reports on member behavior and congressional actions allow voters to evaluate the acceptability of governmental action taken on their behalf. Relevant information alerts constituents of the need to contact their representative to express opinions and serves as a basis for determining the level of electoral support or opposition the constituent is willing to give. Even if the media message never emerges or fails to get through to voters, the very anticipation of an expected media story helps keep public officials on their toes. Media attention is eagerly watched by congressional offices to anticipate upcoming electoral problems.[2]

The sensitivity members of Congress show to media coverage may seem irrational given the high reelection rate. Just enough electoral defeats occur to harbor a healthy fear of retribution at the polls among career-minded members. Losers become poster children for members anticipating, "that is what could happen to me with too much negative press."

It is also important to remember that elected officials operate in one of the rare career patterns where one is very publicly judged as an individual. It is hard to blame others if one loses, or if one's electoral margin declines. Like the eager would-be pick-up sports team members on the school yard, candidates usually jump up pleading "pick me, pick me," and then carry along with them the public expectation that they are as good as *they* think they are. They then allow that assumption to be put to a public vote at regular intervals.

Monitoring media becomes part of most members' self-image verification. "Most Washington politicians have egos of sufficient size to want to see how their comments are being used in the press."[3]

The Care and Feeding of Relevant Audiences

With limited resources of time and energy and differing definitions of news harbored by different media, a major choice for most members is whether they should focus their efforts on gaining local or national media attention. For the vast majority of members, getting good local attention is a necessary condition for staying in office, with national attention a luxury reserved for the few.

All P.R. Is Local?

Congressman David Price (D-NC) pointed out that "the political landscape is littered with fallen members who assumed that their work in Washington would speak for itself." He argued that "at its best [effective] communication conveys a sense of *partnership* – bringing constituents in on what is happening in Washington and what their representative is thinking and doing."[4]

While members of Congress prefer communicating through local media, the local media, especially television, fail to reciprocate through extensive coverage of politics and government. Over 40 percent of local news deals with traffic, weather, and sports. In an analysis of 2012 coverage, only 3 percent of local coverage dealt with politics or government, a decline from a 2005 study, even though 2012 was an election year.[5] Congressional offices send out a myriad of messages, many of which find few or no receivers on the other side. Either the media fail to pick them up for transport, or the receivers fail to absorb them.

The value of good media coverage back home might seem like little more than a job security ploy reflecting David Mayhew's assertion that members of Congress are single-minded pursuers of reelection.[6] A more charitable interpretation sees good local media relations as a method of securing for the member more leeway in his or her decisions on Capitol Hill. Good media coverage gives the member credibility and some "cover" when tough decisions require compromise. Members of Congress do not have to follow every wish or whim of their most vocal constituents, but do need to be in a position to explain their behavior. Good local media coverage bestows credibility on their explanations. In a 2011 survey of congressional staff, 80 percent characterized local media coverage as "very important," almost three times the percentage for national media and four times that of any social media.[7]

The New Congressional Breed

Individual members of Congress emerged from shadows of institutionally focused coverage of Congress by necessity. The weakening of political parties in congressional campaigns from the 1960s onward led to the arrival of more members who saw themselves as "independent contractors beholden to no one."[8] Launching candidate-centered campaigns, raising their own funds and hiring their own consultants, these members arrived on Capitol Hill, often having run for Congress by running against it. The revival of party voting in recent years does not seem to be associated with loyalty to the party organization and particularly not to Congress as an institution. Party voting comes more from ideological commitment forged by the members' ideological base back home. That base of voters seldom has much good to say about the Congress, and disparaging remarks by the member are received with favor.

Receiving good media coverage involves considerable effort. Many local newspapers lack direct access to congressional information, especially stories with a local twist. Members attempt to get their stories out by writing weekly or bi-weekly columns which the news-starved papers use unedited under the member's by-line. David Price (D-NC), a political scientist turned politician, offered his strategy for gaining positive local media coverage. On trips back to the district he makes sure to stop by the local radio stations for interviews. He is not above "staging" events such as ride-alongs with local police to emphasize the need for police funding, or visits to a day care center to talk about federal funding for such facilities. He also attempts to create human interest stories such as photos with local high school groups visiting Washington.[9]

Facilitating Local Media Attention

Getting good coverage involves being a good news source. Members and their staffs alert members of the media of upcoming potential stories with news conferences and personal calls. Members make themselves available after major votes and events such as the State of the Union Message (see Chapter 6) for locally relevant quotes. Good subjects and journalists negotiate agreements as to what is to be covered and how (see Box 3.1).

Box 3.1 Negotiated News: The Journalists/Subject Contract

Members of Congress and journalists participate in an intricate dance where each wants to lead and no one wants to get their toes stepped on. They set up rules that each hopes will serve their conflicting purposes. Members of Congress desire stories that make them, and to a lesser degree, their party and institution, look good. Journalists are more interested in an interesting story which often involves missteps, failure to synchronize actions, and an active "bump and grind" more than a smoothly executed waltz.

At the initiation of an interview journalists and public officials implicitly or explicitly agree on what can be shared and attribution. Four basic agreements emerge:

- "On the record" interviews allow the journalists to quote comment verbatim and attribute them to a source by name and position;
- "Background" interviews cannot result in direct quotes and attribution is by general position ("a senior Senate staffer," "a junior member of the majority," etc.);
- "Deep background" allows no attribution and the use of very general impressions ("many members seem to believe," "everyone seems to understand that," etc.);
- "Off the record" interviews are used to pass information guiding journalists to particular topics, documents, or other interviews sources, but forbid directly using the content in a story.[a]

A non-scientific survey of former members of Congress asked to give guidance to their successors clearly pointed out "a healthy respect for, and general distrust of, the power of the press."[b] Former members suggested three acceptable types of answers to press inquiries:

- I know and can tell you;
- I know and I can't tell you;
- I don't know.[c]

The former members also indicated that there is no such thing as "off the record" when an elected official speaks to the press. Numerous politicians have found that cell phone cameras and other recording devices allow anything they say even to the smallest group of perceived supporters to emerge in the broader media to embarrass them. It is also important to remember that "If you have to explain" you are in trouble, since "the press always has the last word."[d] Reticence, an atypical characteristic of public officials, can be a virtue. As one former member put it, "You'll never regret something you didn't say."[e] Or in a more colloquial way, the politician's prayer: "Oh,

Lord, make my words both tender and sweet, for tomorrow I may have to eat them."[f]

In dealing with the media the cardinal rule for members of Congress is identical to that of other media subjects: Don't lie. The likelihood of getting caught is great in politics since all the participants view their own political survival as so important that they will expose others if necessary.

Sources:

[a] Doris A. Graber, *The Power of Communication*, Washington. D.C.: Congressional Quarterly Press, 2003, p. 244.

[b] Lou Frey, Jr. and Aubrey Jewitt, *Political Rules of the Road*, Lanham, MD: University Press of America, 2009.

[c] Ibid., p. 100.

[d] Ibid., p. 7.

[e] Ibid., p. 103.

[f] Ibid., p. 108.

The Challenge of Geography

The local coverage of members of Congress faces a number of hurdles. Both the delineation of congressional district boundaries and the nature of media markets emanate from geographic considerations. Members of Congress are elected from physically identifiable districts, while traditional media were constrained by geographical limitations on the spread of their electronic signal or their ability to deliver their print product. Unfortunately for both journalists and members of Congress the ease of media coverage related to geographical determinants varies significantly since media markets are seldom identical (congruent) with congressional districts. The Supreme Court cases of the 1960s which mandated population equality over natural geographic boundaries and communities of interest exacerbated the disconnect. New waves of redistricting increasingly ignored the previous political and geographic boundaries around which media markets initially developed. The U.S. contains 210 daily newspaper media markets and 435 House districts guaranteeing that most House members must compete with their nearby colleagues for attention.[10] Local editors and reporters have a greater incentive to cover a member of Congress when the bulk of their readers reside in the same state or congressional district. The lack of market–district congruence between congressional districts and media markets make it difficult (and non-productive) for a television station or newspapers to commit too much time or space to a particular member of Congress.[11] With a limited (and shrinking) news hole, newspapers covering a large number of districts have to choose who to cover, and often end up simply giving local members of Congress short shrift, ignoring them completely.[12]

A second geographical influence could arise when a member's district covers more than one media market resulting in each of their media initiatives (press releases, press conferences, etc.) reaching only a portion of their constituents. About a quarter of congressional districts cover only one media market, while over half of the members of Congress need to get coverage in more than two media markets to reach the bulk of their constituents. In such low congruency districts, members focus a larger portion of their attention on more narrowly distributed dailies or weekly papers which reach their own constituents efficiently. In the "old days" a cozy relationship developed between a newspaper or television station that had only one member to report on and a member who had only a few outlets with which to correspond. While symbiosis still emerges to the benefit of some members, much of the local media coverage "is mostly neutral or ambiguous in its evaluations ... and [is] not as overwhelmingly favorable as past studies have suggested."[13]

The amount of resources members individually commit to publicizing their efforts in Congress depends on the degree to which they believe their actions are already adequately and correctly reported by the media. Members whose electoral district fails to mirror the configuration of media markets have a greater incentive to fight their way into media consciousness via independent efforts. To the degree that the void of local coverage gives members the choice of what to promote via alternative media strategies (particularly newsletters), the power of disclosure shifts in the direction of the member of Congress.[14] Congressional media efforts do seem to make a difference. When members of Congress put forth an effort to publicize their votes through newsletters, their constituents do learn more about those positions.[15] Research as to whether increased information about the incumbent helps or hurts their image results in no consensus.[16]

Since the marginal costs of sending out additional press releases or informing more journalists of a press conference are minimal, congressional offices show little hesitancy to blanket all potential media markets.[17] Members of Congress prepare careful statements in committee or on the floor. The staff pound out well-stated press releases or schedule press conferences. All is often for naught, since local coverage emerges much more from market–district congruence than from the press gyrations of the congressional office. On the other hand members from high market–district congruence have coverage almost fall into their laps by default.[18]

Congruence between congressional districts and media markets has a potential influence beyond the amount and nature of coverage. Research has shown that members representing districts congruent with media markets behave in less ideological and less partisan ways in Congress.[19] With district and media market congruity it may well be that members recognize their behavior will be publicized and adjust their proclivities in anticipation.

The impact of media market congruity clearly emerges from studies assessing voter knowledge. Polling data shows that voters in congruent districts are significantly more likely to receive news and to recall and recognize the name of the representative from their district.[20]

It would be wrong to assume that members of Congress participate in a full court press for local media coverage all the time. Despite the old public relations dictum, "I don't care what they say about me, just so they spell my name right," members of Congress are somewhat more strategically conservative, pointing out, "it is better to have no coverage at all than to lay an egg and have it covered."[21] Former House member Barney Frank (D-MA) points out that for a member with a safe seat, media inattention is often a political blessing.[22]

The Changing Media Environment

Receiving the desired local coverage has become more and more of a challenge. A number of current members and staffs look back at their memory of a "golden age" of congressional coverage. The arrival of communications satellites and the existence of high profits led to expanded coverage of Congress by local stations. Having a Washington bureau became both a possibility and a status symbol. Between 1979 and 1987, the members of the Senate Radio and Television gallery increased from 750 to 2300.[23] Members of Congress fed stories to their local news bureaus which enhanced them and sent them back to the home stations. The experiment was relatively short-lived. By the late 1980s, recession had cut into industry profits, while news directors found relatively little public interest in their Capitol Hill reporting. More and more local newspapers and television stations closed their Washington bureaus and began relying more on national news services or reporters back home covering Congress from afar.

The growth of national chains owning local newspapers also dampened journalists' ardor for covering local members of Congress. Chains often employ a single correspondent to cover Capitol Hill who sends packaged stories back to the local paper. It is a more efficient use of the journalist's time (and the chain ownership's money) to write general stories about Congress and eschew the local angle.[24]

Going National

Most members of Congress accept with resignation that with very few exceptions national news coverage is beyond their reach. As one member put it, "Unless you are a recognized leader, key player or producer of outrageous quotes, it is better to focus on the local media, who control your destiny to an even greater degree."[25]

Why Try the National Scene?

Seeking media attention, especially outside one's district, is a strategic choice emanating from the member's career goals and the nature of the issue. House members aspiring to the Senate often signal that intent by communicating with constituents and media outlets beyond their current geographic constituency. A member's interest in policy issues of high saliency (those that draw the attention of the public and the media) encourages those members to use the national media in hopes of becoming part of the public debate.[26]

"Members of Congress are not equal in the eyes of the national news media, which tend to gravitate toward leaders, committee chairs and others who are understood to be key players in the continuing script of how-a-bill-becomes-a-law."[27] Lack of national media coverage is not that worrisome for most members. Numerous studies have shown that members and congressional press secretaries alike rank local coverage as their ultimate goal.[28] Members with the luxury of good coverage back home can broaden their goal of national coverage, especially when they are more senior, serve on committees dealing with hot policy conflict, and/ or who harbor the goal of running for higher office. Becoming an "issue spokesperson"[29] is not a wise expenditure of effort for many members. As one member admitted, "it may be self-gratifying, and you can tell your mother you were on national television or something, [but] in terms of your career, local media is far more important."[30]

Members of Congress are rational when it comes to media strategies. Those members who believe in the power of the media, especially on the national level, expend more of their efforts, and that of their staffs, on media outreach.[31] Unrewarded initiatives fall by the wayside. If insanity is repeating the same behavior and expecting different outcomes, the most "sane" members of Congress are those who have followed media success with subsequent initiatives, and those whose initiatives were rebuffed and who redirected their efforts in other directions. Some members are clearly "media hogs" absorbing and producing a great deal of content on both the national and local level. They develop opinions on policy having broad public appeal and then seek to make their views heard through the media. More emphasis on national media generally does not come at the expense of maintaining a strong local media initiative.[32] In a twist on the general conclusion that members who take a Burkean view of representation as a delegate would focus on local concerns alone, media entrepreneurs "seem to be more concerned with their constituents *and* [author's emphasis] the general public than the rest of

Congress."[33] In fact, members seeking national media coverage may have to increase their local media efforts to ward off criticism that they have "gone Washington" and thus lost touch with their district.[34]

Media entrepreneurs tend to be younger (although not necessary junior) liberal, non-southern Democrats, a finding that "fits with the picture of an aggressive young generation of politicians who wish to influence policy through many means."[35] Since the major study in this realm occurred when the Democrats controlled both Congress and the White House, the partisan difference may be due to the fact that the party in control has more to "sell," controls the key leadership positions, and has an increased expectation of promoting its program.[36] More than anything, the emergence of media entrepreneurs reflects a generational change in Congress ushering in new members with broader views on media strategies.[37] Certainly the arrival of Newt Gingrich's Conservative Opportunity Society in the 1990s and the Tea Party Republicans in the 2000s reveal the dangers of assuming one party has a monopoly on media strategies. For some members, media entrepreneurship in Congress signals the larger goal of running for national office where national media coverage is a necessity.[38]

Getting National Media Coverage

Media entrepreneurs must employ innovative ways to capture media "as an important mechanism to influence the very legislative process in which they are personally engaged."[39] Entrepreneurs use tactics such as controversial speeches on and off the floor, appearance on national interview programs, calls to the media offering unique insights, frequent use of one minute speeches at the beginning of each session or "special orders" speeches at the end of the day, press conferences on issues both in Congress and their district, and orchestrating "pseudo events" meant to draw attention to an issue in a clever way (see Box 3.2).

Box 3.2 Pseudo Versus Real Events

Although the line is often difficult to draw, a pseudo event is one staged solely for the benefit of the media. Debates on the floor of Congress are "real events" in the sense that they are part of the legislative process. Press conferences represent pseudo events since they are not required for members of Congress to perform their required task of passing legislation. Props serve as valuable methods for gaining attention and providing audiences with a visual image to remember.[a] For example, transporting a wrecked car to a spot on the Capitol grounds with the Capitol dome in the background to comment on the need for tougher drunk driving laws is a pseudo event with a highly recognizable prop.

Frustrated with the lack of attention to issues in which they firmly believed, some members of Congress have resorted to "stunts" to enhance the potential of coverage. Fearing his position as a non-major leader in the chamber, Representative Tony Hall (D-OH) staged a 22-day fast to encourage congressional action on hunger, the subject of the select subcommittee he chaired. His efforts led to positive news stories, a promise for national and international summits on hunger, and the promise of a congressional task force.[b]

Freshman Representative Jim Nussle (R-IA) garnered considerable media attention by going on the floor to give a speech about the House banking scandal wearing a paper bag over his head.[c]

To celebrate National Bike to Work Day, a number of members of Congress stood in front of the Capitol with a wide variety of bicycles and posters promoting riding in the background (see Photo 3.1). The bicycles served as visual props to remind people of the cause at hand.

Photo 3.1 Senator Dick Durban (D-IL) and Other Members of Congress Speak at a Press Conference in Front of the Capitol to Promote Bike Safety and Bike Lanes on National Bike to Work Day

In a battle over protecting Social Security, Democratic members held a press conference reminiscent of the movie *Mr. Smith Goes to Washington*, to showcase the 890,000 signatures they had on a petition, providing visual evidence of the public's concern.[d] In an attempt to initiate an investigation of the attack on the U.S. embassy in Benghazi, Republican members of Congress rolled out a huge petition over a hundred feet long on the grounds of the Capitol to reinforce their case. In 2014, members of the Iraq and Afghanistan Veterans of America delivered over 58,000 petitions to Congress urging action on a suicide prevention bill.

Not all pseudo events result in the intended outcome. In one of the most controversial attempts, House minority leader Nancy Pelosi (D-CA) sought to show Democratic commitment to women by providing a photo op of Democratic women representatives in front of the Capitol. When four failed to make it on time, they were photoshopped into the distributed pictures leading to considerable criticism. Pelosi defended the photo as "an accurate historical record of who the Democratic women of Congress are." Others saw the photo as a fraud (see Photo 3.2).

Photo 3.2 From Representative Pelosi's Website with the Four Added Women Circled

Sources:

[a] See "How to Hold a Press Conference," www.worc.org/userfiles/ Hold-a-Press-Conference.pdf

[b] Timothy Cook, *Governing With the News*, Chicago, IL: University of Chicago Press, 2005, p. 153.

[c] www.american-partisan.com/cols/2004/fiore/qtr4/1123.htm

[d] Donald R. Wolfensberger, *Congress and the People: Deliberative Democracy on Trial*, Baltimore: Johns Hopkins University Press & Woodrow Wilson Center Press, 2000, pp. 36–37.

Congressional travel (the so-called "junkets") often serves as legitimate ways for members to oversee the application of the laws they have enacted. Press conferences or reports from journalists following the entourage provide members the opportunity to comment on past and future policies building directly on the "real world" setting. Having their sound bites in the news establishes media entrepreneurs as "players" even if they lack the leadership positions to which the media are often drawn.[40] Once a member establishes himself or herself as available and willing to forcefully represent a conflicting opinion on an issue, they become a "go to" person for future news stories where a good quote is needed. A member known as someone "always available for a good quote" becomes a good source to go to time after time.

Danielle Vinson posits the "Goldilocks Principle" of coverage to represent the dilemma of both members of Congress and the media.[41] For the national media (or local media doing a national story) both Congress and in particular any individual member of Congress, represent too small a portion of the story to merit much, if any, coverage. For the local media, congressional activity is too big a story to fulfill their perceived role of filling the coverage gap of larger outlets who often ignore city councils, school boards, and neighborhood governance. Just like Goldilocks, some media outlets see their roles as too big, some as too small, and a few as "just right" to serve either the congressmen's or the public's needs.

Reaching One's Colleagues Through the National Media

We normally think of journalists attempting to inform and influence an outside audience. While the media serve as a key tool for connecting with one's constituents, members of Congress often use the media to communicate directly with their colleagues and other Washington policy-makers. Alternatively, a media initiative may seek to send a message to the general public in the hopes that the public's response will reverberate back to Capitol Hill colleagues.

The utility of using the media, especially on the national level, to inform and influence colleagues, must be tempered with reports from Capitol Hill consumers. According to their staff, very few members of Congress (10 percent) take much stock of national news outlet editorials endorsing an issue. Assessment of significant impact by the national news media is dwarfed by techniques such as personal visits from constituents (46 percent), personal letters or e-mails from constituents (20 percent), and comments during town hall meetings (17 percent). Direct messages from colleagues fail to make the list of potential influences.[42] Most members do not seek national attention nor seemingly pay much attention to its content. This helps explain the fact that the vast majority of national media opinion across the ideological board on the 2013 government shutdown expressed strong support for coming to a compromise, while many members were receiving the opposite marching orders from the sources on which they depend most.

Proven General Media Strategies

No matter the audience a member of Congress is trying to reach, a number of proven strategies are available for improving one's chances of not only receiving coverage, but also receiving the type of coverage one desires.

Getting Some Help: The Rise of the Press Secretary

Few members have the skill, interest, or time to compete in the contemporary media environment. The reaction was to call for help. In the 87th Congress (1961–1962) less than 3 percent of House members had full-time press aides and only 41 percent of senators had press secretaries. Today every member of the Senate and 95 percent of House members have press secretaries (called "Communications Directors" in some House and Senate offices). Most Senate offices have two or three people on their communications staff.[43] When the Republicans took control of the House in 1995 they revealed their fiscal conservatism by cutting congressional staff, but noticeably absent from those cuts were personal staff, especially in the media relations realm.

To the degree that press secretaries populated Senate and (much less often) House offices in earlier times, much of their potential was marginalized by their having to deal with mundane information after the fact. Their goals lay in tempering bad news coverage after a decision was made. Today, press secretaries are more likely to play a proactive role in promoting coverage. They and their bosses hope to be in on the policy "take-off" not just as backup players if there is a possible "crash landing." Members hope to interject political considerations up front in the hope that the negative fallout will be avoided.[44]

Press secretaries readily admit that their primary duty involves "spinning" stories so they are framed in the way that reflects best on their boss and his or her priorities.[45] The negative connotations of "spin" as providing a false image leads press secretaries to add a spin on their own job as one of putting events and issues into perspective. Press secretaries see an advantage to a system where proponents on each side of an issue engage in spin tactics with the result that the public is better informed because of the competing viewpoints.[46] While facts are often not difficult to acquire in the policy realm, it is in the interpretation of those facts that Congress plays its most critical role.

Capitalizing on Existing Resources

Members of Congress have provided themselves with a wide variety of public relations resources with which to communicate messages to desired media targets. Using the strategy "if you can't fight them, join them," both the House and Senate offer their members well-equipped recording studios for press conferences, interactive satellite hookups with local television stations, and/or the production of member-created programs to be sent back to their districts.[47] The studio "set" features moveable backdrops, allowing the member to look as if they are in a book-lined office, or standing in front of the Capitol. The American flag is often prominently displayed and the podium often features the seal of the chamber, with such icons intended to impress the public.

Keeping up with new technology the House and Senate created YouTube gateways (House hub and Senate hub) which allow congressional offices to create their own personal video channel on which they can post material they choose (see Chapter 11).[48]

Building Relationships and Anticipating the Needs of Journalists

Members of Congress and the media do more than talk "at" each other. They also talk "with" each other. We often see a kind of mating dance, in which members attempt to sell a story in a certain way and reporters try to tease out stories members have little interest in promoting. One observer called selling a story to reporters the "negotiation of newsworthiness."[49] Members of Congress are in a symbiotic relationship with journalists; each needs the other to do its job. When one journalist was asked, "don't members of Congress 'use' you," he frankly admitted, "we use each other all the time, my concern is when representatives of all points of view don't get a chance to use us."

Successful politicians are strategic communicators. Rather than relying on the content of their message alone, they try to improve the success of their endeavors by attempting to understand the attitudes, preferences structures, cultural tendencies, and organizational and decision-making patterns of the media.[50] Little things such as timing of hearing or press conferences, the line-up of witnesses, and the tone of questioning may lead to very different types of news stories.

Much effective congressional news-making is proactive rather than reactive. Creating fertile ground for positive coverage involves members of Congress and their staffs choosing and honing their public statements in anticipation of how the media might react to different versions.[51] Knowing journalists' deadlines, the inherent needs of their particular medium (sound, pictures, timeliness, human interest, financial implications, etc.) give journalists more motivation to cover a member's preferred story in the most positive way.

A member whose background was in the media pointed out that "as a former reporter, I had the good sense to write my own press releases."[52] He bemoaned the fact that the biggest problem was not distortion of the media's stories, but rather attracting any attention at all. Recognizing the penchant of the media for out-of-the-ordinary stories, he relied on odd-ball things, such as inviting basketball great and then Senator Bill Bradley (D-NJ) to his district to challenge the best player at a local community center to a free-throw contest. The story led the local news that night, with the congressman figuring prominently in most of the visuals. He also made sure that he had a photographer with him at all times to snap pictures with local notables, whose presence almost guaranteed a place in local newspapers.[53]

Each medium brings its own needs. Television ushered in the age of sound-bite politics, with a one-minute quote a virtual tome in the television world. Former Representative Lee Hamilton (D-IN) lamented the sound-bite constraints of television by pointing out, "Politicians must play the game by the rules of television, so they cannot delve into the subtleties and nuances of issues."[54]

Emphasizing the Positive

Good public relations involve associating the congressman's name with positive initiatives while avoiding negative ones. Co-sponsoring popular initiatives and speaking out for them during floor debate allows basking in the reflected glory of a popular idea. Members gravitate toward popular issues and solutions and avoid intractable problems and undesirable solutions. Public opinion is filtered through the perceptions of members of Congress who find ways to associate themselves with the issues and solutions the "relevant" public desires. For most members, the "relevant" public means their constituents, particularly those who voted for them. While government employees and more liberal members of the public bemoaned the government shutdown in 2013, many members of

Congress came from districts where the shrillest voice cried out, "close it down." In a blanket expansion of Ronald Reagan's assertion that the "solution isn't government, the problem is government," the Tea Party component of the Republican constituency saw little value in most government programs. David Mayhew pointed out the important roles of "position taking" and "credit claiming"[55] as key strategies in members' electoral security. To make that work, members gravitate toward issues and actions with "traceability,"[56] the ability to trace a positive outcome back to a member's sponsorship, support, or vote.

Members play it safe by using every possible venue to insert an appropriate comment. The morning after the Boston Marathon bombing, a number of members began their committee questions with a reference to the event, even if the hearing had little or no relation to the issue.

Using Visuals

Visuals have become an important part of communicating political messages. Presidents and members of Congress often choose symbolic settings to announce policy preferences or use backdrops to provide a subliminal message. When the heads of the seven major tobacco companies testified to a congressional committee that they had no knowledge of the dangers of smoking, Representative Henry Waxman (D-CA), a strong proponent of regulating tobacco, had his staff place a placard behind the witnesses reading "One American dies every 80 seconds from tobacco use."[57] The placard undermined the testimony of the tobacco proponents.

Not all visual tricks benefit members of Congress. In negotiating his testimony on the Iran-Contra affair, Oliver North convinced the committee to use low-to-the-ground robotic cameras to "avoid visual disruption." In reality, the cameras resulted in "power shots" of North with his chest full of medals and showing him as a personality dominating the hearings. Broader shots showed members of Congress in raised seats looking down upon their "victim."[58] Public opinion revealed him as "winning" against his detractors among a significant number of citizens. Consternation with positive feedback led the partisan groups on the committee to caucus after the first session to contemplate the power of camera angles.[59]

Frames and Names

The actual titles of legislation are often complex and/or boring. Since research in a variety of media realms indicates the movement toward "sound-bite journalism" where short and simple monikers carry more weight than detailed outlines, members of Congress have adopted another example of "if you can't beat them, join them." Congressional leaders increasingly frame messages using simple, short, and snappy phrases, instead of detailed discussion of policy alternatives and their consequences.[60] Legislation is christened by its proponents with names associated with positive outcomes, while opponents attempt to attach negative labels. Market research has shown that subjects given stories with different titles interpret the articles in different ways.[61] Assuming much of the public (or even the journalists) will not look into the detailed substance of legislation, promoters apply the importance of titles to legislation.

The framing process begins with the numbering and titling of legislation. Securing the number H.R. 1 or S. 1 subconsciously implies that the legislation is more important than legislation with a higher number. H.R. 1776 or S. 1776 carries with it an implication of freedom and democracy irrespective of the content of the bill. The titles of bills are laden with symbolic words such as "freedom," "justice," and "equality": transcendent values with which it is hard to argue against in the abstract (see Box 3.3). Portions of bills receive pejorative labels also. Fighting against limits on inheritances by the wealthy, Republicans began talking about the "estate tax" as the "death tax."[62] In the Affordable Care Act debate, the provision providing for judgments limiting treatment for terminal patients with certain maladies, the decision-making groups were called "death panels."[63] On the other side of the issue, the Obama administration originally eschewed calling the health insurance legislation "Obamacare," but shifted their terminology after President Obama won reelection in 2012, and claimed a mandate for his healthcare initiative (see Box 3.3).

Box 3.3 A Rose by Any Other Name

In biblical history, naming an individual implied a degree of control. Jews were admonished not to say the name of God in respect for divine power. In the secular world, names carry with them both cognitive and emotional content. Members of Congress attempt to grease the skids for their proposed legislation by clever names and acronyms. These acronyms often become much better known than the actual titles.

The Currency Optimization, Innovation, and National Savings (**COINS**) Act proposed doing away with paper dollar bills. Its official name: "To improve the circulation of $1 coins, to remove barriers to the circulation of such coins, and for other purposes" lacked excitement.[a]

Using the title the Development, Relief, and Education for Alien Minors (**DREAM**) Act implies more of the American spirit and promise than its official title: "A bill to authorize the cancellation of removal and adjustment of status of certain alien students who are long-term United States residents and who entered the United States as children and for other purposes."[b]

The **HAPPY** Act (Humanity and Pets Partnering through the Years) would have allowed individuals to deduct pet care expenses from their taxes.[c]

Perhaps the granddaddy of all name gimmicks was the USA **PATRIOT** Act. Its official name: "An Act to deter and punish terrorist acts in the United States and around the world, to enhance law enforcement investigatory tools, and for other purposes" lacked much appeal. It received significant panache through the amalgamation of a series of positive buzz words it would be hard to oppose. (Uniting and Strengthening America by Providing Appropriate Tools Required to Intercept and Obstruct Terrorism Act of 2001.[e])

Once associated with a positive moniker, the media tends to sign on, turning the shorthand title into a descriptive term in the public dialogue.

Adjectives to describe bills sound appealing. Calling something a "clean bill" (without unrelated amendments) sounds much better than a "dirty" bill. Avoiding the "death tax" was preferred rather than simply increasing the amount of taxes on a person's estate. When former Speaker Nancy Pelosi (D-CA) talked about "passing a budget in the dead of night," she implied nefarious activity and the assumption that individuals make better decisions during daylight hours. Even a member such as Senator Daschle (D-SD), a clever wordsmith himself, took on President Bush's stimulus package as "a sham, wrapped in a spin, shrouded in deception."[e]

Sources:

[a] www.pretenseofknowledge.com/2013/08/22/watch-for-laws-with-clever-names/

[b] www.govtrack.us/congress/bills/111/s3992

[c] www.pretenseofknowledge.com/2013/08/22/watch-for-laws-with-clever-names/

[d] www.acronymfinder.com/Uniting-and-Strengthening-America-by-Providing-Appropriate-Tools-Required-to-Intercept-and-Obstruct-Terrorism-Act-of-2001-(USA-PATRIOT-ACT).html

[e] Patrick Sellers, *Cycles of Spin*, New York, NY: Cambridge University Press. Examples available at: http://cyclesofspin.davidson.edu

Framing aspects of the political process is a two-way street used both by members of Congress and the media. A member changing his or her position on a bill could be seen as "giving up one's principles," or "agreeing to a compromise in order to accomplish a higher goal." The fairness of particular frames leads to heated discussions about media bias. Much of the media coverage of Congress is framed in terms of conflict. While disagreements are an important part of representative government, the focus tends to be on those participants who not only disagree, but do so in a disagreeable manner. Conflict is often presented in simplistic terms, failing to fully explain the basis for the conflict and bowing to objectivity by including a few of the more extreme quotes from each side. Without disagreements we would not need a political process to determine the outcome. If everyone agreed an administrative process could simply carry out the will of the people. Politics involves lining up support for one's preference and attempting to win the necessary votes to turn one's preference (or a compromised version) into law. The media need to point out that politics is a messy process where one seldom gets everything wanted, but with a decision the majority can accept, at least for the moment. When anyone asks, "Why can't we just get rid of the politics," the appropriate response of the journalist or well-informed citizen must be, "What would you replace it with?"

Media Coverage from the Congressional Perspective

If Congress and its members fail to get positive media coverage it is not for lack of trying. Significant staff and member time is absorbed by public relations efforts. To a large degree, the choice of what to cover and how to cover it remains in the hands of journalists. As we will see in the next chapter, some members do draw significant attention to themselves, but much of it tends to be negative. Later chapters will discuss the uniqueness of various media venues and the opportunities and challenges they present Congress.

Notes

1 Timothy E. Cook, "Press Secretaries and Media Strategies in the House of Representatives: Deciding Whom to Pursue," *American Journal of Political Science*, vol. 32, no. 4, 1988, p. 1059.
2 See R. Douglas Arnold, *Congress, the Press, and Political Accountability*, New York, NY: Princeton University Press, 2004, pp. 1, 12.
3 Elaine Povich, *Partners and Adversaries*, Arlington, VA: The Freedom Forum, 1996, p. 94.
4 David E. Price, *The Congressional Experience*, Boulder, CO: Westview Press, 2000, p. 196.
5 Mark Jurkowitz et al., "The State of the News Media 2013: The Changing TV News Landscape," available at: http://stateofthemedia.org/2013/special-reports-landing-page/the-changing-tv-news-landscape/
6 David Mayhew, *Congress: The Electoral Connection*, New Haven, CT: Yale University Press, 1974, passim.
7 Congressional Management Foundation, "Communicating with Congress: Perceptions of Citizen Advocacy on Capitol Hill," 2011, p. 7.
8 Povich, p. 20.
9 Price, p. 196.
10 Brian F. Schaffner and Patrick J. Sellers, "The Structure and Determinants of Local Congressional News Coverage," *Political Communication*, vol. 20, no. 1, 2003, pp. 43 and 45.
11 Danielle Vinson, *Local Media Coverage of Congress and Its Members: Through Local Eyes*, Creskill, NJ: Hampton Press, 2003, p. 11.

12 Schaffner and Sellers, p. 53.
13 Vinson, p. 169.
14 See Daniel Lipinski, *Congressional Communication*, Ann Arbor, MI: University of Michigan Press, 2004, pp. 83 and 108.
15 Daniel Lipinski, "The Effect of Messages Communicated by Members of Congress: The Impact of Publicizing Votes," *Legislative Studies Quarterly*, vol. 26, no. 1, 2001, pp. 81–100.
16 Ibid., pp. 83–84.
17 Schaffner and Sellers, p. 52.
18 See Vinson, p. 97.
19 James M. Snyder, Jr. and David Stromberg, "Press Coverage and Political Accountability," *Journal of Political Economy*, vol. 118, no. 2, 2010, pp. 355–408.
20 Richard Niemi, Lynda Powell, and Patricia Bicknell, "The Effects of Congruity Between Community and District on Salience of U.S. House Candidates," *Legislative Studies Quarterly*, vol. 11, 1986, pp. 187–201; Vinson, passim.
21 Author's interview.
22 Bill Kovach and Tom Rosentiel, *Warp Speed*, New York, NY: The Century Foundation Press, 1999, p. 47.
23 Stephen Hess, "The Decline and Fall of Congressional News," in Thomas E. Mann and Norman J. Ornstein (eds.), *Congress, the Press, and the Public*, Washington, D.C.: American Enterprise Institute and The Brookings Institution, 1994, pp. 145–146.
24 Schaffner and Sellers, pp. 43 and 53.
25 Author's interview.
26 Christine DeGregario, *Networks of Champions*, Ann Arbor, MI: University of Michigan Press, 1997, p. 45.
27 Timothy Cook, *Governing with the News: The News Media as a Political Institution*, Chicago, IL: University of Chicago Press, 2005, p. 151.
28 Ibid., p. 151.
29 Ibid., p. 269.
30 Povich, p. 98.
31 Karen M. Kedrowski, *Media Entrepreneurs and the Media Enterprise in the Congress*, Creskill, NJ: Hampton Press, 1996, p. 163.
32 Ibid., p. 166.
33 Ibid., p. 166.
34 Ibid., p. 202.
35 Ibid., p. 50.
36 Ibid., p. 192.
37 Ibid., p. 193.
38 Ibid., p. 50.
39 Ibid., p. 4.
40 Ibid., pp. 1–6.
41 Vinson, p. 203.
42 Congressional Management Foundation, p. 3.
43 Gary Lee Malecha and Daniel J. Reagan, *The Public Congress*, New York, NY: Routledge, 2012, pp. 49–53.
44 Cook, 2005, p. 168.
45 Kedrowski, p. 91.
46 Ibid., p. 96.
47 Malecha and Reagan, p. 17 and Povich, p. 51.
48 Malecha and Reagan, p. 63.

49 Cook, 2005, p. 12.
50 Jarol Mannheim, "The News Shapers: Strategic Communications as a Third Force in News Making,' in Doris Graber et al. (eds.), *The Politics of News*, Washington, D.C.: CQ Press, 2008, p. 106.
51 Patrick Sellers, *Cycles of Spin: Strategic Communications in the U.S. Congress*, New York, NY: Cambridge University Press, 2010, p. 3.
52 Author's interview.
53 Author's interview.
54 Quoted in Richie, p. 226.
55 Mayhew, passim.
56 Douglas Arnold, *The Logic of Congressional Action*, New Haven, CT: Yale University Press, 1992, pp. 72–74.
57 David Paletz, *The Media in American Politics*, New York, NY: Longman Publishers, 2002, p. 245.
58 Ibid., p. 255.
59 Author's interview with committee staff member.
60 See Todd Belt and Marion Just, "The Local News Story: Is Quality a Choice?" *Political Communication*, vol. 25, no. 2, 2001, pp. 194–215.
61 Emily Heil, "How Names of Bills Aim to Sell Legislation," *Washington Post*, July 25, 2013.
62 Walter Oleszek and C. Lawrence Evans, *Congress Under Fire*, Boston, MA: Houghton Mifflin, 1997, p. 115.
63 www.westernjournalism.com/obamacare-death-panels-illegally-with holding-treatment/

Chapter 4

Catch Me If You Can

News Hooks and Nobodies

Just another "Who done me wrong song"
> Classic country western refrain

Classic training in journalism expects each story to cover the five Ws (who, what, where, when, and why) with primary emphasis on who. The "who" of a story serves as the news hook around which the story is developed. With the multiplicity of potential congressional voices, journalists are often overwhelmed with a cacophony of messages emanating from Congress, many of which are either not relevant to their audiences or unlikely to move the story forward. Journalists are thus forced to focus their attention on a subset of political players.

Competing Voices from the Outside: The President and Congress

Contemporary media with their limited news holes gravitate toward the president, who is almost universally recognized and who speaks with one voice (see Figure 4.1). Following the five Ws dictates of a good story, the president is the big "who." The public knows so much about him that little of the story has to use up time or space discussing his party, political proclivities, and behavior patterns. A brief mention of the president's name allows the journalist to get on with the heart of the story. Most members of Congress lack widespread name identification. Stories about members of Congress require the journalist to provide biographical background before they can dig into the story or else the reader will have no idea of whom they are discussing. Stories out of the White House are coordinated to avoid conflicting perspectives and the image of disunity. When congressional reaction is reported it often appears as a cacophonous barrage of competing perspectives. Journalistic dictates of fairness and balance send them hustling for competing perspectives, even when

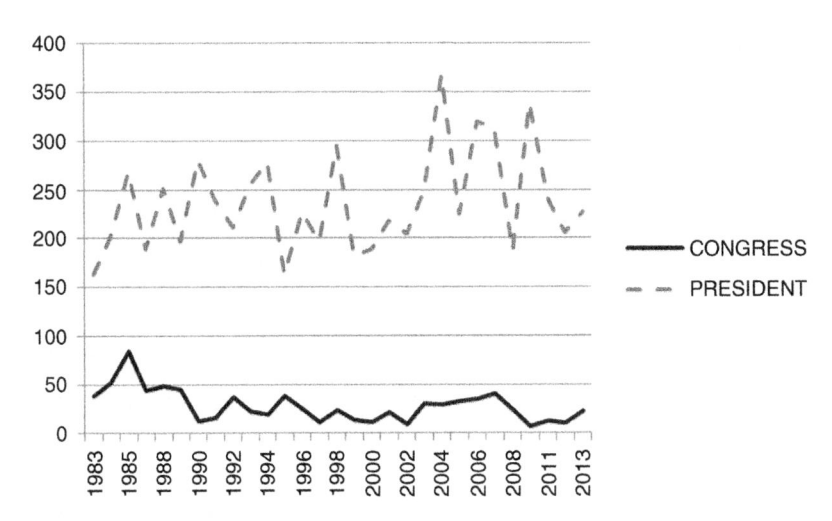

Figure 4.1 Speak Softly, But Get the Word Out: Presidents and Congress in the Media. Number of presidential and congressional stories on the network evening news during the month of April. Calculated by the author from the Vanderbilt Television News Archives

antagonistic reactions are unrepresentative and few and far between. When all perspectives are given equal weight, Congress comes off as a squabbling debating society, lacking discernment and rational judgment. The wacky and weird flow out of Congress as easily as the wise and judicious.

Presidents offer the media a good story with clear events marking a challenge (a president proposing the solution to a problem), negotiation (the president meeting with political leaders to develop a compromise), and a conclusion (a presidential bill-signing ceremony). In comparison, Congress looks like a disorganized multi-ring circus with overlapping events. The White House's clear and unified message emanates either directly from the president or from surrogate spokespersons whose variation from the official line threatens their job security. A public relations expert with experience both in Congress and the executive branch explained the difference this way:

> In the executive branch, in order to coordinate a media message with an office parallel to yours, you go up your chain of command three or four levels to get approval, and then it goes down your recipient's chain for their "chop" on the message. The result is a media message everyone can approve, but the message is often pretty bland

and unlikely to get many headlines. In Congress you have some 400 odd admirals, each of whom runs their own ship the way they want. Coordination is possible, but neither required nor likely. Individual members have little interest in looking out for the institution as a whole and the message it projects.[1]

In such an environment, Congress speaks with a barrage of shrill voices, each of whom is trying to out yell the others, especially for attention back in their own district. The range of coverage individual members of Congress receive from the national media varies dramatically. It is not atypical for the most covered member to receive over a hundred times more mentions than the least covered members.[2] The media gravitates toward senators and institutional leaders as their names, states, and party affiliations are more likely to be part of the public's knowledge base.

The Senatorial Soap Box

Individual senators receive more national media attention than House members for a variety of reasons. As the smaller chamber, the Senate offers fewer "news hooks" on which to hang a story. Senate rules such as the filibuster (even in its current weakened form) allow more potential to individually tie up Senate proceedings and determine the fate of legislation. As former Senator Alan Simpson (R-WY) put it, "One person can tie this place into a knot, and two can do it even more beautifully."[3] Senatorial media outreach efforts (press releases, bill sponsorship, and press conferences) tend to draw more members of the media. The decision to attend an event or search a document almost automatically results into turning acquired content into an actual news story. In both the House and Senate most press conferences include multiple members in the hope that numbers and geographic spread will overwhelm the inherent draw of the president for attention.[4] Getting a reporter to show up at a press conference is the key step. Assignment editors and journalists alike don't want to be seen as "wasting" precious resources by going to an event or studying a document with no story emerging. Finally the Senate serves as a common breeding ground for presidential candidates (although not winners in recent years), whose presidential media strategies receive significant coverage that is hard to separate from their roles as senators. Media attention paid to senators versus House members shows up in public knowledge. While over 90 percent of the public report had read about their senator in a newspaper or seen him or her on television, that is true of only about 60 percent of House members. When it comes to an election, voters could almost universally recognize their senator's name, with House members lagging about eight percentage points behind. The gap is even greater when voters are asked to recall the name.[5]

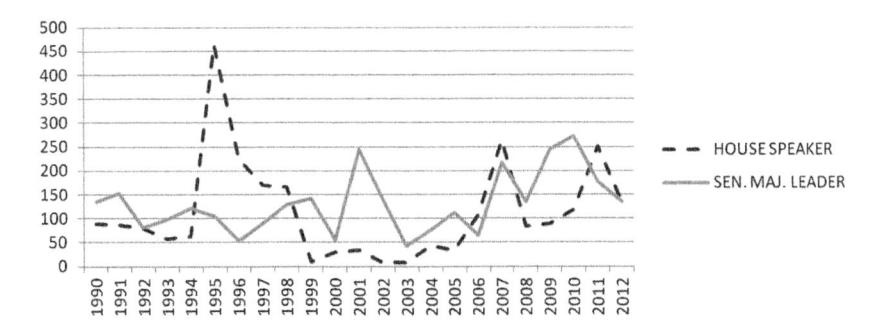

Figure 4.2 Who Speaks for Congress: Media Coverage of the Speaker of the House and Majority Leader in the Senate. Yearly total of stories referring to the Speaker or Senate Majority Leader by name. Calculated by the author from the Vanderbilt Television News Archives

While news attentiveness to the unique and extraordinary might lead one to expect greater coverage of the more extreme members of the Senate, research findings indicate a nuanced reality. If one takes into account the generally accepted findings that the media pay most attention to majority party leaders and senators running for higher political office, more media attention is granted to senators in the ideological center of their party, at least in non-election years. It seems that the media recognize when their stories focus on legislation that these "median" senators use as crucial bridges for actual legislation passage.

The Personality News Hook

While the Senate as an institution and individual senators tend to get more media attention, the situation becomes more nuanced when looking at individual leaders. Outspoken leaders can often draw the attention of the media above and beyond what their position might entitle them. As Figure 4.2 reveals, Speaker Newt Gingrich (R-GA) dominated individual coverage during the 1994–1997 period. Nancy Pelosi (D-CA) garnered significant attention as Speaker 2007–2008 as did John Boehner (R-OH) from 2009 to the present.

Committee Leaders

In order to narrow the number of members to cover, journalists tend to gravitate toward committee and party leaders. Committee and subcommittee chairs are deemed to have both expertise and the power to shape legislation. Chairs, and to a lesser degree ranking minority party members on a committee, dominate its activity by choosing the timing of meetings, formulating lists of witnesses, framing policy discussions through opening statements, and presiding over hearings. Each of the chair's powers has a potential impact on media coverage. Scheduling a committee meeting when there is little competition from other hearings increases its chances for coverage. Selecting individuals with significant notoriety draws the media toward a hearing (see Chapter 6). Opening statements in committees carry more weight since journalists tend to wander away as hearings drag on. Since hearing protocol prescribes a questioning order from the most senior to the most junior members, junior "backbenchers" find that the most newsworthy questions have often already been asked by the time they get their turn. Through controlling the gavel, the chair retains the right to determine whose voice is heard and whose is not (see Box 4.1). Committee chairs and ranking minority members also gain exposure by serving as the spokespersons for their committees during floor debate. They manage the time and order of speaking, often reserving for themselves the right to open and close the argument, thereby giving the media key sound bites to describe their support or opposition to the bill at hand.

Box 4.1 Backfire

Representative Daryl Issa (R-CA) Chair of the House Oversight Committee and Elijah Cummings (D-MD) agree on very little. As committee chair, Issa controls committee sessions, and, perhaps most importantly, the microphone, but does not control the media coverage. During a hearing on alleged IRS targeting of conservative political groups, Issa called the session to a halt when the IRS representative refused to testify. Ranking minority member Cummings sought to ask a question and Issa began to leave, reiterating that the session was over. Cummings quickly pointed out, "Mr. Chairman, you cannot run a committee like this. You just cannot do this. We're better than that as a country, we're better than that as a committee." Issa reached over and muted Cummings' microphone, eventually turning the mike back on, telling the rest of the chamber they were free to leave. "We've all adjourned, but the gentleman may ask his question," Issa said. After several seconds Issa cut off Cummings' microphone again saying "We're adjourned." He then ordered "Close it down." The Chairman complained that Cummings was making a speech, not asking a question. Cummings finished his thoughts without the mike. Issa's attempt to dampen Cummings' message failed to pan out, as the media picked up the seeming high-handedness of Issa.[a] Chairman Issa eventually had to apologize after media coverage was almost universally negative.[b] Issa and Cummings also got cross-wired over the hearings about the attack on Benghazi. Issa's strong partisan leadership style has not gone unnoticed by political humorists on venues such as *Saturday*

Night Live whose skits parodied his battles with Representative Cummings.[c]

Sources:

[a] www.msnbc.com/hardball/issa-cummings-clash-irs-hearing

[b] www.msnbc.com/hardball/issa-cummings-clash-irs-hearing and www.politicususa.com/2014/03/07/darrell-issa-slithers-punishment-apologizing-cutting-democrats-mic.html

[c] http://articles.latimes.com/2013/may/21/nation/la-na-issa-profile-20130522 and www.newsmax.com/Hirsen/SNL-Benghazi-Hearings-Issa/2013/05/13/id/504141/

The Nature and Potential for Party Voices

Another obvious counterbalance to the president are the opposition party leaders in Congress. They have procedural powers, personal following, and the potential to provide a more limited set of coherent messages. Since the 1950s, much of the literature has emphasized members of Congress acting as individualized entrepreneurs, promoting themselves and their causes without the organized support of their parties. As the labor-intensive nature of election campaigns, the bailiwick of party organizations with small armies of foot soldiers, shifted toward media initiatives, the parties were slow to provide candidates with the money or tools necessary to communicate with larger, more diverse, and harder-to-reach constituents. Candidate-centered campaigns replaced contests controlled by disciplined parties with the ability to control nominations and deeply affect electoral contests.

Traditional Party Leaders

Just imagine a major legislative leader unwilling to appear on national television interview shows, who banned recording of committee and chamber deliberations, who invited select reporters back to his office for drinks and off-the-record discussions many afternoons, and then received protection from those reporters, who avoided asking tough questions during his brief daily press conferences. We are not talking about a less democratic country or a long-gone era. This pretty much describes Speaker Sam Rayburn's (D-TX) relationship with the media in the 1960s.[6] Rayburn worked on the premise that, at least for hand-picked members of the media, "to know us is to love us." Echoing the consequences of instituting "embedded reporters" during the Iraq War in the 2000s, the situation was described as "a little like being a war correspondent: you really become a part of the outfit you are covering."[7] In both cases, coverage reflected a positive slant on the motivations and behavior of the participants.[8]

Up until the 1970s, the press tended to be "respectful" of the political establishment, if not downright subservient.[9] Journalists of the day decried allowing in negativity and saw reporting on scandal as lowering their standards "from serious and fair-minded coverage of the issues to a frivolous and sensational focus on political sideshows."[10] While unduly protecting members of Congress, or any political official, fails to serve the public's need for oversight, the dramatic pendulum switch in the other direction carries with it its own dangers.

New Leaders for a New Era

Congressional leaders are not shy about the importance of using the media to attain their goals. Representative John Boehner (R-OH), then House Minority Leader, told a closed session of his Republican colleagues in 2009, "we are no longer in the business of legislating and should focus almost solely on communicating our message with voters."[11]

Despite assertions that the "party was over,"[12] during the 1970s and 1980s with the new norm of "candidate-centered campaigns" emerging, political parties refused to die. They fought their way back to relevancy by strengthening congressional fundraising committees, creating their own leadership political action committees, and amplifying the leadership role in committee assignments. As the media discovered these tools, party leaders were thrust back into the spotlight, and often criticized for not demonstrating the strong leadership the media attributed to their new resources. To some degree, the regeneration of congressional parties emerged from the provision of communications and media resources for their candidates. As the cost of communicating effectively was reduced with the availability of new technologies, members of Congress found their messages competing with an ever-growing glut of information. The result was often to turn back to the political parties to serve their traditional role as "interest aggregators" and broad-based communicators of simple but effective messages with the potential to influence a broad base of voters.[13] The leaders took on two tasks, setting the legislative agenda and creating a recognizable "brand name" for their party.

Agenda Setting

For those who fault Congress for failing to discover the correct answer to significant problems and then force the proper decision, the role of party leaders and their press secretaries causes heartburn. Even congressional leaders "perceive themselves as foot soldiers in a partisan war to determine and interpret the agenda."[14] Their role lies in getting the public and their colleagues to interpret problems and potential solutions in the way they see it and use the media to win the other players over to their cause. If there were a "right" answer, the process would involve applying some formula, calling on some undisputable higher value, or pointing to an incontrovertible set of facts. Solving problems with such obvious correct answers could be done at a much lower level than Congress. There is no universally accepted answer to how much we as a nation should spend on schools versus roads, or when human life begins. We call on Congress to produce decisions a majority of its 535 members can live with, even if they do not like all of its provisions. Facts are important, but largely as "ammunition" to persuade colleagues to join legislative coalitions and can often be presented in ways to support different interpretations. Seldom are the facts so overwhelming that agreement on a course of legislative action is a foregone conclusion. Policy leaders pick and choose among facts, emphasizing some and discarding others. To the degree that their colleagues depend on constituents' opinions, leaders attempt to use the media to create a public mindset. Even if the public is not paying attention, media efforts may deliver messages about the policies directly to congressional colleagues.

Words and presentation are important. Political strategist Frank Luntz points out that "it is not what you say but what the audiences hear that counts."[15] In order to have maximum effect both individual members and party teams recognize the need to present homogeneous, simple, and consistent messages. Ralph Waldo Emerson argued that "consistency is the hobgoblin of little minds."[16] But Emerson never won political office. Mixed messages or change over time leads to charges of insincerity or flip-flopping.

Recognizing the power of unity and numbers, both parties in the House and Senate have created "communications enterprises" or "theme teams" to craft and distribute coordinated party messages on the House and Senate floor and in other forums.[17] Closely associated with the party leadership, staffs in leadership offices develop talking points for both leaders and followers, react to actions by the opposing party, and seek opportunities to spread the party message through developing a press-booking operation. With titles like the "GOP Theme Team" and the Democratic Message Group," these squads of members organize coordinated speeches on the floor, offer seminars on the use of new media technologies, and organize informal "salon" sessions bringing together members of the media, members of Congress, and subject matter experts.[18]

The initial attempt to provide coordinated party messages involved a joint effort by Minority Leader Newt Gingrich (R-GA) and Haley Barbour, Chair of the Republican National Committee. By the early 1990s "CommStrat," housed in Gingrich's office, was distributing the "message of the day" and following Barbour's goal of getting "everyone saying the same thing." Barbour advised, "Repeat it until you vomit" and "The only way you can get market penetration is through repetition, repetition, repetition."[19]

The Big Step Forward: The Contract with America

Seeking majority status in the House, Gingrich and his COS (Conservative Opportunity Society) colleagues hatched a strategy of differentiating themselves from the Democrats by creating a mid-term party platform they called the "Contract with America." Its ten items went through a series of focus groups and carefully avoided issues like abortion on which the party was split. Over three hundred Republican congressional candidates gathered in front of the Capitol to launch the initiative which Republicans hoped would lead to majority status in less than a decade. The media showed up in large numbers, but largely saw the contract as a gimmick by a set of pipe dreamers.

As evidence of television in the early 1990s as the big dog in the mass media pack, the Republicans purchased the back page of *TV Guide* to outline the contract. On the surface the contract looked like a media flop. On Election Day, 71 percent of the voters claimed they had never specifically heard of it.[20] Much to the surprise of everyone, the Republican leaders included, many voters saw the contract in different terms. Although polls showed considerable disagreement with particular commitments, voters seemed to have picked up the vague impression that, "at least the Republicans have a plan, something missing from the Democrats who have held the majority in Congress for forty years." Not one incumbent Republican House member lost his or her seat in 1994, and Republicans picked up enough seats from Democrats to win a majority. Democratic House Speaker Tom Foley (D-WA) became the first Speaker to lose his congressional seat in 130 years. Far from looking back at the 1994 election as a good first step, Newt Gingrich was faced with taking over partisan control of the House, with no sitting Republican ever having been part of the majority.

By and large, the media did not report the election as an endorsement of the Republicans or a mandate for specific change. The media were quick to point out polls revealing the vote as against Congress in general, with the Democrats taking the brunt for being in charge.[21] Reality is often in the mind of the beholder. More conservative writers looked at the results in a different way, seeing a mandate for the conservative policies proposed by speaker Newt Gingrich and his new majority.[22]

Procedural changes made by the new Republican majority did garner significant media approval. Placing term limits on the Speaker and committee chairs was seen as tempering the arrogance of power. Subjecting Congress to the same laws required of the private sector removed one of the largest set of congressional perks. The media showed less support for substantive promises in the contract such as balancing the budget and limiting product liability.

Unlike previous elections with vague promises and divided party platforms, the Contract with America gave journalists an explicit set of goals against which to measure congressional performance. Journalists developed contract "scorecards" to measure progress. Although Republicans only promised to take the ten items up in the first 100 days, the measure of success soon became passage into law. The Senate proved to be the greatest stumbling block to enacting the items in the contract, with many of the Republicans opposing the changes. Shortly after the Republicans took over, the majority of coverage of Congress by newspapers was negative, even among more conservative papers such as the *Wall Street Journal*.[23]

Speaker Gingrich Attempts to Ride the Wave

As a media "darling," Gingrich decided to capitalize on their attentiveness by giving them unique access. Speaker Tip O'Neill initiated the idea of brief "bullpen" press conferences before each daily session in the 1980s as an antidote to President Reagan's success with the media. Basking in the glow of his electoral success in taking over the majority, Gingrich took the position that "to know me is to love me" one step further assuming that the bad press emanated from the dearth of access and coverage. As we will see (Chapter 10), such a view earlier helped propel allowing television coverage of congressional proceedings. After his election as Speaker, Newt Gingrich acted on this presumption by allowing television coverage of the Speaker's daily press briefings. In a "live by the camera, die by the camera" phenomenon, the experiment proved short-lived as the media questioning became more pointed.[24] He found that far from "love," the sessions led to bad press. Shifting to the view that "familiarity breeds contempt," he scrapped the practice after a short time.

Contemporary Efforts at Agenda Setting

The contemporary party caucuses in Congress are motivated to present their party in a positive light and to speak with one voice. To this end, party leaders attempt to facilitate and encourage common themes. The party leaders convene weekly meetings of press secretaries and suggest topics and approaches. The weekly meetings of the Democratic Caucus and the Republican Conference[25] result in establishing party priorities and discussing methods of promoting them. "Theme Teams" of well-spoken members are sent out to drive the message home.

The Democratic Policy Committee provides each member of their party with the *Weekender*, which includes key points to be made when talking to the media. The Republican Conference packet is called the *Boarding Pass*, with its suggestions of themes and quotes.[26] About half the members indicate they use the prepared materials in dealing with the press. Others point out they know what might appeal to their local media and constituents much better than the party leaders.[27]

Once a consensus is reached, however, Republicans have traditionally marshaled their coordinated message efforts with centralized control and precision strikes. Democrats, on the other hand, tend to operate in a much more informal way,[28] harkening back to humorist Will Rogers' famous statement, "I am not a member of any organized political party. I am a Democrat."[29] Today, both parties not only use traditional approaches such as press conferences and press releases, but also offer a partisan portal website (GOP.gov and dems.gov) designed to disseminate the party message.[30]

Branding

Political leaders in Congress not only seek to control the day-to-day agenda and promote favored policies, they also seek to "brand name" the party label with policy content on issues that differentiate them from the opposing party in an attempt to draw voters to their candidates.[31] Republicans have tried to use the media to brand themselves as the tax cut and national defense party, while Democrats have sought to be seen as the party of the little guy working together with government to provide social program benefits. To the degree that a party "owns" an issue area, they can frame policy debates in a way that favors their preferences and identifies their party as the only one able to pursue particular goals. Republicans talk about tax cuts in terms of "protecting the fruits of one's hard work and encouraging individual initiative." Democrats talk about government expenditures as "cooperative efforts to promote fairness, equality and personal development." While Republicans cringed at Barack Obama's seemingly demeaning comments to successful businessmen that "you didn't build that," Democrats focused on the assertion that the cooperative efforts in providing schools, roads, and other government programs undergirded economic development.

The ability of the leaders to sell their party images to the media and eventually to the public is enhanced when the party caucus is unified in its legislative actions and message to the public. An analysis of press releases by party leaders shows their hesitancy to encroach on the "home

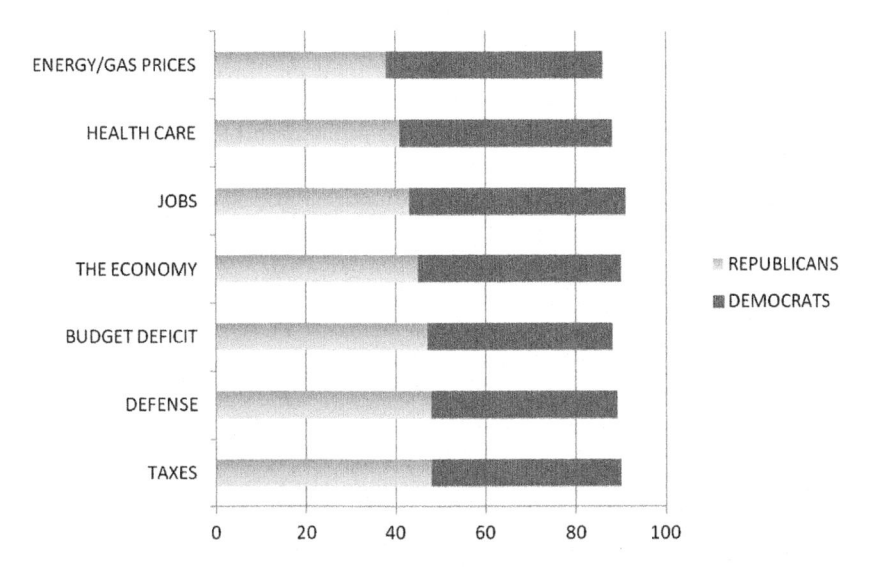

Figure 4.3 The Party Brand: % Viewing Party as Best to Handle Issue
Source: New Models National Brand poll of 1000 registered voters, September 2013,
Roper Center for Public Opinion iPOLL database.

field advantage" of their opponents. While the dominant theme for both parties in this 1997 study was macroeconomics (with each party leader taking a different approach), the issue focus of the two leaders varied widely. Then Democratic Majority Leader, Tom Daschle (D-SD), focused on health, education, and banking, while then Republican Minority Leader, Trent Lott (R-MS), stressed defense and government operations. Both leaders attempted to expand attention to "their" issues by enlisting the help of other members of their caucus.[32]

In order for issue branding to work a large proportion of the party must be "reading from the same page." When this happens the media have little chance to miss the intended message. The problem for leaders lies in the fact that they "have little wherewithal to contain deviations in message."[33] The political life and death of members is controlled by the voters back home, not the leaders in Washington. During the 2013 run-up to the government shutdown, House Speaker John Boehner (R-OH) could not control either the votes or public pronouncements of a significant portion of his party. The media were quick to latch on to the most uncooperative statements of the party's Tea Party contingent unwilling to seek a compromise and openly rallying to "shut it [the government] down."[34]

Each party maintains legitimate "bragging rights" concerning the issues the public perceives them as best to handle (see Figure 4.3). Party leaders attempt to "prime" the media and the public by framing a myriad of issues under the umbrellas of issues on which they are viewed positively. Even if a specific policy proposal fails to neatly fit under a party's favorable frame, clever packaging may draw it in. In its role of simplifying complex issues, the media often uses the policy frames promoted by the parties and helps implant these in the public mind.

Promoting issues closely aligned with a party has two benefits. On the aggregate level it reinforces the party image and provides a collective benefit to all candidates running under the party label. Individually members of Congress can claim credit for the initiatives of their party and their contribution to it, thus revealing their commitment to their political base and the veracity of their own campaign promises.

Branding goes beyond evaluating the issues "owned" by each party. Harkening back to earlier media reports of the 1995 government shutdowns and branding the Republicans as the "party of no,"[35] former Representative Thomas Davis (R-VA) feared guilt by association. Speaking as a key strategist for congressional campaigns as former chair of the National Republican Congressional Campaign Committee he bemoaned that "the Republican brand is in the trash can ... If we were a dog food, they would take us off the shelf."[36] Democrats also have not been immune to negative branding. Charges of irresponsible spending and "throwing money at problems" dog the Democrats at regular intervals.

The Challenge of Coordinated Messaging

A major role of leaders in the contemporary Congress revolves around creating, promoting, and protecting the party message. Since disparate and conflicting messages undermine a clear party definition, leaders attempt to avoid issues on which their fellow partisans disagree.[37] The ideal issue is one that unifies one's party and divides the opposition.[38] There are few ultimate rewards or sanctions leaders can impose on their colleagues.

Broadening Support

Clever leaders attempt to expand their influence by "dealing in" members starved of media attention. On issues around which one of the parties coalesce with a united view, party leaders serve as "megaphones" exploiting the issue and encouraging non-leaders to reinforce the commonly held perspective. Dampening dissent, the leaders grant more junior members a share of news coverage at press conferences and other events.[39] Since local media outlets show great interest in what "their" members have to say, non-leaders can serve as relevant reinforcers of the national message on the local level. While Ralph Waldo Emerson's "consistency is the hobgoblin of little minds" seems eminently reasonable in a changing world, Emerson never ran for political office, where "flip-flopping" is often seen as a cardinal sin. Congressional leaders may secure support by asking wavering members to join them at a press conference announcing support for a new policy. Once they are on the public record for their support, it locks in their vote and may send a message to similarly minded members.[40]

Party leaders face a classic problem when trying to create and promote a common message. The collective benefit of the common message will presumably help all members of the party, whether they expend any effort or not. Members of Congress out of step with their party will simply go it on their own, either ignoring or even opposing particular party policies. Leaders try to decrease the number of "free riders" who do not pay for their benefits by taking an electoral risk and backing the party position. When push comes to shove, district political necessities tend to prevail.[41] Sellers concluded that "in the legislator's decisions about whether to promote their party's message, individual benefits seemed paramount."[42]

Less Cooperative Targets

Not all members play the "follow the leader" game. When calling for a coordinated message, electorally secure members are more likely to take up the preferred cause than are those with more concern about their future electoral fortunes.[43] Not surprisingly, members consistently in the middle of the party's ideological pack find it more comfortable to support the party message than those on the party's ideological fringes.[44]

The more a member feels dependent on the Republican or Democratic Party for electoral support back home, the more they are likely to support the party media messaging attempts. The more members feel they "made it on their own," by challenging the favorite of the local party organization in a primary, or by depending on a non-party group such as the Tea Party, the less likely they are to feel beholden to the national party, to which they give only pro forma support.

For the dissident member, the best defense may be a good offense. If a member's personal values or constituency needs are in conflict with the party position, it is possible to use the media to send a message to party leaders and other members, touting oneself as "independent of party control." One former member outlined the proper way to do this, saying,

> party leaders don't like surprises. Inform the party whips once you have made a decision and then stick by it. Call a press conference and lock in your position. This will protect you from becoming a target of party leaders in the days leading up to the vote and on the floor.[45]

Coordinating messages from senators has proven more difficult. With their smaller numbers, media deference, and tradition of working on their own, senators challenge attempts by party leaders to coordinate their messages. Both parties in the Senate have communications operations attempting similar actions to their counterparts in the House. Republican message coordination lagged behind that of the Democrats until they lost control of the Senate in 2006. As is often the case, reform comes when things are not going as one wishes. Believing they did not lose on merit, but based on the inability to get their message out, the Republicans beefed up their public relations efforts by expanding staff and challenging other leaders to take a more active role in communicating messages in their area of responsibility.[46]

Dealing with Dissidents

When the party is divided on an issue, the leader's media options are less robust. Attempts to change the minds of a colleague, especially when their position is publicly known, are rarely successful. A member might be allowed to vote with their conscience, but asked to discourage media attention to the fact. At times, leaders can imbed a divisive issue in a larger package of issues on which the party is united. Members (and the party as a whole) thus have some "cover" when they go to the press, emphasizing the broader issue.[47] Recognizing that not every piece of legislation a member votes on is perfectly attuned to their liking, accepting a minor undesirable component with a much broader package of benefits is widely understood by both the members and the media on Capitol Hill.

When party leadership and individual member goals collide, personal and constituency benefits tend to prevail. Few members seem willing to sell out their constituency or disavow a deeply held personal belief in favor of the collective benefit of the party presenting a united front. The best the party leadership might hope for is that the opposing members might remain silent and that the media would not pick up on the break in party ranks. For example during the 2003 decision on banning partial-birth abortion, a number of moderate Democrats voted for the Republican ban, but did not use the media to advertise their desertion.[48] In the aftermath of natural disasters which target particular districts, Republicans from affected districts often find themselves torn between the party preferences for limited government spending and non-governmental relief efforts, and the needs of their constituents. After Hurricane Sandy, Representative Peter King (R-NJ) took an active role in challenging his party to unleash government aid. On national television King accused the leaders of his own party of sticking "a knife in the back of New Yorkers and New Jerseyeans" after the GOP-led House delayed a vote on desperately needed Sandy disaster aid. Calling the move an "absolute disgrace," King urged voters to hit the GOP where it hurts – in the wallet. "They're in New York all the time filling their pockets with money from New Yorkers," King thundered on CNN. "I'm saying right now, anyone from New York or New Jersey who contributes one penny to congressional Republicans is out of their minds."[49] King, normally a limited-expenditure Republican, was joined by a number of fellow Republicans from the Northeast. While calling for a "clean" relief bill lacking more offensive measures, aid in any form trumped other hesitations. In an interesting case of predicting the future, King argued "your turn will come." Only a few months later a devastating tornado hit Oklahoma and its congressional delegation from both sides of the party aisle began the pursuit of federal funds. Weakening their positions was the fact that a number of Republicans who had opposed similar aid to their Northeastern brethren drew considerable media attention.

Unanticipated Consequences of Coordinated Messages

Speaking with one voice to the media and eventually the public sounds like an unvarnished positive in a political system where numbers count and power is related to unity. While seeking to control the message they send to the media and the public, the parties lack the ability to control what the media or public will do with those messages. An analysis of the 1994 election indicated significant pressure on Democratic members to present a positive message about their stewardship as the majority party. The media viewed the majority Democrats as frittering away the superior position and failing to get much done. Despite low congressional approval, many of the party stalwarts heeded the leadership call to defend the party's stewardship and faced recall on Election Day. In a case of "guilt by association," those Democrats most willing to defend Congress and its actions reduced both their own and the Democratic Party's electoral chances. Democrats *said* good things about eliminating gridlock and passing key legislation in the future, while the voters *heard* a more negative message and asked "why didn't they do it when they had a chance." It was that message that seemed to carry the day in the voting booth.[50]

As we moved into the Congresses of the 2010s, another consequence emerged. The encouragement of united messages by leaders looked like a key contribution to gridlock, as the media perceived the problem as too much loyalty among two relatively even competitors. The loyalty of individual members led the media to see them as inflexible party hacks unwilling to compromise enough to get anything done.

Unheard and Misheard Voices

The media are not an equal opportunity provider of coverage. They pick and choose among potential sources, favoring some and ignoring others. Few in public life complain about too much coverage, while being ignored or misrepresented engenders frustration and resentment.

The Minority Party Speaks Up

Serving the minority in Congress often results in frustration. The majority party controls congressional procedures to a degree greater than their numerical percentage. Key committees are stacked in favor of the majority party. Leadership positions, unlike a number of state legislatures, are populated totally by members of the majority party. Nothing is scheduled in committee or on the floor without majority party backing. It is no surprise that the media gravitate toward majority party members like moths to a flame.

Lacking desired power and visibility members of the minority party seek to take their policy battles outside the halls of Congress by promoting their agenda and policy positions in the media.[51] In fighting for their place in the media's sun, members of the minority depend on, and sometimes remind journalists of, the "pro and con" model of reporting which potentially blunts charges of media bias. In order to increase the newsworthiness of stories, reporters are tempted to quote more extreme members taking widely divergent positions.[52]

Stifled in committee and on the floor, the minority party often chooses an "outside" media strategy to maintain their position as a player in the legislative process. Newt Gingrich and his supporters used the televised coverage of Congress to build a name for themselves and a broader constituency (see Chapter 10).

Kuklinski and Siegelman found that despite their complaints and the fact that they were the minority in the 1990s, Republicans actually received more coverage in the Senate than did Democrats.[53] They and others[54] also found that ideologically extreme senators received more coverage than their more moderate colleagues. The dampening of this effect in the later (Reagan) years of their analysis is explained by the fact that support for Reagan and his conservative backers served to silence some of the more liberal Democrats.[55]

Profiling and the News

Faced with covering a story, journalists look to those who seem most obviously affected by and interested in the issue at hand. Their judgment call on this may well reveal significant bias. Stereotypes take often common characteristics or interests of a group of people, generalize them to the entire group, and emphasize them to the exclusion of other, often more relevant, characteristics.

LWB: Legislating While Black

African-American members of Congress might want to shout, "I am a member of Congress first and an African-American second," after reflecting on their representation in the media. The media seek out African-American members on issues relating to minorities, but not on other issues, thus denying them the ability to be seen as a member widely competent on a variety of issues and deserving of higher office.[56] Local television stations cover African-American members more than their non-African-American colleagues, but focus on race-oriented issues regardless of the member's legislative record.[57]

Will the Gentlelady Yield

Women in Congress face a similar challenge. Once an extreme rarity in Congress, women now hold 18 percent of the seats in the House and 20 percent in the Senate. Unlike a few decades ago, once nominated, women no longer face disadvantages in terms of fundraising and the ability to win.[58] Despite progress, female legislators point out a more subtle form of stereotyping both during campaigns and once in office. Descriptions of women members of Congress in the news often lead with comments about what they were wearing and/or their family status, topics that generally get bypassed in descriptions of male legislators. As one press secretary to a female member stated in exasperation, "A reporter once asked me, 'How does she have time for kids and Congress?' I asked him if he had ever posed the same question to a man."[59]

They are sought out by the media for comments on "women's issues," but are often "bypassed when stories revolve around meatier issues both of more general importance and often more importance to the female member and her constituents."[60] Content analysis of media initiatives of female members of Congress showed they did not heavily emphasize an interest in women's issues or unique personal characteristics, indicating that the stereotype emanated from the media, not the source. Women "are subject to being viewed by the media as women representatives, rather than as a representative who happens to be a woman."[61]

The Bottom Line

The renewed attempts to use political parties as vehicles for breaking into the media seem to work. Content analysis shows that the more congressional parties do in a coordinated manner to inspire media attention, through such things as multi-member press releases, the more coverage they receive. The media focus on congressional and party leaders' efforts at disseminating a desired message seem to pay off for the parties. "The public hears national leaders' explanations of developments in Washington sooner and more frequently in the national media than they hear the explanations offered by their own individual senators and representatives."[62]

Effort, though, is not the only variable. The partisan tilt of the medium makes a difference; Democrats win more coverage in liberal media for their efforts and Republicans do the same in conservative outlets.[63] As we will see in Chapter 7, individual misbehavior can overwhelm the party message.

Notes

1 Author's interview.
2 R. Douglas Arnold, *Congress, the Press, and Political Accountability*, New York, NY: Princeton University Press, 2004, p. 245.
3 www.nytimes.com/1987/05/21/us/washington-talk-senate-the-new-improved-filibuster-in-action.html?pagewanted=2
4 See Patrick Sellers, "Winning Media Coverage in the U.S. Congress," in Bruce I. Oppenheimer (ed.), *U.S. Senate Exceptionalism*, Columbus, OH: Ohio University Press, 2002, p. 134.
5 Gary C. Jacobson, *The Politics of Congressional Elections*, New York, NY: Longman, 2009, pp. 124 and 129.
6 Joseph Foote, "Rayburn the Workhorse," in E. E. Dennis and R. W. Snyder (eds.), *Covering Congress*, New Brunswick, NJ: Transaction, 1997, pp. 139–146.
7 D. R. Matthews, *U.S. Senators and Their World*, New York, NY: Vantage Books, 1960, p. 214.
8 See Michael Pfau et al., "Embedding Journalists in Military Combat Units: Impact on Newspaper Story Frames and Tone," *Journalism and Mass Communications Quarterly*, vol. 81, no. 1 (Spring), 2004, pp. 74–88.
9 J. E. Zaller, "Without Restraint: Scandal and Politics in America," in M. S. Carnes, *The Columbia History of Post-World II America*, New York, NY: Columbia University Press, p. 230.
10 Katherine Fink and Michael Schudson, "The Rise of Contextual Journalism, 1950s–2000s, *Journalism*, 2013, p. 2.
11 www.renodiscontent.com/2009/02/01/boehner-republicans-are-no-longer-in-the-business-of-legislating
12 See David Broder, *The Party's Over*, New York, NY: HarperCollins, 1972.
13 See Patrick J. Sellers, "Congress and the News Media: Manipulating the Message in the U.S. Congress," *Press/Politics*, vol. 5, no. 1, 2000, p. 22.
14 Karen Kedrowski, *Media Entrepreneurs and the Media Enterprise in Congress*, Creskill, NJ: Hampton Press, 1996, p. 195.
15 Quoted in Christine DeGregario, "Lawmakers and Lobbyists," *The American Review of Politics*, vol. 31, 2010, p. 113.
16 He actually said "*foolish* consistency," but that qualifier is often dropped in the quote's use.

17 Gary Lee Malecha and Daniel J. Reagan, *The Public Congress*, New York, NY: Routledge, 2012, p. 73 and C. Lawrence Evans and Walter Oleszek, "The 'Wired Congress'," in James A. Thurer and Colton C. Campbell (eds.), *Congress and the Internet*, Upper Saddle River, NJ: Prentice Hall, 2003, p. 112.
18 Malecha and Reagan, pp. 78–81.
19 David Mariness and Michael Weisskopf, *Tell Newt to Shut Up*, New York, NY: Touchstone, 1996, pp. 131–133.
20 CBS/*New York Times* Poll, November 3, 1994.
21 Mark Rozell, *In Contempt of Congress*, Westport, CT: Praeger, 1996, p. 105.
22 Ibid., p. 106.
23 Center for Media and Public Affairs, "Media Won't Sign On to G.O.P. Contract," April 20, 1995, p. 7.
24 http://articles.baltimoresun.com/1995-05-03/news/1995123187_1_speaker-newt-gingrich-daily-news-briefing-cameras
25 Both organizations are similar, existing as the meetings of members under each party label. Since their origin the Republican meetings have never fit the caucus definition as a "partisan legislative group making decisions binding on its members." Republicans see their sessions more as information sharing than decision-making. Some argue that Republicans eschew the "caucus" terminology seeing it as having socialist overtones.
26 Daniel Lipinski, *Congressional Communication*, Ann Arbor, MI: University of Michigan Press, 2004, p. 61.
27 Lipinski, p. 62.
28 DeGregario, p. 129.
29 www.brainyquote.com/quotes/quotes/w/willrogers122697.html
30 Malecha and Reagan, pp. 78–81.
31 Sellers, 2002, p. 134.
32 Sellers, 2002, pp. 138 and 149.
33 Malecha and Reagan, p, 73.
34 http://firstread.nbcnews.com/_news/2011/03/31/6384346-tea-party-ralliers-shut-it-down?lite
35 Michael Grunwald, "The Party of No: New Details on the GOP Plot to Obstruct Obama," *Time*, August 23, 2012.
36 Quoted in Malecha and Reagan, p. 69.
37 Patrick Sellers, *Cycles of Spin: Strategic Communication in the United States Congress*, New York, NY: Cambridge University Press, 2010, p. 13.
38 Ibid., p. 205.
39 Ibid., p. 74.
40 Timothy Cook, "The News Media as a Political Institution: Looking Backward and Looking Forward," *Political Communication*, vol. 23, no. 2, 2006, pp. 167–168.
41 Sellers, 2010, p. 23.
42 Ibid., p. 206.
43 Douglas B. Harris, "Orchestrating Party Talk: A Party-Based View of One-Minute Speeches in the House of Representatives," *Legislative Studies Quarterly*, February 2005, p. 134.
44 Ibid., p. 136.
45 Author's interview.
46 Malecha and Reagan, pp. 84–85.
47 Sellers, 2010, p. 74.

48 www.senate.gov/legislative/LIS/roll_call_lists/roll_call_vote_cfm.cfm?congress =108&session=1&vote=00402
49 www.nydailynews.com/news/politics/rep-peter-king-gop-sandy-aid-snub-knife-back-article-1.1231448
50 Lipinski, p. 100.
51 Sellers, 2000, p. 23.
52 See James H. Kuklinski and Lee Siegelman, "When Objectivity Is Not Objective: Network News Coverage of U.S. Senators and the 'Paradox of Objectivity'," *Journal of Politics*, vol. 54, no. 3, 1992, p. 815.
53 Ibid., p. 821.
54 See Peverill Squire, "Who Gets National News Coverage in the U.S. Senate," *American Politics Research*, vol. 16, no. 139, 1988, p. 44.
55 Kuklinski and Siegelman, p. 830.
56 Brian Schaffner and Mark Gadson, "Reinforcing Stereotypes? Race and Local Television News Coverage of Congress," *Social Science Quarterly*, vol. 85, no. 3, September 2004, p. 619.
57 Ibid., p. 619.
58 www.politicalparity.org/research-inventory/money-and-women-candidates/
59 David Niven and Jeremy Zilber, "How Does She Have Time for Kids and Congress," *Women and Politics*, vol. 23, nos. 1–2, 2008, p. 154.
60 Author's interview.
61 Niven and Zilber, p. 160.
62 Lawrence R. Jacobs, Eric D. Lawrence, Robert Y. Shapiro, and Steven S. Smith, "Congressional Leadership of Public Opinion," *Political Science Quarterly*, vol. 113, no. 1, 1998, available at: www.jstor.org/discover/10.2307/2657649?uid=3739704&uid=2&uid=4&uid=3739256&sid=21103379202947
63 Sellers, 2000, p. 28.

Chapter 5

From Props to First Responders

Congress and the State of the Union Message

> He [the president] shall from time to time give to the Congress
> Information of the State of the Union, and recommend to their
> Consideration such Measures as he shall judge necessary and expedient.
>
> U.S. Constitution, Article II, Section III

The chamber is impressive, dripping with tradition and widely recognized by the American public. The setting seems like a Hollywood set and the spectacle a well-choreographed ceremony. The amphitheater seating focused on a raised dais directs one's attention to the speaker. Virtually the entire top echelon of government[1] arrives early and almost universally shows the president deference. The size of the television audience rivals some of the most popular sports and entertainment events. The president arrives to hearty applause and is ushered through the crowd like a conquering hero. Even members of the opposing party in Congress generally honor the office if not the man, recognizing he is "our" president also. The media play their role, anticipating the upcoming message, commenting on congressional reaction, and offering a member of the opposing party – usually a member of Congress – time for live rebuttal.

While the Constitution requires that the president report to Congress, it fails to designate the time, place, or format. The "tradition" of presidents speaking in front of Congress began with George Washington's inaugural address and succeeding annual messages (which would not become known as the "State of the Union Message" [SOTU] for over a century). Following the presidential speech, the president received formal replies from each house of Congress expressing their commitment to the president's goals. Washington gave all of his eight messages orally and Adams followed suit with his four. The emerging tradition of presidents speaking personally to Congress assembled came to a grinding halt with Thomas Jefferson who saw the custom as "an English habit, tending to familiarize the public with monarchial ideas." Jefferson feared that the president's physical presence would intimidate Congress, waste time, and relieve its members of "the embarrassment of immediate answers on subjects not yet fully before them."[2] It is also possible that ego and harsh reality entered the equation; the acclaimed writer of documents such as the Declaration of Independence was known as "one of the least effective public speakers to hold the nation's highest office."[3] Jefferson simply communicated his views to Congress in writing. Whether he spoke or not, Jefferson would be remembered for his prowess with the written word more than his oratorical skill. Subsequent presidents followed Jefferson's guidance since "the habit of writing to Congress was convenient, especially to presidents who disliked public speaking" or who spoke with a lisp.[4]

The tradition of written reports to Congress solidified over the next hundred years until Woodrow Wilson revived the practice of presidents speaking to Congress directly, while dropping the practice of a direct congressional reply. Wilson saw going to Congress as less speaking *to* Congress and more as a method of speaking *directly to* the public at large through a speech in the chamber of Congress.[5] Choosing to speak in such a setting seemed to add importance to the words spoken. While it would be a number of years before technology would allow such speeches to be heard and then seen in real time, the print media of the day picked up on the excitement.

As the spokesperson-in-chief of the American people, presidents use the congressional venue at times of crisis to reveal national unity and express human emotion. Lyndon Johnson stood before the members of Congress a few days after John Kennedy's assassination to proclaim, "All I have I would have given gladly not to be standing here today."[6] Johnson called for the help of Congress and the American people. The television networks cleared their schedules for the speech, and media attention was extensive. Almost forty years later, George W. Bush spoke before a joint session of Congress expressing outrage at the 9/11 terrorist attacks and soliciting congressional and public support for retaliation.[7] Again there was no question that the major television networks would clear their schedules and the media would heavily cover the event. Since Lyndon Johnson's speech, the media environment had changed considerably. The proliferation of cable channels with neither a legal requirement nor financial incentive to cover public affairs gave viewers other options. Up until the late 1970s, a presidential speech in prime time with the existing limited number of channels could be expected to reach about 50 percent of U.S. households. By the 1990s that had dropped to about one-third.[8]

Empirical research shows that the SOTU message is the most watched of all presidential speeches. Despite growth of the U.S. population, though, the size of the audience has declined slightly in recent years. While Bill Clinton and George W. Bush garnered over 45 million viewers, President Obama's figures were about 2 million less.[9] The SOTU is memorable for its audience. Almost 70 percent of those watching the speech could recount at least one point the president made and 26 percent could remember three or more points.[10]

As a scholar of Congress and the presidency, Wilson had definite ideas about the presidential role, feeling that modern presidents can and should lead through public rhetoric. He sought to be a "man of real power and statesmanlike initiative," so he promoted the "purpose of the nation so in the quick in what he urges upon Congress that the House will heed him promptly and seriously."[11] Wilson chafed at calling the speech "The President's Annual Message to Congress," and began referring to it as the "State of the Union Message" (SOTU).[12]

A Televised Happening

The arrival of television merged communications capabilities with America's new cultural vehicle. Harry Truman's 1947 SOTU was the first delivered to the public via television. Lyndon Johnson shifted the speech from its midday tradition to an evening event designed to garner a larger television audience.[13]

Typically, in their front-row seats, well within camera range, Supreme Court justices and members of the Joint Chiefs of Staff sit like stone-faced effigies expected to seemingly hear nothing, see nothing, and especially say nothing. In 2010 President Obama called the Court's recent Citizens United case, which defined corporations as "persons" and allowed them to make campaign contributions, a decision that "reversed a century of law" and would "open the floodgates for special interests, including foreign corporations, to spend without limit in our elections." Justice Alito had had enough and mouthed "not true," just as the television cameras, cued by the speech draft, panned to the justices. Later Alito described the address as "a very political event" and "very awkward," adding, "We have to sit there like the proverbial potted plant most of the time."[14] The revenge of the "potted plant" became a significant news story.

Cognizant of their role as props, members of Congress consider when or if they should applaud specific presidential initiatives. The White House distributes speech drafts so members can follow along and not be embarrassed by failing to show appropriate support or opposition. At times attempts are made by groups of congressmen to make an impact using visual clues.

If you are going to be a prop, you might as well use the opportunity to send a message. Members of Congress supporting President George W. Bush's Iraq policy and celebrating its recent free election followed the lead of freshman Bobby Jindal (R-LA) in wearing purple or dying their fingers purple, the dye used to make sure Iraqi voters only voted once.

The fingers were waved in the air each time the president mentioned success in Iraq.[15]

Seating in the House chamber is traditionally by party, with Republicans on one side and Democrats on the other. The growing partisanship in Congress became visually clear with the speech punctuated by a series of standing applause demonstrations from the president's fellow party members, while the opposition party members seemed glued to their seats while sitting on their hands. Such obvious demonstrations of support and opposition provided a common theme of media stories. In 2011 a number of members picked out "buddies" in the opposition party and took up seats across from them in a symbolic representation of bipartisanship. The action was not missed by the media, but largely viewed as a public relations gimmick.[16]

With the television cameras capturing the SOTU for media distribution back home, a number of members attempted to use the event to their own advantage. The way members of Congress commit their time and priorities indicates the strategies they deem most useful. In recent years, a regular contingent of members show up in the House chamber to claim the unassigned seats along the main aisle the president will enter. Knowing that the television networks and still photographers will capture the slow walk through grasping hands and beaming smiles, these members seek a moment or two for a picture in close proximity to the president or even a chance to pass on a short message. Some members have become known for their consistent successful photo ops which they hope will show up in their district papers to legitimize their claim of being close to the president.

Presidents are announced to the chamber in a booming voice by the House Sergeant-at-Arms, and the president walks down the aisle accompanied by House and Senate Leaders. It looks like a campaign event with the president grabbing hands and having short conversations with selected members picked up by the microphones. Members of the president's party tend to get the lion's share of face time with the president.

Television is a very personal medium that invites the stories of individual effort and valor our individualistic culture seeks. Corporate America encourages us "to focus on individual responsibility rather than collective responsibility."[17] We traditionally analyze success by looking for extraordinary heroes and investigate failures as the result of individual shortcomings. In politics, idealistic Americans tend to avoid identifying problems as structural, beyond the control of any one individual, and seek a person to blame. The SOTU is the chance for the president to identify societal problems, and more importantly outline how he would go about solving them. If blame must be assigned, it usually is directed at the president's predecessor or the opposite party. American life is characterized as a set of "heroes and zeroes." We are

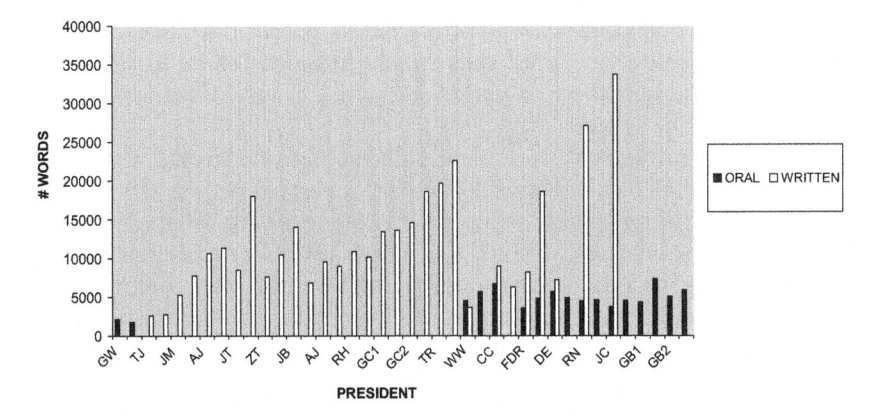

Figure 5.1 Length of Presidential Speeches to Congress
Source: John Woolley and Gerhard Peters, *The American Presidency Project*, available at: www.presidency.ussb.edu/sou_words.php

drawn more to the "great man theory" of history, rather than a perspective that men and women are raised to greatness or dashed to disgrace by forces largely out of their own control.

The shift from oral to written speeches unleashed a torrent of words. Wilson's shift back to the oral format led to an acceptable length of an oral speech of about five thousand words (see Figure 5.1). Recognizing the growth of sound-bite journalism and limited public attention span on television, SOTU speeches became significantly shorter during the television era. Modern audiences would not sit through the earlier messages, which averaged about 15,000 words (www.presidency.ucsb.edu/).[18] With such a limited window of opportunity, presidents must express care in how they shepherd the resource. Taking a hundred words or so to humanize the speech comes at the cost of other content.

Over time, the content of presidential speeches also varied. Earlier speeches remained relatively formal, with the president outlining legislative initiatives. As the president's words spread more directly to the population, the public began to see the human side of the president as he played the role of "reactor-in-chief" commenting on crises facing the nation. The human connection received another spin with modern presidents over four times more likely to include words such as "we" and "our" in their speeches than were their nineteenth-century predecessors, thus drawing the public into presidential speeches more as co-participants than as simple audience.[19] Ronald Reagan proved transparent in his strategy explaining, "I have the word 'they' and 'their' in speaking of these heroes, I could say 'you' and 'your' because I'm addressing the heroes of whom I speak – you the citizens of this blessed land."[20] When presidents use the pronoun "you" in their speeches, they are often not talking to the assembled audience of legislators, who now seem to be "relegated to the role of studio audience."[21] The "you" refers to the viewers. Telling us stories of our friends and neighbors as heroes seems like a natural progression of personalizing the speech.

The SOTU provides the president with the most consistent vehicle by which the president can connect with the American people. The SOTU has shifted from reporting *to* Congress to reporting *from* Congress. The audience in the chamber is much less important than the media and the public, whom the president is really trying to reach. The congressional setting adds seriousness and legitimacy; its members are not particularly amenable to persuasion since most have already taken stands on the key issues that they are unlikely to change.

The audience among the public is impressive, giving the president access to a larger percentage of the public than most other initiatives. Polls indicate that 40–70 percent of the American public report having seen all or part of the SOTU each year since the Reagan administration.[22] The SOTU serves as a tool through which the president attempts to shape the policy agenda by setting out his preferences and priorities. Research results are mixed as to whether the media shape the president's choice of topics as opposed to presidential priorities shaping subsequent media content.[23] A challenge for the president lies in the personality bias of modern media. The abstract and complex nature of policy initiatives is harder to write about than the exploits of individuals. The speech is more of a launch pad than a landing. Presidents follow up the State of the Union with speeches around the country reinforcing the core messages.[24]

Refining the Rhetoric

After reviewing presidential speeches from Washington to Reagan, Jeffrey Tullis concludes that "in Ronald Reagan, America found the rhetorical president."[25] While criticized for detachment in many realms of presidential responsibility, Reagan took a hands-on approach to the development of a speech. The process was described as one where "His writers supply the substance; he adds the homespun paragraphs … he sees himself as less an originator of policy than as the chief marketer of it."[26]

As one of the key weapons in a president's arsenal of persuasion weapons, subsequent presidents have paid careful attention to strategies that work to draw positive media attention and public acceptance. Personalizing the speech through the insertion of hero stories seems to work.

A Tradition Begins

The leader of the free world stood before the Congress outlining his priorities and pleading for support. Looking the assembled legislators directly in the eye, he asserted, alleged, and argued his case. Just as his audience became accustomed to being the focus of his attention, the president's glance went over their heads and in a moment he was saluting a surprised and rather nondescript young government worker with an unknown name lacking a clear pedigree sitting beside the president's wife in the gallery. Legislators craned their necks to see what was happening behind their backs wondering who deserved such fealty. Neither members of Congress nor the cameramen recording the event for posterity knew whether they should laugh, cry, applaud, or ignore the president's singling out one person as "the spirit of American heroism." No one in the chamber knew how to react. Cameramen accustomed to following gestures of speakers eventually broadcast his picture worldwide. The young man, who at first assumed Ronald Reagan's salute was meant for First Lady Nancy Reagan, awkwardly rose to his feet at the urging of his seatmates and began what was to become much more than his allotted fifteen minutes of fame. Few in the chamber or in the large television audience realized they had just experienced a unique historical event, the birth of a tradition.

As Ronald Reagan tilted his head toward the first lady's box in the House chamber no one was prepared for the tradition he was about to create out of whole cloth. Flipping through the television channels a few weeks before his 1984 SOTU Message, Ronald Reagan saw Lenny Skutnik risk his life in the icy winter waters of the Potomac to save the life of a struggling flight attendant whose plane had crashed into the river. As others looked around, hesitated, and chose not to act, Skutnik "instinctively ripped off his overcoat, kicked off his shoes, dove into the river, and pulled 22-year old flight attendant Priscilla Tirado to safety."[27] She would become one of five survivors of the seventy-nine people on the plane. The crash of Air Florida Flight 90 just after take-off from National Airport resulted in many heroic acts, with Lenny Skutnik's unselfish act topping the list since it was captured on tape and was successful. Preparing for his SOTU message, Reagan, the actor, saw the potential of humanizing the complex concepts of volunteerism and individual initiative as opposed to government action. For a leader who believed that the "solution is not government, but the problem is government," an average citizen with no legal responsibility to act was too good a symbol to pass up. In his world view individuals had a moral obligation to voluntarily contribute to the betterment of society. Helping others is the way we "justify the brief time we spend" here on earth.[28]

A New President Adopts the Strategy, with a Twist

Television images of the SOTU often reflect the schizophrenic nature of partisan political support. In 1995, recognizing the tendency of the president's partisans to publicly show their support during the SOTU, Bill Clinton set the Republicans up for a political fall. He found a hero the Republicans would be hard-pressed to ignore.

Only a few months after the attack on the Murrah building in Oklahoma City, Social Security worker and Vietnam veteran Richard Dean found himself in the House gallery as a heroic honoree. On that fateful morning in April 1995, Dean had just finished a conversation with an old friend he would never see again, when the bomb rocked the building. After seeing a brilliant flash and hearing a huge noise, he was buried in ceiling tiles, shattered glass, and furniture pieces. After a deathly silence, the cries for help began.[29] Dean became a one-man rescue squad, helping the injured and searching through the rubble for his long-time girlfriend. Reality struck hard when he realized that the dampness seeping though from above was not from broken pipes, but from crushed bodies in the daycare center and offices on the next floor. He would soon be joined by Oklahoma Police Sergeant Jennifer Rodgers, who also risked her life on the upper floors comforting and saving victims. The death toll would eventually climb to 168, many of them not the government workers against whom Timothy McVeigh had turned his anger, but children and innocent citizens. Dean's story would have a happy ending when he found his girlfriend uninjured after more than an hour of searching.[30]

The heroism touched the hearts and minds of Clinton's congressional audiences without regard to political stripe. The applause crossed the House of Representatives aisle which separated Republicans from Democrats. Embarrassed, "Dean swallowed hard and clasped his hands together, untwining them to rub them across his pants and shake the hands of well-wishers, including Mrs. Clinton."[31]

But Clinton was not through with Richard Dean, or the Republicans in Congress. After establishing Dean's credentials as a hero, Bill Clinton offered his follow-on, a one-two punch to make a point and embarrass the Republicans. As the standing ovation began to die down, Clinton dropped the other shoe. When the Republicans forced the shutdown of the government by refusing to agree to Bill Clinton's budget, Dean continued to help social security beneficiaries from home even though he had been forced from his office and was working without pay. Clinton pointedly looked at the glum and now seething Republicans and challenged them never to allow such a shutdown again.[32] As it became clear that the government shutdown cost both additional money and considerable disruption in public services, Republican electoral fortunes diminished, with Bill Clinton giving the wheel another turn in the name of Richard Dean.

The Tradition Goes On

Virtually every SOTU message since Reagan has included a reference to heroes in the gallery. There is no clear definition of what exemplifies a hero in politics. In general Democratic presidents tend to focus on heroes who made new and/or expansive uses of government programs, while Republican presidents honor heroes who eschewed government programs and attempted to bring about social change on their own.[33]

In order to create an "all knowing" image, the "talking heads" of the media attempt to predict what the president will say and who he will recognize in the gallery prior to the SOTU. Even before the final applause dies down, the on-air reporters engage in instant analysis critiquing both the content and the presentation, often exuding an "I told you so" attitude.

Congress Responds

Although imprecisely, the media attempt to gauge general presidential approval and/or possible success for specific proposals by the congressional response to the speech. Media coverage often indicates the amount of time it took the Speaker of the House to regain order or the number of times the speech was interrupted by applause. In the age of extreme partisanship, the image often takes on the aura of two competing teams cheering on their captain.

The physical set-up of the House reinforces the image of competition, placing the Republicans in seats to the left of the presiding officer and Democrats to the right, separated by an aisle. This designation may seem strange, since we normally associate Republicans with the right and Democrats with the left. The right- and left-wing terminology began with the French Parliament where the ordinary people (more liberal) sat to the left of the *presiding officer*.[34] The American right and left terminology looks at the chamber from the *perspective of the members* elected by the people. This fits more clearly with American political philosophy that all sovereignty comes from the people, rather than the European view that kings and other political leaders give up sovereignty as a system becomes more democratic.

If imitation is the sincerest form of flattery, members of Congress have attempted to insert their own heroes into the media spotlight. In 2006, peace activist Cindy Sheehan accepted an invitation from Representative Lynn Woolsey (D-CA) to sit in the gallery as a symbol of opposition to the war in Iraq. While President Bush spoke, she was escorted from the chamber and later arrested because she wore a t-shirt opposing the war. In Congress' drive toward the image of bi-partisanship, that same evening the wife of Representative Bill Young (R-FL) was asked to leave for wearing a shirt supporting the war.[35] When the stories hit the news, the Capitol police were forced to apologize, admitting the improper application of an archaic rule that flew in the face of free speech.[36]

At times members of Congress fail to play their expected role. When policy issues deeply divide the parties, the media focus their commentary on the number of applause lines the president receives from Congress and/or the standing ovations presidents get from members of their party while the opposition sits on their hands. Standing ovations and feigned indifference by opposition party members of Congress have increased in recent years.[37] During the 2009 SOTU speech, Representative Joe Wilson (R-SC) used a loud stage whisper of "you lie," challenging President Obama's assertion that illegal immigrants would not be insured under his healthcare plan. The president ad-libbed, "that is not true," giving the outburst more visibility and guaranteed media coverage. In the short run, Wilson's outburst was replayed hundreds of times by media providing a vivid image of a policy conflict between the president and the opposing party.[38] Wilson's website traffic exploded after the outburst and he raised thousands of dollars from supporters.[39] The longer-term consensus was that Wilson had overstepped his bounds. In a more subtle protest, a number of Republicans held out stacks of papers to indicate they had a better and more specific healthcare plan and had been shut out of the policy development process.

As soon as the speech concludes many members dash from the chamber to do interviews with the media, trying to spin the story either in a positive or negative direction. Journalists stake out the hallways for reactions from members all too willing to insert their two cents' worth. The House and Senate recording studios see a line of members attempting to get a sound bite into the media mix. Other members begin tweeting even before the speech has concluded. As in all their media relations, members must constantly be on guard. After the 2014 SOTU, Representative Michael Grimm (R-NY) got so mad at a reporter who strayed from the script of asking about his reaction to the SOTU message and inquired about a tax fraud charge against the congressman that he threatened to throw the reporter over the Capitol balcony. The video went viral and the congressman had to apologize for overreacting.[40] Grimm ran for reelection in 2014 and retained his seat but later resigned.

The Official Congressional Rebuttal

For much of recent history, fairness in media coverage was defined as equal time. Although equal time no longer serves as the benchmark for evaluating fairness, it remains so in the congressional realm. Immediately following the SOTU message the opposition party is given a block of time to make its case.

Being asked to officially respond to the president's SOTU by one's party is a mixed blessing. It marks one as a player by both the media and the public, but one's performance is fraught with potential dangers. For one thing, the president sets the agenda and as responder-in-chief, the party representative gains little if he or she has not anticipated what the president has just said will say and make a cogent counter-argument. Second, while the president "performs" with all the trappings of office and gains the advantage of having his rhetorical "juices" stimulated by the setting and the crowd, the responder is tucked away in a small room on Capitol Hill with only the camera crew and a few staff members around. Third, the response comes after the speech and in the later portion of prime time television for many Americans. Drawn to the once-a-year attraction of the SOTU, less interested voters are likely to have "had enough of politics" and either turned off the television set or switched to an entertainment program by the time the opposition party spokesperson has a chance to speak.

There is no guarantee that the response to the SOTU will capture the fancy of the media, or that if it does what the media will focus on. In 2013, Senator Marco Rubio (R-FL) received considerably more attention for his awkward on-camera snatching of a bottle of water than for the substance of his comments.

Being "Used"

Politics often involves being "used" both by one's friends and one's opponents. In the SOTU, the president uses the congressional setting to add legitimacy and drama to his attempt to set the national agenda. Members of Congress, on the other hand, recognize that in serving as the audience-in-chief they gain the status of being the ones who deserve being informed first – even if the president is often talking over their heads to the American public and even the international community. The media serve as the bridge to analyze the president's thoughts and the tool for expanding the president's audience beyond the confines of Capitol Hill.

Notes

1 Traditionally, one member of the Cabinet is absent, in order to maintain a line of succession should a tragedy occur.
2 Quoted in Jeffrey Tulis, *The Rhetorical Presidency*, Princeton, NJ: Princeton University Press, 1987, p. 56.
3 Loch K. Johnson, "Thomas Jefferson: Third President of the United States," in Bernard K. Duffy and Halford B. Ryand (eds.), *American Orators Before 1900*, Westport, CT: Greenwood, 1987, p. 245. See also www.monticello.org/site/research-and-collections/public-speaking

4 Henry Adams, *History of the United States During the Administration of Thomas Jefferson*, New York, NY: Scribner's, 1989, vol. 1, pp. 247–248 and "State of the Union Trivia," Gannett News Service, January 25, 2008.

5 See Tulis, p. 133.

6 www.history.com/shows/jfk-specials/videos/lyndon-johnsons-address-to-congress-after-kennedy-assassination

7 www.c-spanvideo.org/program/166196-1

8 Samuel Kernell and Laurie L. Rice, "Cable and the Partisan Polarization of the President's Audience," *Presidential Studies Quarterly*, vol. 41, no. 4 (December) 2011, p. 695.

9 PBS News Hour, "Obama's SOTU TV Audience Numbers Continue to Drop, Now Lower than Bush's Lowest," transcript, available at: http://cnsnews.com/news/article/obama-s-sotu-tv-audience-numbers-continue-drop-now-lower-bush-s-lowest

10 George C. Edwards, *On Deaf Ears: The Limits of the Bully Pulpit*, New Haven, CT: Yale University Press, 2003, pp. 197, 198, and 208.

11 Woodrow Wilson, *Congressional Government*, Boston, MA: Houghton Mifflin, 1885, p. 161. Quoted in Tulis, p. 133.

12 David Muir, "Historically Speaking," *ABC News Now*, January 23, 2007.

13 Ryan Teten, "Evolution of the Modern Rhetorical Presidency," *Presidential Studies Quarterly*, June 2003, p. 233.

14 Adam Liptak, "For Justices, State of the Union Can Be a Trial," *New York Times*, July 23, 2012, available at: www.nytimes.com/2012/01/24/us/state-of-the-union-can-be-a-trial-for-supreme-court-justices.html?_r=0

15 www.foxnews.com/story/2005/02/03/red-white-and-blue-city-sees-purple/

16 www.washingtonpost.com/wp-dyn/content/article/2011/01/24/AR 2011012405382.html

17 Bert Rockman, *The Leadership Question*, New York, NY: Praeger, 1984, pp. 177–178.

18 Richard Nixon did break the norm, giving the longest speech on record of over 33,000 words (www.presidency.ucsb.edu/).

19 Teten, p. 342.

20 Ronald Reagan, Inaugural Address, 1981, www.presidency.ucsb.edu/ws/index.php?pid=43130

21 Geoffrey Nunberg, "And, Yes, He Was a Great Communicator," *New York Times*, June 23, 2004, p. 5.

22 Martha Joynt Kumar, *Managing the President's Message*, Baltimore, MD: Johns Hopkins University Press, 2007, pp. 12–13.

23 See Maxwell McCombs, *Setting the Agenda*, Cambridge, MA: Polity Press, 2004, p. 101.

24 Kumar, p. 12.

25 Tulis, p. 189.

26 "How Reagan Stays Out of Touch," *Time*, December 8, 1986, p. 34.

27 Michelle Malkin, "The Importance of a Ronald Reagan Moment," *Human Events Online*, June 9, 2004.

28 See David S. Adams, "Ronald Reagan's 'Revival'," *Sociological Analysis*, 1987, p. 17.

29 Stephen Barr, "A Presidential Salute," *Washington Post*, January 24, 1996, p. A14.

30 John Farrell, "Checking in with Clinton's 'Heroes'," *Boston Globe*, January 27, 1998, p. A12.

31 Macon Morehouse, "State of the Union," *The Atlanta Journal and Constitution*, January 24, 1996.
32 Glenn Kessler, "Clinton Took Advantage of Opportunities," *Charleston Daily Mail*, November 4, 1996, p. 1A.
33 See Stephen Frantzich, *Honored Guests: Citizen, Heroes, and the State of the Union*, Lanham, MD: Rowman and Littlefield Publishers, 2011.
34 www.encyclopedia.com/topic/Left_Wing.aspx
35 www.cnn.com/2006/POLITICS/01/31/sheehan.arrest/
36 Ibid.
37 www.washingtonpost.com/wp-dyn/content/article/2011/01/24/AR2011012405382.html
38 Jocelyn Noveck, "A Weekend of Ugly Discourse," *The Virginian-Pilot*, March 23, 2010, p. A9.
39 Jody Yager, "Lawmaker Acknowledges Shouting Out 'Baby Killer'," *The Hill*, March 23, 2010, p. 1.
40 www.politico.com/story/2014/01/reporter-rep-grimm-was-so-angry-102799.html

Chapter 6

Mr. Chair and My Loyal Fans

Celebrity Testimony on Capitol Hill

The face was familiar, but it seemed out of place. Comedian Stephen Colbert, or his faux alter-ego, the conservative spokesperson, was testifying on migrant workers, marshaling his experience of an afternoon working in the fields. The event was not without controversy. Some members criticized the event and questioned the loss of respect for Congress such a gimmick might have on Congress produce. Representative Steve King (R-IA) challenged Colbert's role as a policy spokesperson, arguing that he supported American workers who "prefer the aroma of fresh dirt [more] than the sewage of American elitists."[1] In the long run, the gimmick did garner significant media attention for both Colbert and the issue.

Congressional testimony serves a number of purposes. Witnesses can provide the benefit of their expertise, contributing new facts and/or interpretations to the congressional decision-making process. As a political strategy, witnesses garnering the attention of the media have the potential to expand the terrain of political battle, drawing in other media, interest groups, and the general public. As a more defensive strategy, a full lineup of witnesses potentially stifles complaints that all positions were not heard, even if one alternative eventually wins out. The right to express one's views carries with it the possibility of cooptation wherein the dissenter mollifies other opponents by asserting, "at least our position got a hearing."

Members of Congress struggle for the eyes and ears of the public. Media attention is important both for the advancement of personal political careers and the promotion of preferred public policies. Members have found that America's fascination with celebrity can be used to their advantage, by using sports and entertainment stars as spokespersons for legislative causes during congressional hearings. Senator Arlen Specter (D-PA) drew the attention of the media and titillated the viewers on the issue of pornography's impact on women by inviting Linda Lovelace and two other porn stars to testify.[2] A well-known celebrity draws the media to a congressional hearing like a light attracts bugs. When well-known celebrities swoop onto Capitol Hill with their personal entourages, the cry "xx is in the building" sweeps through the Capitol e-mails and phone lines. Star-studded staff and media "groupies" follow the action and enlarge the crowd.

The Early Years of Celebrities on the Hill

The call to testify on Capitol Hill, now accepted with relish by celebrities, was not always received positively. In the early days of film, stars associated with a studio were discouraged from political activism for fear that it would harm the bottom line at the box office.[3]

During the red scare of the late 1940s the call to testify before Congress became more ominous. Being charged as a potential communist disrupted and at times killed careers. The House Un-American Activities committee called dozens of Hollywood writers and actors. Youthful indiscretions and innocuous comments or behavior were dredged up and laid on the committee table for all to see. The very fact that someone refused to answer a question (using their constitutional right against self-incrimination) was enough to "prove" their guilt. Running scared, the leaders of the entertainment industry largely failed to come to the aid of their professional compatriots. Showing up on the studio blacklist led to losing one's celebrity status and/or foregoing one's means of employment.[4] A number of entertainers ended up serving jail terms for failing to cooperate with the congressional investigations. Looking back, it is hard to imagine the paranoia of the era and the excesses of the committee, but they led to a chilling effect on testimony in front of Congress. It would take a generation or more for celebrities to turn giving testimony from being a detriment to a benefit.

The Nature of Celebrity

The word "celebrity" comes from the Latin *celebritas* which relates to "multitude" or "famous." Celebrities in a society are those who are "much talked about." With a bit of a swipe at the legitimacy of their status, Daniel Boorstin defines a celebrity as "a person who is known for his well-knowness."[5] As opposed to a hero who gains that status by acts of bravery or unique effort, celebrity emerges from a less solid grounding. Heroes risk their lives, fortunes, or reputations for a higher cause. For the celebrity, they are their own cause. We even talk about a "cause célèbre" which draws inordinate attention. Heroes wear their mantles through many generations by mentions in folklore, sacred texts, and history books. Celebrity status is more transitory being granted by gossip, contemporary public opinion, and less serious media.[6] Parents urge their children to emulate heroes much more than celebrities. Most celebrities are there because of a good dose of luck, more than personal ability or effort. Many work hard to create and maintain their celebrity status, a set of behaviors which marks them as particularly self-serving. Most celebrities fade or fall into anonymity within a generation, while heroes have their images enhanced by repetition and/or exaggeration. Celebrities thus enter the policy arena with a major detriment: limited legitimacy. Most members of the public feel a little guilty about the attention they personally give celebrities and are particularly critical when their friends and neighbors become "star struck."

The Contemporary Search for Legitimate Spokespersons

Commentators on celebrity testimony tend to fall into four camps. The *idealists* assert the right of every citizen to express their point of view in a democracy and argue that celebrities should not be denied this right. Life is seldom fair. When questioned about his use of celebrity status, actor Paul Newman argued, "Just because I can sway more people than I have a right to, does that mean that I'm not entitled to my opinions or to voice them? The world situation affects us, as movie people, as much as it does others."[7]

Some idealists see celebrities as role models, whose civic activism may well spur on general citizen involvement. Some go so far as to imply that life experiences of celebrities may well be superior to those of others since they have often overcome disadvantages to reach their current notoriety and can now look back with unique insight into life's challenges which the government may try to alleviate.

The *pragmatists* point out that in a celebrity-focused society such as the United States, celebrities, with their publicity-drawing power and often well-honed communications skills, have the potential for drawing attention to problems shared by their unknown fellow citizens. By acting instead (in the place or "stead") of others, celebrities can give voice to the silent majority lacking the skills, slack resources (time and money), and the platform to make their case.

The *cynics* see celebrity promotion of political viewpoints as public relations gimmicks in which the celebrity attempts to burnish their image by supporting popular causes. Cynics see celebrities as largely minimally talented individuals who caught a break and garnered the attention of a gullible citizenry, public officialdom, and media. Living vicariously through their celebrities, many members of the public are seen as psychological groupies, accepting largely uninformed and vacuous celebrity musings. Looking for a good story that will guarantee them print space or television time, the media are seen as pandering to the public with its fascination with celebrities, their families, and pets. Public officials are not immune to celebrity worship, at best using them to promote the officials' own perspectives, and at worse treating them with unwarranted deference, never giving their testimony the critical evaluation it deserves.

Going a step further, the *critics* see celebrity testimony as thwarting objective analysis of critical issues. Celebrity agendas do not necessarily reflect public interests or societal needs. Living in a rarified world, most celebrities are seen as lacking realistic perspectives. Stacking the deck in favor of celebrity perspectives gives the celebrities more power than they deserve. From an institutional perspective, lowering the bar in defining "experts" has the potential for demeaning the entire legislative process based on gathering the best information and making the wisest legislative decisions.

Passing the "Laugh Test"

It is important for celebrities to pass the "laugh test," and create the legitimacy of having their testimony seen as something worthy of listening to. Having the testimony seen as nothing but a cynical joke undermines both the value of the testimony and the legitimacy of Congress' committee system for gathering information. Legitimacy emerges in a number of ways. Some celebrities "live" the issue, having personal experience with a disease or consequences of a public policy. Others "learn" their way into the policy process, becoming substantive experts. Celebrity endorsements simply add their status as a star to an issue, requesting both Congress and the public to come to the conclusion that if the issue is good enough to be of concern to the celebrity, it is good enough for their attention.

Legitimacy is not simply granted or denied, but exists along a continuum. The celebrity visibly struggling with a disease has more credibility (see Box 6.1) than one relaying experiences with a relative. Someone directly harmed by a public policy generates more concern than someone speculating on the possible impact of policy change. Celebrities who have observed problems and are attempting to place them on the policy agenda carry less weight than those having felt the sting of purportedly bad policy (see Box 6.2).

Box 6.1 Testimony from the Heart

In the early stages of his Parkinson's disease, Michael J. Fox was not ready to face public scrutiny. He described the trick he used to hide the symptoms medication could not cover. Moving around when he talked, Fox could hide the tremors, and did a number of interviews walking around, leading the interviewers to comment on his nervous energy, but failing to discover the actual cause. He was so nervous about mumbling or shuffling at the Golden Globe awards, he had the chauffeur drive around the block three times while he got his nerve up to face the crowd.[a] It was a seemingly lonely seven-year battle of wits and courage until he decided he could go public on his own terms in an interview with Barbara Walters. Fox's revelation upset the storyline of both his professional and personal life as a young, handsome, and invincible person with courage (the conservative offspring of liberal hippies in *Family Ties*) and the flexible hero in *Back to the Future*. All of a sudden a member of the young and beautiful crowd had an "old person's disease" accompanied by increasing incapacity. In a Hollywood ending, Marty McFly would time-travel to the future, cure Parkinson's disease, and return to live happily ever after. In the real world, though, Fox feared he would be written off "as a tragic figure, a helpless victim."[b] As it turned out, his revelation led to media discussion of young-onset Parkinson's. Perhaps unwittingly, Fox was drafted into a larger movement to increase public awareness and change public policy relative to Parkinson's disease. Fox recognized that it was no longer "a mission to save myself."[c]

Sources:
[a] C. S. Beck, "Personal Stories and Public Activism: The Implications of Michael J. Fox's Public Health Narrative for Policy and Perspectives," in E. Ray (ed.), *Case Studies in Health Communication*, Mahwah, NJ: Erlbaum, 2005, p. 337.
[b] Michael J. Fox, *Happy Man*, New York, NY: Hyperion, 2002, p. 228.
[c] Ibid., p. 26.

Box 6.2 Some Recent Celebrity Testimony

CELEBRITY	SUBJECT	LEGITIMACY	YEAR
Lance Armstrong (athlete)	Cancer funding	Cancer survivor	2008
Roger Clemens (athlete)	Steroids	Defending himself	2008
Linda Ronstadt (singer)	Funding for the arts	Personal cause	2009
Usher (pop star)	Community service	Foundation founder	2009
Bill Corgan (entertainer)	Performer compensation	Affected party	2009
Kevin Costner	Oil spill clean-up	Clean-up company owner	2010
Louis Gosset Jr. (actor)	Prostate cancer funding	Cancer survivor	2010
Rashard Mendenhall (athlete)	Childhood obesity	Personal commitment	2010
Nick Jonas (singer)	Childhood diabetes	Victim	2011
Richard Gere	Human rights in Asia	Personal cause	2011
Mickey Rooney (actor)	Elder abuse	Victim	2011
Martin Sheen	Creation of drug courts	Former drug user	2011
Ben Affleck (actor)	Aid to the Congo	Personal interest	2014

Stretching the bounds of legitimacy are celebrities simply using the congressional platform to push a personal policy preference which in the ideal world would have no more legitimacy than the preferences of any ordinary citizen. Celebrities have no magic ability to choose the best preferences for society. Most criticism is reserved for celebrities who either mislead congressional committees or who view their testimony as a performance in which truth and real commitment are lacking. For many, the low point in celebrity testimony (perhaps after the appearance of *Sesame Street*'s Elmo) came with Stephen Colbert's testimony as his on-air conservative persona on farm workers after the "experience" of spending an afternoon working alongside them (see later discussion).

The Celebrity Mediated World

In one sense, public fascination with celebrities and their political views does not make a great deal of sense. They live in a unique world few of us can imagine. The daily pressures of paying our bills, disciplining our kids, and calling in the plumber to fix a leak seem to pass celebrities by. Considerable evidence exists, though, that major segments of the public look at celebrities as role models for fashions, lifestyle, and even political outlooks. Commercial entities have long used celebrities to endorse their products. An emerging field of communications research looks at "entertainment-education" as a strategy with the potential to "increase audience member's knowledge ... create favorable attitudes, shift social norms, and change overt behavior."[8]

The public creates para-social relationships with celebrities, respecting their views and aspiring to be like them. Even absent any direct personal contact, members of the public may create strong "friendship" ties and mimic the behavior of celebrities who they adopt as role models. The ties are "analogous to the real interpersonal relationships that people have in a primary face-to-face group."[9] The celebrity may become a "counselor, comforter, and model."[10] Television is seen as a uniquely powerful medium for developing para-social interaction by combining stimuli (audio and visual), repetitive and familiar settings, and intimate camera angles.[11] The intimacy of television relationships and television in general has deepened through the increased use of first names as surrogate titles and salutations in both conversation and official business. Early television gave us "Jackie" (Gleason), "Uncle Miltie" (Berle), and "Jack" (Benny). Today no one flinches at familiar salutations such as "Bono," "Oprah," or "Dr. Phil." Politicians may well have led society in attempting to build personal ties by not publicly objecting to monikers such as "Abe," "Teddy,"[12] or "Barack."

Who Wins?

A celebrity's arrival on the Hill is an "event" drawing the attention of the denizens of the Capitol building and the media alike. The celebrities generally enhance their careers by serving as responsible citizens interested in the body politic.[13] On arrival, celebrities are generally treated with deference and subject to less critical questioning than the typical stable of experts.[14]

Political consultant Robert Squire used his experience in Washington to place the issue of celebrity testimony in Congress in stark relief saying,

> It's very simple. Some people are draws and others aren't, and you coddle the people who will draw audiences for you and beat up on the rest ... When politicians invite celebrities to come to a hearing and speak, and then are uncomfortable with the relationship they have established, it is because they feel they cannot draw the cameras themselves. So the politicians need the celebrities.[15]

His words were echoed by a member of Congress who described the purpose of celebrity testimony,

> You raise awareness of the issue. You get the American people to care about it, you get TV, you get the press; there's nothing wrong with that. Now, I wouldn't just take testimony from movie stars, but for publicity, it's okay.[16]

Since all media have a limited news hole, editorial decisions as to who and what to cover is often a zero-sum game – covering one thing or person means not covering someone or something else. Former Chief Justice of the Supreme Court, Charles Evans Hughes, pointed out, even if unintentionally, an insightful analogy. In a eulogy to Charles Lindbergh, he compared the pilot and later political story to a ship, explaining, "We measure heroes as we do ships, by their displacement. Colonel Lindbergh has displaced everything."[17] The news stories covering Lindbergh displaced possible stories of other newsworthy people and topics about which we will never know. The same can be said of contemporary celebrity testimony. It pushes aside other voices in the media.

Celebrities often serve as "door openers," giving access to themselves and other activists in the cause they which to promote. Once in the room, the celebrity must have some real substance in his or her comments or they will hurt the cause more than help it.[18] Once a celebrity has brought the issue to the table, it is generally politically more effective to step back and allow the substantive experts to dominate the conversation.

Push Back

Not all members of Congress gladly welcome celebrities, especially when they come to testify against the member's position on an issue. Stephen Colbert set the cynical tone for his 2010 testimony before a House Judiciary subcommittee on farm workers by asserting, "I certainly hope that my star power can bump this hearing all the way up to C-SPAN 1."[19] Colbert pushed the envelope even further and titillated the audience by showing pictures of his colon while explaining the importance of roughage.[20] When asked about the bill in question, Colbert shot back, "like most members of Congress, I haven't read it."[21] Zoe Lofgren (D-CA), chair of the subcommittee, drew the ire of the full committee chair for inviting Colbert to testify, especially on live television.[22] Members of the committee "shifted on the dais"[23] during the testimony. Republicans on the committee objected to Colbert, whose faux conservatism hits home with many, but had less of a leg to stand on about celebrity testimony since the Republican majority welcomed Elmo the puppet to testify in 2002 on the importance of music education.[24] Media reports on the Colbert appearance were largely negative, although it is important to point out that they relished the story and spread the issue far and wide.

Over in the Senate, celebrity witnesses have also received mixed reception. When Back Street Boys singer Kevin Richardson testified on mountaintop mining, Senator George Voinovich (R-OH) refused to attend, stating "It's just a joke to think that this witness can provide members of the United States Senate with information on important geological and water quality issues ....We're either serious about the issues or we're running a sideshow."[25]

Senator Joe Lieberman (D-CT) defended his invitation of Richardson by asserting, "Mr. Richardson is here as more than a well-known celebrity ... He is knowledgeable on this issue and has in fact worked to protect the environment in his home state. I believe his voice will add to our understanding of the issue."[26]

Who Cares?

Celebrity testimony on behalf of a political issue is directed at a number of audiences. In the proximate and pragmatic sense, the members of Congress before whom they testify maintain the primary position for only they have the right to vote on policy. When media pay attention to an issue, others tend to follow for fear of being seen as out of touch and irrelevant. The potential impact may well be more indirect. Celebrity testimony may be designed to garner media attention, which in turn is designed to influence the public. Stories covered by the media touch the hearts and minds of other members of Congress and the public. No member wants to face a reporter or constituent with "Gee, I have never heard about that issue." Thus agenda setting facilitated by celebrity testimony ultimately may create direct or indirect pressure on the members of Congress when they face a vote in committee or on the floor.

Notes

1 Dan Zak, "Stephen Colbert Brings Truthiness About Farm Workers to Capitol Hill," *Washington Post*, September 25, 2010.
2 Shanto Iyengar, *Media Politics: A Citizen's Guide*, New York, NY: W.W. Norton, 2011, p. 222.
3 For an in-depth look at celebrity testimony, see H. C. Strine, "Stars on Capitol Hill: Explaining Celebrity Appearances in Congressional Committee Hearings," Ph.D. dissertation, Purdue University, December 2004.
4 www.history.com/this-day-in-history/the-red-scare-comes-to-hollywood
5 Daniel J. Boorstin, *The Image: A Guide to Pseudo Events in America*, New York, NY: Antheum, 1972, p. 57.
6 See ibid., p. 63.
7 *Playboy* interview quoted in Ronald Brownstein, *The Power and the Glitter*, New York, NY: Pantheon Books, 1990, p. 231.
8 Arvind Singhal et al. (eds.), *Entertainment Education and Social Change*, Mahwah, NJ: Lawrence Erlbaum Associates, Publishers, 2004, p. 5.
9 Ibid., p. 366.
10 Ibid.
11 See Donald Horton and R. Richard Wohl, Communication and Para-Social Interaction," *Psychiatry*, vol. 19, 1956, p. 217.
12 When Theodore Roosevelt spoke at rallies, people began to chant "Teddy" at rallies; perhaps it is because it rolls off the tongue a little easier than "Theodore." TR embraced the nickname publicly, but privately did not like being called "Teddy" (R. Matuz, *The Presidents Fact Book*, New York, NY: Black Dog and Leventhal Publishers, Inc., 2001, p. 402.
13 P. David Marshall, *Celebrity and Power: Fame in Contemporary Culture*, Minneapolis, MD: University of Minnesota Press, 1998, p. 85.
14 Strine, p. 149.
15 Quoted in Len Sherman, *The Good, the Bad and the Famous*, New York, NY: Carol Publishing, 1990, p. 146.
16 Ibid., p. 149.
17 Quoted in Boorstin, p. 68.
18 Brownstein, p. 270.
19 Matea Gold, "Colbert's Through-the-looking-glass Moment in Congress," available at: http://articles.latimes.com/2010.sep/25/nation/la-na-immigrants-colber-20100925
20 Richard Sisk and Corky Siemaszko, "Steve Comes Colon," *Daily News* (New York), September 25, 2010 and Ashley Parker, "A Comic Twist on Political Chatter," *New York Times*, September 25, 2010.
21 Sara Afzal, "The Top 10 Political Quotes of 2010," *Christian Science Monitor*, December 19, 2010.
22 "Colbert's Corny Report: Democrats Invite Satirist to Make a Farce of the Lawmaking Process," *Washington Times*, September 17, 2010

23 Michael A. Memoli, "Colbert Delivers Congress the 'Whole Truthiness'," *The Gazette* (Montreal), September 25, 2010.

24 www.washingtonpost.com/wp-dyn/content/article/2010/09/28/AR 2010092804802.html?wpisrc=nl_most

25 www.billboard.com/articles/news/75515/senator-boycotts-backstreet-boys-testimony

26 Ibid.

Chapter 7

Bombasters and Buffoons

Making Congress an Easy Target

Every family has the oddball aunt or the strange cousin whose behavior brings disrepute on the entire clan. While there is little evidence that Congress as a whole has a greater percentage of inappropriately behaving individuals, the transgressions of the few make news for a variety of reasons. In the first place, members of Congress are public officials whose behavior is monitored and who are expected to behave in particularly virtuous ways in the eyes of their paymasters, the American public. Second, individuals in politics are expected to make pronouncements of grand principles about appropriate behavior in the ideal society, but whose own personal behavior often fails to stand up to those principles. Finally, rather than viewing inappropriate behavior by members of Congress as personal failures, there is a significant temptation on the part of the media to generalize the entire institution, to tar and feather every member for the sins of a few.

The media tendency to cover controversy, scandals, and gaffes increasingly pushes out more substantive news. To a degree the definition of a gaffe or a scandal is in the eyes of the beholder. For our purposes, we will consider a "gaffe" as a self-inflicted statement or action which portrays the perpetrator as uninformed, stupid, or insensitive, while a scandal involves violating widely held values of morality, legality, or failing to uphold the public trust. Opponents often attempt to elevate a gaffe into a representation of a moral failing. For example, when Virginia Senate candidate George Allen referred to a student of Sri Lankan heritage who had been monitoring his campaign for his opponent, as a "Maccaca" (unfortunately for Allen caught on videotape), the gaffe created a "perfect storm." Allen's first (and rather delayed) statement that he never said it, set him up for charges of lying. The later interpretation that he did not know what the term meant sent reporters out to investigate. They found the word was a common derogative term (literally for a monkey) in the section of Morocco where Allen's mother grew up. The alleged lying heightened either the impression of Allen's insensitivity, or his assumptions about the stupidity of journalists whom he felt would not know or learn the term.

In the final analysis, the outburst struck deep at an alleged lack of moral reprehension toward racism. Being known for having a confederate flag in his office, and for other statements differentiating the kinds of people in Virginia led to defeat in a race he was expected to win easily.[1]

Perhaps it is a positive reflection on normality, but scandals draw a great deal more attention from the media than do the more common serious and competent handling of the expected tasks of a member of Congress. Creating a "scandal frame" to besmirch one's political opponents has become a common strategy. Democratic oriented members and media see the "speck" in Republican legislators' "eyes" more than the "log" in the "eyes" of Democrats, while Republican-leaning newspapers and members show a similar pattern of forgiveness for fellow partisans and contempt toward their partisan opponents.[2]

The Draw of Personal Failure

Virtually all observers point to the increased emphasis on scandal stories about Congress. While it is impossible to determine whether modern members are more venal or stupid than their predecessors, a number of factors associated with increased media demand and ease of supply help explain some of the reasons for the fascination with congressional scandal.

Changing Norms and Needs: Increased Demand

The expansion of media outlets, increased competition for stories, and the reduced impact of professional norms facilitates the dissemination of stories that once might have remained hidden. For much of the history of covering Congress and other political institutions, journalists accepted the rule that behind-the-scenes personal behavior with no direct impact on a member of Congress' official role was out of bounds. From the pragmatic perspective, journalists saw that allowing members of Congress wide leeway would protect their future access. Under such constraints, personal shortcomings seldom left Capitol Hill. The general movement toward investigative journalism accelerated by rewards for the Watergate reporters (see Chapter 2), facilitated moving beyond investigating policy shortcomings and illegality to personal failures.

In the latter part of the twentieth century, a new breed of journalists, less subject to socialization and training in the traditional norms, arrived on the scene. The decline in local media coverage of Congress made long-term access to specific members less important, making more members targets for stories about intemperate statements, womanizing, and drinking. The muddying of the line between "on" and "off stage behavior" occurred across the political board. On the presidential level the prohibition about showing Franklin Roosevelt in the wheelchair or reporting John F. Kennedy's sexual encounters was replaced by the media playing and replaying Bill Clinton's answer to a student's question of whether he wore boxers or briefs.[3] Few of the new journalists questioned covering the barrage of explicit stories about the president's sexual proclivities. On Capitol Hill, the threshold for news coverage of personal proclivities dropped considerably. The old advice of former Louisiana Governor Edwin Edwards, that a politician was only vulnerable if he "got caught in bed with a dead girl or a live boy"[4] was superseded by the reporting of charges involving adultery and texting sexual messages.

Television, regulated by the Federal Communications Commission (FCC), adhered to a relatively prudish set of criteria as to what was acceptable on the air. Entertainment programs instituted a seven-second delay, to allow in-house censors the opportunity to "bleep" out words that might get them in trouble. *The Smothers Brothers*, one of the most popular comedy shows of the 1960s, was eventually canceled because some guests made anti-war comments and there was a joke about children playing doctor.[5] George Carlin mocked network television with his "seven dirty words you cannot say on television."[6] While still banned on broadcast television, they reverberate on cable and the web regularly.

The deregulation of the 1980s turned the FCC into a toothless tiger and the arrival of cable television whose content was not controlled encouraged the broadcast networks to loosen their limits. When the Supreme Court defined the Internet as a publishing vehicle, rather than a broadcast medium (ruling the Communications Decency Act unconstitutional), purveyors and consumers of previously questionable material now had another outlet and source.[7]

In the era of fixed publication times and broadcast schedules, politicians could use strategic timing to either increase or decrease coverage. Richard Nixon's famous "Saturday Night Massacre," when he fired the special prosecutor investigating the Watergate break-in, was timed to miss the Sunday morning paper deadlines. When a number of House members got in trouble for overdrawing their accounts at the House credit union, the House waited until after midnight to vote and reveal the names of the offenders, again trying to reduce coverage in the morning newspapers (see Chapter 2).[8] With the arrival of the 24-hour news cycle, such strategies have lost much of their utility. With no "down time," and a huge news hole to fill, anything publicized at out of the ordinary times is likely to get *more* attention. In addition, as the media have increased their role as interpreters as much as reporters of the news, speculation about the motivation behind behavior becomes news in and of itself.

Discovery and Shelf-Life: Increased Supply

The new media environment differs not only in the creation and dissemination of news, but also in its shelf life and potential for archiving and retrieving. In the print era a lead from someone's (perhaps faulty) memory might result in a frustrating odyssey of discovery of the rightful source. Since most newspapers were not indexed, access to past editions of most papers required retreating to a dingy newspaper "morgue" where one needed to know information such as date of publication to find the key quote or action one was looking for. It was a task one would not wish on one's worst enemy. Dead ends were the norm. Even the official proceedings of congressional actions, the *Congressional Record*, provided only limited indexing and clumsy searching. Access to radio or television clips was even more difficult, with very limited indexing and retention.

Today, sources such as LexisNexis provide full text access to hundreds of newspapers, the *Congressional Record*, and transcripts of national news programs. YouTube indexes provide access to both mainstream electronic program segments and unofficial recordings of members of Congress. It is no longer wise to say one thing to one set of constituents and the opposite to another. Members of Congress are now held accountable for what they said months or years before. The "I can't remember" or "I never said that" excuses receive little validity when compared with retrieved records. What a member says on social media or in an e-mail may generate more news than what they say in a floor debate.

Finding television clips was even more difficult until recently and depended on serendipity and luck. Most events were not saved to tape. Today archives such as the Vanderbilt Television News Archives (national news programs), and the Purdue Public Affairs Video Archives (C-SPAN coverage of Congress) provide searchable databases of congressional statements. Such sources have been supplemented by YouTube where viewers become editors, providing official news segments with amateur footage of politicians and others in action. The sophisticated ability to edit YouTube submissions creates a whole new level of potential jeopardy for public officials. Spoof pictures and videos reside along with the legitimate. Once a picture or video enters the blogosphere it is impossible to rein it back in. Once a bell is rung, there is no mechanism to un-ring it. Not only do such sources provide the media with more raw material, but denying gaffes and inconsistencies is increasingly difficult in modern politics since much more is recorded, preserved, and archived in ways it can be found.

Making the Scandal "Cut"

There is no clear bright line defining inappropriate behavior. The media retain the right and power to elevate particular behavior patterns into various categories. At times factors other than objective standards applied uniformly dramatically affect those decisions. For example, about the same time the public lost billions of dollars through laws giving savings and loan organizations publicly funded insurance to cover bad investment practices, the media almost ignored this story in favor of a more simple one about the House of Representatives "bank" in which no public money was lost (see Chapter 2).

Changing Standards

At times members of Congress must feel "damned if they do, and damned if they don't." Once ignored or even heralded behaviors become black marks of shame over time. In 1950, the venerable American Political Science Association published a position paper entitled, "Toward a More Responsible Two Party System."[9] It endorsed the goal of creating more distinct parties with candidates pledged to their principles and elected officials committed to carrying out the party goals. Today both academics and the media criticize such party distinctiveness and partisanship as a major flaw in congressional behavior leading to partisanship and gridlock.

Certain issues tend to upset the contemporary press corps more than in the past. In 1946, when Congress included pay increases for its members, major newspapers such as the *New York Times* and the *Washington Post* applauded the move as a way of attracting the best candidates to perform the important task of Congress.[10] Today that talk of a pay increase brings almost universal condemnation. Distrust of Congress and its members led to the passage of the 27th Amendment in 1992 making it illegal to apply congressional pay increases until after the next election. In order to further insulate themselves from media and public opposition, congressional pay is now determined by a formula based on economic indexes and the pay of other federal workers. The adjustment goes into effect the next Congress, unless Congress votes to prohibit it. In about two-thirds of the cases in recent years, Congress has allowed the adjustment to take place.[11]

Outbursts and Misbehavior

In scanning congressional behavior, the media searchlight tends to fall on members whose behavior seems inappropriate or inconsistent. They challenge the norms of civility and rational debate.

Bombasters

Angry and intemperate language draws the attention of the media. Touted by its members and supporters as great deliberative bodies, ad hominem outbursts and personal challenges having little to do with the issue at hand are almost too good for the media to ignore. The rules of Congress attempt to buffer political passion with expectations of courtesy. Members can be called out of order for criticizing fellow members by name or questioning their motives. On the societal level expectations of courtesy in everyday interactions have declined dramatically. It is impossible to know whether the harshness of talk radio and the popularity of conflict-based news programming is a cause or result of societal conflict, but the new tone spills over to both the coverage of Congress and the behavior of its members.

The loosening of societal norms of what is acceptable behavior reflected in the media was accompanied by reduced civility in the House and Senate. During President Obama's 2009 State of the Union message, Representative Joe Wilson (R-SC) inappropriately yelled out "It's a lie" when the president made a point about his healthcare plan (see Chapter 5).[12] Speaking on the House floor about abortion policy in 2010, Representative Randy Neugebauer (R-TX) yelled about "It's a baby killer" while Representative Bart Stupak (D-MI) was speaking; so much for reasoned debate.[13] With the 24-hour news cycle, such outbursts get national attention (much more than the tepid or misleading apologies) and the speaker becomes a hero among some groups in the population. Lacking other congressional news, the video clips of inflammatory comments are repeated over and over again.[14]

Buffoons

Lest one think that inappropriate congressional behavior is a new phenomenon, selected episodes did reach the media through the public in the past. Behavior showing a member skating close to the line of illegality, or acting in strange ways has been part of Capitol Hill lore from the beginning. The impact of such stories was limited by the fact that the local media of most importance to the member's political well-being often downplayed the stories. Many of the most outrageous characters in Congress continued to gain reelection (see Box 7.1).

Box 7.1 A Flood of Criticism

In the 1970s, Representative Dan Flood (D-PA), a colorful former Shakespearian actor known as "Dapper Dan," based on his waxed mustache and his flitting around Capitol Hill in a black cape, was convicted of conspiracy and bribery in federal court and later brought before the House ethics committee. Throughout his career Flood created a close tie with local newspapers, especially the *Wilkes-Barre Record* and *Times Leader* (both owned by the same company). When Flood called with a story, senior editors took the call and wrote glowing stories. As one former editor put it, "We idolized him in the press."[a]

During a series of trials and hearings and charges of perjury associated with illegal contributions, the *Pittsburgh Post-Gazette* was quick to point out the criminal connections of Flood's accusers.[b] On the other hand, local newspapers in the area simply reprinted Associated Press articles on the trial and published a series of letters to the editor supporting Flood. No local newspaper initiated any investigative journalism to determine the validity of the charges against Flood.[c]

While on the national level, Flood was being "excoriated ... both in print and cartoon,"[d] the local media and his constituents stood by him. Despite the charges, the local citizens thumbed their noses at the national media and Flood's accusers selected him as "Citizen of the Year" in 1978, well after the charges had been filed. Although under indictment during the 1978 campaign, and found guilty of three charges a few weeks before the vote took place, Flood again won reelection easily. A grateful constituency emblazoned his name throughout his district. There is a Daniel J. Flood Elementary School, a Daniel J. Flood Rural Health Center, and a Daniel J. Flood Industrial Park.[e]

Facing ill health, a new round of accusations and review by the House Ethics Committee, Flood resigned. He maintained his innocence and gave credence to the assertion of locals that "Flood was being used as a 'scapegoat' by the Carter administration because [of his] 'opposing giving up the Panama Canal' or by the 'all powerful abortion lobby'."[f] Whatever the case, the local media undoubtedly lengthened his congressional career and strengthened his resolve, while the national media played a key role in one of the first cases where a member of Congress was held responsible for alleged ethical and legal violations.

Sources:

[a] William C. Kashatus, *Dapper Dan Flood*, University Park, PA: The Pennsylvania State University Press, 2010, p. 151.

[b] http://downfalldictionary.blogspot.com/2009/04/daniel-j-flood-dapper-briber.html

[c] Kashatus, p. 270.

[d] Ibid.

[e] www.nytimes.com/1994/05/29/obituaries/daniel-flood-90-who-quit-congress-in-disgrace-is-dead.html

[f] Kashatus, p. 270.

In all forms of media and for all public officials there was once a relatively bright line of distinction between public and private life. Sexual improprieties, drinking problems, or other untoward behavior might be bandied around the bar or in the press room by journalists, but reports seldom found their way into the news. By the 1990s "no one – not the media, not the politicians, not the public – sees a line anymore between what should be public and what should be private in a public servant's life."[15] Hard visual evidence makes it difficult to sweep inappropriate behavior under the rug.

Wise members of Congress evaluate potential behavior by speculating, "How would this look on the front page of the *Washington Post*?" Public officials are "often misled by the adulation of those around them and the misperception that their position will make them invulnerable to outside criticism."[16] Some congressional behavior is simply dumb, such as Anthony Weiner's (D-NY) "sexting" via Facebook (see Box 7.2). Other behavior borders on illegality, such as Dan Flood's (D-PA) illegal fund-raising (see Box 7.1). Both examples drew the media toward members, who before, seldom saw their names in national outlets.

Box 7.2 Hot Dog, a New Technology

In 2012, former Rep. Anthony Weiner (D-NY) was forced to resign after texting a provocative picture ("sexting") of himself on the Internet. The picture went viral, with the media unable to restrain itself after being handed such a funny juxtaposition of a name and a behavior. As the story developed, he was mocked by a man, dressed as a hot dog, singing

Oh I wish I'd been an Oscar Mayer "wiener,"
Instead of the big stud I tried to be!
Then I'd still have my seat in Congress,
And no one would be making fun of me.[a]

The story might have ended with his congressional resignation, if Weiner had not tried to make a comeback by running for the Mayor of New York. During the campaign, it came out that Weiner had done similar sexting *after* his resignation from Congress. The repeated inappropriate action offended both the media and past supporters, leading to the end of his political career.

[a] http://blogs.courier-journal.com/politics/2012/03/26/democrats-collect-the-barbs-at-gridiron-club-dinner/

Congress is filled with human beings who strive for greatness, live mundane lives, and/or make mistakes. The mistakes garner more news coverage. Some mistakes emerge from human weaknesses reflected in inconsistency between public policy positions and personal. The conservative espousing family values and then carrying on an affair becomes fodder for the media, as does the liberal criticizing public education, only to send his or her own children to private schools. Other mistakes fall more clearly in the category of crime (see Box 7.3). There is no clear evidence that members of Congress have more criminal tendencies than others in high-level positions, but it is clear that they operate under a more unforgiving media microscope.

Box 7.3 "To Faithfully Discharge the Duties of the Office on Which I Am About to Enter"

This portion of the oath of office for members of Congress at least implies that members remain law-abiding citizens and do not use their public office for illegal gain. The temptations of public office have led some members astray, giving the media a spate of stories about human weakness.

James Trafficant (D-OH) was expelled from Congress in 2002 after being convicted in federal court of bribery.

Bill Janklaw (R-SD) resigned from Congress after a conviction for vehicular manslaughter resulting in the death of a motorcyclist.

William Jefferson (D-LA) was caught with $75,000 hidden in his freezer in what he claimed was a sting operation. A conviction on racketeering and money laundering led to his 2008 defeat.

Jesse Jackson Jr. (D-IL) resigned from Congress in 2012 after pleading guilty to using $750,000 in campaign funds to buy personal items.

Trey Radel (R-FL) was caught in 2013 purchasing cocaine and sentenced to one year's probation. He later resigned from the House.

Michael Grimm (R-NY) was indicted for tax evasion and perjury after hiding more than $1 million in business revenues. He ran in the 2014 election but resigned after his indictment.

Source: Martha Moore and Kevin Johnson, "N.Y. Rep Charged with Tax Fraud," *USA Today*, April 28, 2014, available at: www.usatoday.com/story/news/politics/2014/04/28/michael-grimm-indicted-congress/8386217/

Implications of Focusing on the Negative

Optimists see the focus on the personal foibles of members of Congress as a deterrent warning other members to hold in check their more base motivations and personal peccadilloes. On the other side of the spectrum media fascination with personal shortcomings may well drive more important stories out of the news, contribute to the lack of trust in Congress, and discourage potentially good office holders from placing their lives under the microscope.

Notes

1 Stephen Frantzich, *O.O.P.S: Observing Our Politicians Stumble*, Cremona, CA: ABC-CLIO, 2012, pp. 139–141.
2 Ricardo Puglisi and James M. Snyder, Jr., "Media Coverage and Political Scandals," http://ssrn.com/abstract=111//16

3 http://content.time.com/time/specials/packages/article/0,28804, 2007228_2007230_2007258,00.html

4 www.brainyquote.com/quotes/quotes/e/edwinwedw111998.html

5 www.dead-frog.com/comedians/comic/jackie_mason

6 www.theatlantic.com/entertainment/archive/2012/05/the-7-dirty-words-turn-40-but-theyre-still-dirty/257374/

7 http://partners.nytimes.com/library/cyber/week/062697decency.html

8 Mark J. Rozell, *In Contempt of Congress*, Westport, CT: Praeger, 1996, p. 97.

9 www.apsanet.org/~pop/APSA1950/Ranney1951.pdf

10 Mark J. Rozell, "Press Coverage of Congress, 1946–92," in Thomas E. Mann and Norman J. Ornstein (eds.), *Congress, the Press, and the Public*, Washington, D.C.: American Enterprise Institute and The Brookings Institution, 1994, pp. 59 and 110.

11 Ida A. Brudnick, "Salaries of Members of Congress: A List of Payable Rates and Effective Dates, 1789–2008," Congress Research Service, 97–1011 GOV, updated February 21, 2008.

12 David Lightman and William Douglas, McClatchy-Tribune News Service, March 24, 2010.

13 "Discourse Gives Way to Loud Rhetoric," *The Oklahoman*, March 29, 2010, p. 12a.

14 Jocelyn Noveck, "A Weekend of Ugly Discourse," *The Virginian-Pilot*, March 23, 2010, p. A9.

15 "The Love-Hate Relationship Between Politicians and the News Media," *American Journalism Review*, September 1994, available at: www.the freelibrary.com/The+love-hate+relationship+between+politicians+and+the+news+media.-a015853974

16 Author's interview with a legislator.

Chapter 8

Congress, the Houses of Ill Repute

Cartoonists Take on the House and Senate

In the contemporary era, with Congress' public approval at about 10 percent, the lowest of all national institutions, it is tempting to conclude that Congress' fall from grace is a recent phenomenon. Looking back for some golden age of congressional approval remains elusive. In fact, since the beginning of the republic, Congress has been the butt of jokes and derision. Some of the most abiding vehicles for making fun of Congress are cartoons. Since the earliest days, Congress and its members have stood out as fodder for cartoonists' pens. A number of reasons stand out for the appeal of Congress. Taking on Congress as a whole fits with the biases against it as an institution and results in few repercussions. Congress lacks a coherent collective voice to object to even the most outrageous charges. Furthermore, the inherent nature of Congress invites derision when related to appealing but unrealistic standards such as efficiency and rational compromise. Congress is filled with fallible human beings who carry out much of their personal and official life in public. Duplicity, illegality, immorality, and stupidity all make news and the raw material for humor. Politics resembles kids on the ball field choosing up teams with the most interested shouting "pick me, pick me." Their very eagerness to be appreciated invites extra scrutiny. Each shortcoming invites derision among those not picked first. The partisan nature of contemporary politics creates two teams, each seeing value in tearing down those on the other team.

Complaints about cartoons focusing on Congress and its members receive few complaints from its targets. The cultural norms of "being a good sport" and willingness to laugh at oneself make it difficult for the target of a cartoon, or their supporters, to object without making the situation worse. Lack of countervailing information tends to give the original assertion more validity.

Cartoonists love nothing better than capitalizing on public shortcomings with national appeal and human characters. It is hard to imagine a laudatory cartoon, except perhaps with the passing of a national hero.

Cartoonists point out failures, justifying their actions as designed to improve the political process by passing it through the force of public criticism.

Comic Strips

Cartoons come in two basic forms, comic strips and editorial cartoons. While categories are not absolute, each operates under different expectations and constraints. Comic strips generally appear on dedicated comics pages, include a number of panels, and tell developing stories by continuing imaginary characters. Only a few cartoon strips take up political issues and even fewer deal with Congress. Since comic strip artists need to syndicate their product to a wide number of newspapers, they need to tread softly on hot political issues. The comics pages are some of the first places people go in a newspaper, seeking the exploits of their favorite characters. Editors tread carefully considering dropping any comic strip, recognizing that each has an important and vocal constituency. Editors signal their evaluation of more edgy cartoon subjects. When a comic strip, such as *Doonsbury*, becomes too political in the editor's eyes, it is often moved to the editorial page or somewhere else in the paper. That said, a number of strips use unflattering caricatures of generic members of Congress to demean the character and behavior of all members. It always seems worth a chuckle to portray Congress as inefficient and individual members of Congress as pompous and prone to improper behavior (see Box 8.1).

Box 8.1 Sticks and Stones May Break My Bones, but Names Will Never(?) Hurt Me

Comic strip cartoonists telegraph their cynicism about Congress through the names they use to label members of the Senate. The regular jabs at the institution and its members could not have improved their images.

Senator Jack S. Phogbound appeared in the comic strip *L'il Abner*, set in the imaginary hamlet of Dogpatch. *L'il Abner* was created by Al Capp, who spent forty-three years teaching the world about Dogpatch, reaching 60 million readers in over 900 American newspapers and 100 foreign papers in 28 countries. The strip ran from 1934 through November 13, 1977.[a]

George Lichty drew *Grin and Bear It* until the 1970s using a pompous, posturing gasbag of a politician by the name of **Senator Snort**. The parody and name continues on with Lichty's replacements.[b]

In the 1950s, Walt Kelly, creator of the comic strip *Pogo*, gave us **Senator Simple J. Malarky** based on Joseph McCarthy (R-WI), the disgraced senator who made unsupported charges about the communist infestation of government.[c]

Senator **Lucias Bedfellow** was the greedy and arguably evil senator in Berkeley Breathed's Pulitzer Prize winning *Bloom County* during the 1980s. The parodied senator frequently came under scrutiny from his constituents in the meadow. Though previously convicted on corruption charges, Bedfellow returned two decades later in Breathed's new comic strip *Opus*, still usually drunk and plagued by reporters.[d]

Senator **Batson D. Belfry** regularly graced the comic strips of Jeff MacNelly's *Shoe* beginning in the late 1970s. Sen. Belfry, the "Beltway blowhard" bore a striking physical resemblance to former House speaker Tip O'Neill. The strip and character continues after MacNelly's retirement with a handpicked team of cartoonists who regularly puncture the pomposity of the senator.[e]

Sources:

[a] www.thegovernmentrag.com/phogbound_the_real_cause_of_the_shut-down.html

[b] http://visualhumor.wordpress.com/2012/06/09/grin-and-bear-it/

[c] www.loc.gov/pictures/item/acd1996004581/PP/

[d] http://tvtropes.org/pmwiki/pmwiki.php/ComicStrip/BloomCounty?from=Main.BloomCounty and www.berkeleybreathed.com/pages/About.asp

[e] www.berkeleybreathed.com/pages/About.asp and www.washingtonpost.com/blogs/comic-riffs/post/of-shoe-and-jeff-macnelly-new-story-celebrates-strips-35th-anniversary–and-its-legendary-creator/2012/09/09/7642bcb0-f97a-11e1-a073-78d05495927c_blog.html

Editorial Cartoons

Editorial cartoons, on the other hand, are usually one panel, with a timely topic, often including caricatures of real politicians. Their efforts appear on the op-ed page with a variety of textual columns in which the editorial writers are expected to express their opinion. Editorial cartoonists build on and amplify stories in the news. Until relatively recently most major newspapers had an editorial cartoonist on salary, with the expectation that cartoons about local topics would generally trump the national. The appeal of a national target such as Congress has increased in recent years as newspapers have dropped local cartoonists in exchange for buying from syndicated sources. Syndicated cartoonists, out of necessity, tend to give short shrift to local issues in order to increase the salability of their cartoons in the national market. A few widely recognized symbols, such as the Capitol dome, send powerful signals to cartoon consumers, aiding their understanding of the cartoon's target. Added to this is the ability to humanize abstract concepts. When focusing on Congress, American media tend to focus on the "who," in the "who, what, when, where, and why" journalistic formula. Cartoonists use caricatures of generic or highly visible members of the House and Senate to send specific messages about the nature of the institution as a whole.

Analysis of cartoons over time clearly points out the limited shelf life of most efforts. Looking at cartoons from previous eras, or even previous months, often leaves the observer scratching his or her head mumbling, "I don't get it." Lacking context created by other arms of the media leads to few cartoons reaching iconic status.

Ready, Aim, Fire

As one cartoonist put it, "I place politicians in my sights and shoot projectiles over their bows revealing hypocrisy, illegality, and stupidity."[1] Editorial cartooning is a process involving determining context, choosing a target, and preparing an assault. While the following tools cartoonists use are important to understand, it is equally important to remember that if a cartoon (like any joke) needs explanation it has failed its most basic task of serving as a stand-alone assertion.

Getting Ready

Few editorial cartoons emerge on their own. Most cartoonists stash away a few "evergreens"; generic cartoons reflecting widely held opinions (i.e., Congress as inefficient, members of Congress beholden to special interests, etc.) to emerge from the drawer when a deadline approaches and no new idea stimulates creativity. Cartoonists, out of necessity, are news junkies, monitoring numerous sources to test the news of the day. With each story, they ask a number of questions. Can I represent this issue visually in a way understandable to a broad segment of the public? Does the story have enough visibility to appeal to a wide audience? Can I turn the issue into something clever and hopefully humorous through tools such as caricature or irony? Can I get the finished cartoon through the editors who make the final decision on what to run?

Source: drawn by Eric Smith.

Source: drawn by Eric Smith.

Identifying the Target

Editorial cartoons are short-hand summaries of complex issues. The cartoonist must make a point with a few strokes of the pen and at most a few words. In order for a cartoon to reflect on Congress, the reader must recognize the target. To assure reader understanding, cartoonists bend over backwards to provide multiple cues. They tend to follow the premise of H. L. Mencken that "No one ever went broke underestimating the intelligence of the American people."[2] In over 50 percent of the congressional cartoons analyzed, cartoonists played it safe and penciled in the word "Congress."[3] The relevancy of a cartoon increases in the consumer's mind when it takes on a decision-maker whose actions are perceived as important. It makes little sense to take on weak targets, especially when there is little they can do about the criticism. About 25 percent of the cartoons present a well-known member by name. In just under 20 percent the Capital dome alone symbolizes Congress.

Tools of the Trade

Editorial cartoonists use a few tried and true techniques in their assault on Congress. Some of the cleverest cartoons combine a variety of approaches to increase the chances that one of them will hit home.

Caricature

Caricatures are built on exaggerations of recognized physical characteristics of individuals or groups of individuals. Above and beyond identifying the target the exaggerations carry with them connotations (usually negative) reflecting personal shortcomings. In order to assure reader understanding, only members of Congress with widely known features to exaggerate become targets. If a cartoon consumer fails to recognize the target, the battle for understanding is lost. Cartoons often show generic members of Congress as fat, wearing atypical clothes, and/or associated with a money bag (supposedly ill-gained).

Source: drawn by Eric Smith.

Source: Steve Sack.

Metaphor

Metaphor involves comparing Congress to a widely recognized symbol while leaving a negative impression. Congress is associated with a number of common metaphors such as animals (tortoise, pigs at trough, herding cats, stealing chickens, bull in china shop), sports (fight, strip poker, bull fight), tools and machines (out of gas, long knives, meat grinder, smoking gun, puppet), behaviors (hand in cookie jar, crossed fingers, in bed with, kids in sand box), historical or literary figures (Pinocchio, Frankenstein, Cookie monster), or job holders (clowns, robbers).

Source: drawn by Eric Smith.

Source: drawn by Eric Smith.

Sarcasm/Irony

Sarcasm portrays the worst possible interpretation of Congress as the norm. The focus falls on questionable motives and consistent behavioral shortcomings.

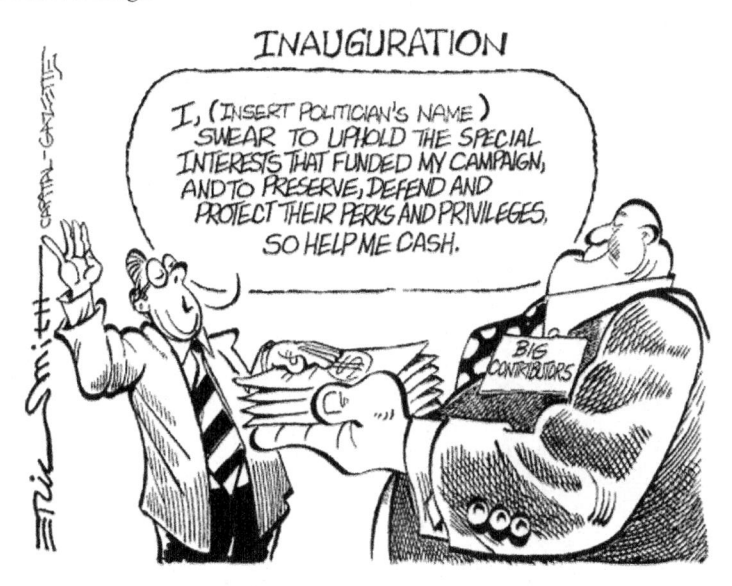

Source: drawn by Eric Smith.

Source: drawn by Eric Smith.

Word Play

Word play involves cleverly using the meaning (or double meaning) of a word to encourage people to see a member of Congress or the institution in a new or different way. While the graphical representation makes the cartoon more interesting, most of the meaning resides in the words used.

Source: drawn by Eric Smith.

Source: drawn by Eric Smith.

Source: drawn by Eric Smith.

Sight Gag

Sight gags take the opposite approach. The words (if any) mean significantly less than the visual picture to present Congress or its members in a critical new and clever way.

Source: drawn by Eric Smith.

Source: drawn by Eric Smith.

Taking Aim

With two chambers, 535 members, and a variety of competing political institutions, editorial cartoonists have a wide variety of targets on which to focus. As they scan the political horizon, cartoonists have considerable leeway as to where to set their sights. Today's top story may be tomorrow's irrelevant sideshow. A number of patterns seem to guide editorial cartoonists as they consider Congress a worthy target.

Context

Congress operates in a complex environment in which the importance of its activity depends to a great deal on what else is happening in the political world. Like the public, cartoonists seem to prefer the efficiency of united government over the supposed advantages of checks and balances. Although at times the public has expressed the desire to have Congress and the presidency controlled by different parties, most polls – especially in recent years – indicate a preference for united government.[4] Congress finds itself in the crosshairs of cartoonists more often during years with divided government as opposed to those with united government. The visual image of gridlock serves as the anchoring graphic in numerous congressional cartoons (see Figure 8.1).

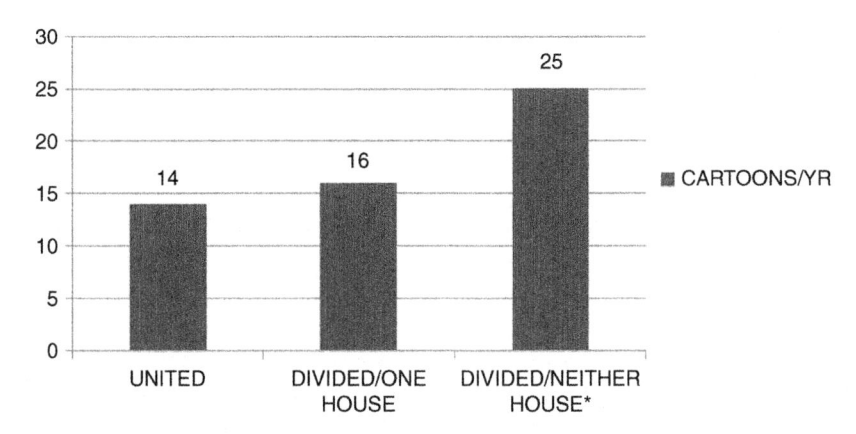

Figure 8.1 Congressional Cartoons and Party Control of the Presidency and Congress
*President's party controlling neither house.

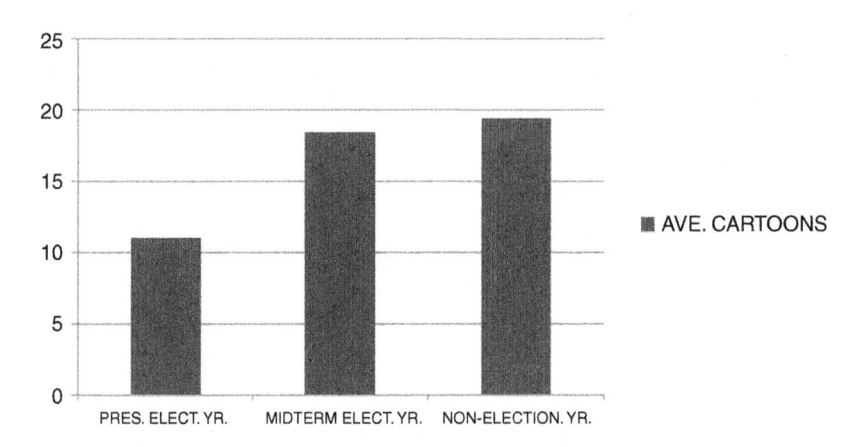

Figure 8.2 Election vs. Non-Election Year Congressional Cartoons

The electoral context also makes a difference. The news hole for cartoons is limited. Cartoons about Congress displace cartoons about other institutions and individuals. During presidential election years, cartoonists gravitate toward the national contest and away from Congress. During non-presidential election years, the relevancy of Congress for cartoonists increases (see Figure 8.2).

Isolating the Target

Editorial cartoons generally target action, looking at some organization or individual doing something, or failing to do something when action seems called for. The status of "public official" makes members of Congress legitimate targets, with cartoonists justifying their role as one of enforcing accountability. Targets generally emerge based on the impact of their behavior on others and/or the degree to which they are known to the public. Cartoonists seldom have the time to create an individual to target and then target them. Most cartoons focusing on individual members of Congress depend on members who have become household names because of their formal positions or based on atypical behavior already seared into the public consciousness by the news media.

In determining likely targets, we might expect that congressional leaders become the surrogates for the rest of Congress. Furthermore, members of the Senate are generally better known, and therefore better targets, than members of the House. It also makes sense that the majority party in Congress, especially when it takes on the role of "loyal opposition" to the president, would appeal to cartoonists, since cartoons, and the media in general, see conflict as legitimate news.

About half of the congressional cartoons focus on a generic member of Congress, often caricaturing him (very seldom her) as overweight, associated with money bags, or wearing particular clothing (often out of date or implying pomposity). Party and committee leaders are the focus of virtually all other cartoons caricaturing members of Congress. Non-leaders are virtually invisible unless they are caught in unethical or immoral behavior. Most cartoons deal with Congress generically, not focusing on a particular chamber. The Senate holds only a slight advantage in terms of the cartoonists' targets.

While a majority of congressional cartoons do not identify a specific member of Congress or a specific partisan group, named Republicans are slightly more likely to feel the wrath of cartoons than Democrats, while Democrats are slightly more likely to be criticized as a group (see Figure 8.3).

Firing the Comical Missile

As one cartoonist put it:

> I see myself like a dentist. When one goes to the dentist, they do not expect him to meet them at the door and say, "What a nice personality and pleasant smile, see you next year." The patient wants the dentist to look into their mouth very carefully attempting to spot existing or emerging problems. While relieved if there are no cavities, it is better to find them than ignore them. As a cartoonist, I am looking for cavities in the body politic.[5]

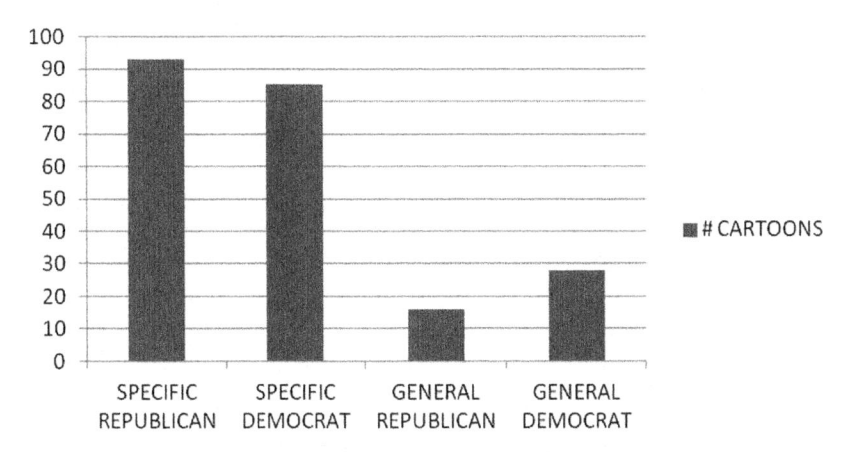

Figure 8.3 Partisan Targets

Editorial cartoons are designed to wound their targets, or at a minimum, warn them that their purported inappropriate behavior or shortcomings will not go unnoticed. The nature of congressional criticism inherent in editorial cartoons over the last forty years indicates two types. On the one hand the undesirable personal characteristics and behavior of individual members draw the cartoonists' fire. Personal shortcomings dominate the slate of personal failures. The cartoonists had a heyday with Representative Tom Delay's (R-TX) illegal fund-raising,[6] Senator Larry Craig's (R-ID) restroom missteps,[7] Representative Anthony Weiner's (D-NY) inappropriate Internet postings,[8] and dozens of other personal foibles. Taking on members for purportedly bad policy choices or the unwillingness to make compromises account for about 40 percent of the personal disapproval reflected in congressional cartoons (see Figure 8.4).

The hammer of criticism falls differently on members of Congress depending on their party. Democrats are seen through cartoons as more immoral and corrupt, while Republicans take the hit for their inflexibility, poorly thought-out preferences, and support for undesirable policies (see Figure 8.5). Whether this results from legitimate behavioral patterns of some members or is the result of cartoonist bias is beyond the scope of this analysis, but non-implicated members of Congress must chafe under the implied guilt by association these generalizations imply.

The cartoonists also take on the Congress for purported procedural shortcomings. Specific procedural criticisms have shifted over time from general complaints about Congress as an inefficient processor of legislation to a more specific complaint of increasing partisanship and lobby

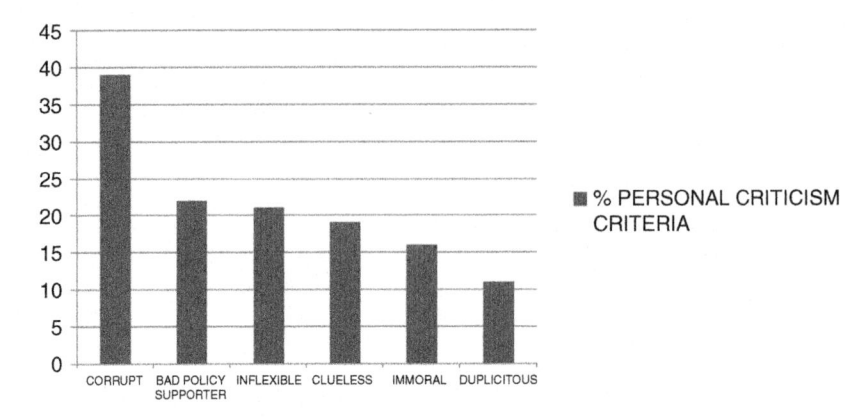

Figure 8.4 Personal Criticism of Members of Congress in Cartoons

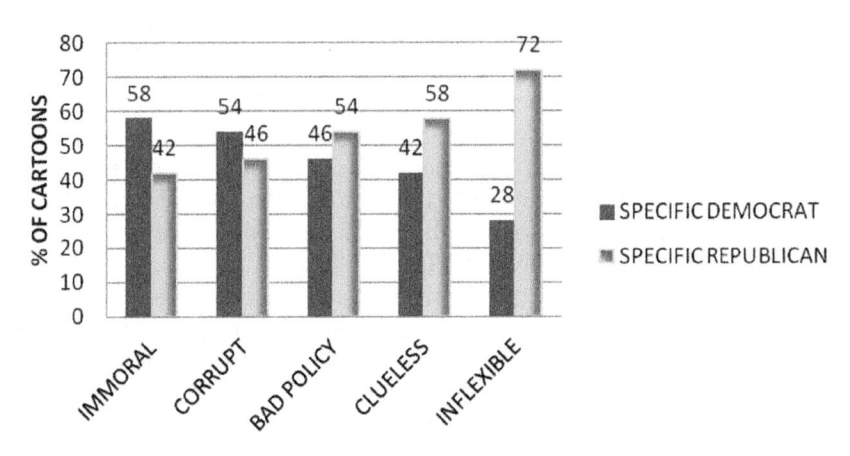

Figure 8.5 Personal Criticisms in Congressional Cartoons by Party

influence as an effective but undesirable cause of legislative gridlock. In earlier years, the president shared more of the blame for the pitched battle between the national institutions of government, with the contemporary criticism more clearly focused on Congress (see Figure 8.6).

The Impact of Cartoons

In the media-rich world of contemporary politics, it is hard to isolate the specific impact of one genre such as editorial cartoons. In the first place, few individual cartoons emerge on their own as significant influences. Most cartoons depend on previous news stories to set the stage and

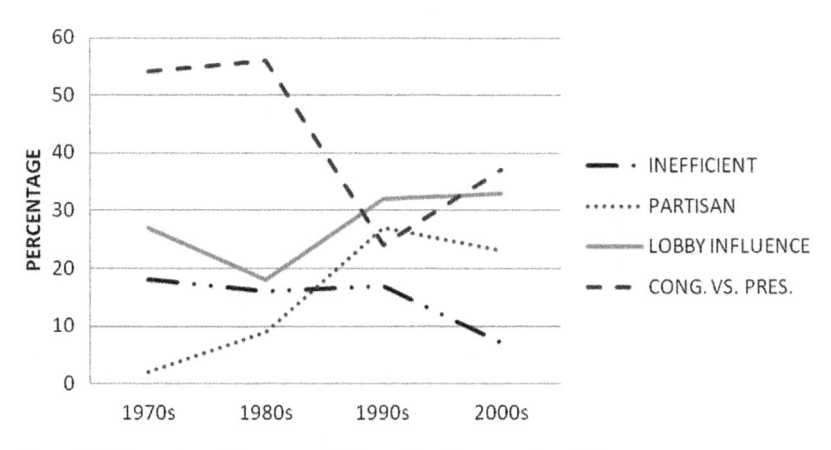

Figure 8.6 Procedural Concerns Reflected in Congressional Cartoons

provide the context consumers need to interpret them. In most cases, a cartoon is part of a package of influences. News stories set the stage and the cartoonist drives home the point, often in an exaggerated manner. In the communications theory view, few cartoons have a "hypodermic" influence, dramatically interjecting a new idea and changing outlooks on their own. More often, editorial cartoons contribute to a "stalagmite" process in which a variety of stimuli each contribute a layer of understanding. The cumulative effect is to create a new or strengthened outlook. A series of news stories talking about increased partisanship in Congress, supplemented by a number of cartoons representing the broad and seemingly insurmountable gap between Republicans and Democrats eventually creates a mindset verifying and vilifying the split. The amalgam of news stories and cartoons helps create conventional wisdom that eventually emerges as undeniable truth. Change is possible, but only over a long period of time with the contribution of many influences. Cartoons both reflect and contribute to conventional wisdom.

While little evidence exists that editorial cartoons *cause* the dismal evaluation of Congress, a more reasonable conclusion is that their negative tone *reflects* and perhaps *reinforces* negative public evaluations. Cartoons may well sharpen the focus of discontent by translating a general level of discomfort on a specific set of actions or shortcomings. Since we often make sense out of politics through "pictures in our heads,"[9] cartoons implant simple, yet dramatic, pictures on which we can hang our opinions. It is hard to imagine that hard-hitting editorial cartoons do Congress any good. They give the wheel of congressional degradation another spin disappointing the public but hopefully challenging

Congress and its members to find ways to move out of the cartoonists' bulls' eye.

Notes

1 Author's interview with a nationally syndicated cartoonist.
2 www.quotationspage.com/quotes/H._L._Mencken/31
3 Since 1973 Charles Brooks has published *The Best Editorial Cartoons of the Year*. Cartoonists submit cartoons of which they are most proud. Each year this collection includes over 500 submissions. Almost 20,000 cartoons were reviewed for any visual or textual reference to Congress or its members. While quite possibly not a random sample, the cartoons do represent the messages the participating cartoonists see as most relevant. A content analysis of over 650 congressional cartoons serves as the basis for the data presented in this chapter.
4 www.gallup.com/poll/157739/americans-preference-shifts-toward-one-party-government.aspx
5 Author's interview.
6 www.washingtonpost.com/wp-dyn/content/article/2011/01/10/AR 2011011000557.html
7 http://usatoday30.usatoday.com/news/washington/story/2012-08-03/larry-craig-bathroom-trip-lawsuit/56759984/1.
8 www.nytimes.com/2011/06/17/nyregion/anthony-d-weiner-tells-friends-he-will-resign.html?pagewanted=all
9 See Walter Lippman, *Public Opinion*, New York, NY: Harcourt, Brace and Co., 1922.

Chapter 9

Congress and Popular Culture
Dissing Congress on a Grand Scale

Laugh and the whole world laughs with you, cry and you cry alone.

When an institution loses trust and respect in the popular culture it is hard to regain its legitimacy. Individuals are willing to say things under the protective canopy of humor they would be hesitant to express as statements of fact. Recipients of biting humorous attacks often find themselves caught in a dilemma between attempting to refute exaggerating or misstatement and coming over as someone who cannot take a joke. With evidence of general audiences, and particularly the young, moving toward entertainment venues for news,[1] understanding how Congress and its members fare in non-traditional news sources looms increasingly large.

Relative to the presidency, popular culture has not found Congress an overwhelmingly fascinating subject. Only about 5 percent of the jokes on late night television targeted Congress as an institution. Most of the jokes related to Congress dealt with misdeeds of a few individual members, but even these targets fell far behind presidents and presidential candidates in their focus.[2] Its complexity and vast stable of key players make it hard to summarize and parody. When popular culture venues do turn to Congress its portrayal tends to ooze disappointment and criticism.

Legacy Comedians

There is a temptation to characterize the era in which one lives as unique. Using Congress as a butt of jokes and editorial cartoons is nothing new (see Chapter 8). The social commentary of classical comedians such as Mark Twain, Will Rogers, and others often placed Congress in their crosshairs with one-liners and other zingers (see Box 9.1).

Box 9.1 Classic Humorists Take Congress to Task

1897 It probably could be shown by facts and figures that there is no distinctively native American criminal class except for Congress. (Mark Twain)[a]

1890s Suppose you were an idiot. And suppose you were a Member of Congress. But I repeat myself. (Mark Twain)[b]

1935 I'm an amateur, and the thing about my jokes is that they don't hurt anybody ... But with Congress – every time they make a joke it's a law. And every time they make a law it's a joke. (Will Rogers)[c]

1947 Congress is so strange. A man gets up to speak and says nothing. Nobody listens – and then everybody disagrees. (Boris Marshalov)[d]

1991 Above the doors [of the House chamber of the Capitol building] are medallions bearing bas-relief profiles of mankind's great and reasonably great lawgivers: Moses, Solomon, Alfonso X, Hammurabi, Pope Innocent III. No U.S. congressmen are included. (P. J. O'Rourke)[e]

Sources:

[a] Rhodes Cook, "Most House Members Survive, But Many Margins Narrow," *Congressional Quarterly,* November 10, 1990, p. 3798.

[b] Richard Morin and Helen Dewar, "Approval of Congress Hits All-Time Low, Poll Finds," *Washington Post,* March 20, 1992, p. A16.

[c] Leslie McAnemy, "Pharmacists Again Top 'Honesty and Ethics' Poll; Ratings for Congress Hit New Low," *Gallup Poll Monthly,* no. 322 (July 1992), pp. 2–4.

[d] Quoted in Alexander Wiley, *Laughing With Congress,* New York, NY: Crown Publishers, 1947, p. 58.

[e] P. J. O'Rourke, *Parliament of Whores,* New York, NY: Atlantic Monthly Press, 1991, p. 50.

Congress Goes to the Movies

If the news media has trouble explaining Congress, filmmakers face an even tougher challenge. They need a fast-moving story, understandable to the public, and resulting in a happy (or at least definitive) ending.[3] Some of the most important realms of the congressional process, such as committee meetings, lack drama and are largely ignored in film representations of Congress.[4] The most common film storyline views Congress as filled with deceitful and barely redeemable politicians engaged in a corrupting process.[5] If a movie about Congress has a hero, it is the unique outsider such as Jimmy Stewart (Senator Jeff Smith) in *Mr. Smith Goes to Washington* (1947), "the classic fable of the unsophisticated Little Man taking on the big, corrupt forces and winning by dint of persistence and pluck"[6] (see Box 9.2).

Box 9.2 Will the Gentleman Yield?

Frank Capra's classic, *Mr. Smith Goes to Washington*, tells the story of a young idealistic senator who faces – and defeats – a crowd of less idealistic colleagues by using the filibuster to gain time to build popular support for his legislation. While the film's criticism of Congress looks tame by today's standards, at the time the movie generated enough controversy that it was almost not made and later faced issues about its distribution.

Joseph Breen, head of the movie industry's self-regulating Production Code Administration, complained that the proposal for the movie should be rejected because of its "general unflattering portrayal of our system [that is] a covert attack on the democratic form of government."[a] Despite the criticism, Capra created a sea change in the level of criticism. "Nothing like it had been seen in an American mainstream movie. No filmmaker had ever before made such massive accusation about the pervasiveness of corruption inherent in the hitherto untouchable hallowed halls of Congress."[b]

At the special premier in Washington, members of the Senate were "writhing in their seats," and some reportedly got up and left. Senate Majority Leader Alben Barkley called the film "silly and stupid."[c] A barrage of speeches in the Senate condemned the film. Washington columnists panned the production, with Frederick William Wile of the *Washington Star* insisting that the film "shows up the democratic system and our vaunted free press and exactly in the colors Hitler, Mussolini and Stalin are fond of painting them."[d] The controversy did not end with the film's premier. U.S. Ambassador to Great Britain, Joseph P. Kennedy, complained that the film would jeopardize "American prestige in Europe and should be withdrawn from European distribution."[e] The criticism from government officials and Washington columnists lost much of its potency when reviewers around the country gave the film rave reviews and the public flocked to theaters.

Once the media and public official dust storm settled, *Mr. Smith Goes to Washington* came to symbolize for many the uplifting theme of American democracy in which an average guy could cleverly exercise the rules to better a questionable group of political manipulators. It left the lasting image of the "good guys" winning despite the corrupt system. Once the movie achieved classic status, subsequent members of Congress often saw themselves, at least privately, as reincarnations of Mr. Smith, while the media largely denigrated these new champions as unrealistic and idealistic dreamers fighting an organizational culture doomed to derail their aspirations.

Sources:
[a] www.sheilaomalley.com/?p=9698
[b] Arc Elliot, quoted in www.sheilaomalley.com/?p=9698
[c] www.tcm.com/tcmdb/title/3771/Mr-Smith-Goes...Washington/notes.htm
[d] www.sheilaomalley.com/?p=9698
[e] www.tcm.com/tcmdb/title/3771/Mr-Smith-Goes...Washington/notes.htm
[f] www.sheilaomalley.com/?p=9698

The same year *Mr. Smith* was taking the box office by storm, *The Farmer's Daughter* told the story of a clever housemaid in a congressman's residence who reacted to corruption by running for Congress and winning herself. *Advise and Consent* (1962) "shows a world replete with ignoble characters and sordid events," eventually revealing how the process finally works by "triumphing over the frailties of individual members."[7] *The Seduction of Joe Tynan* (1979) posits the corruption of power, giving a contemporary example of Lord Acton's famous assertion that "power corrupts and absolute power corrupts absolutely."

With the rise of professionalism in campaign management, Hollywood turned to the dangers of image-based campaigns. In *The Candidate* (1972) Robert Redford played an idealistic Senate candidate who defeats a corrupt incumbent, but at the cost of being manipulated into selling out his values. Eddie Murphy in *The Distinguished Gentleman* (1992) redirected some of the blame onto uninformed voters showing how "a small-time confidence man steals a congressional seat only because he shares the last name of a popular – and ignobly deceased – incumbent."[8] He arrived in Washington to discover that Congress "is full of scheming fat cats (in other words, fellow con artists). That's the entire movie."[9]

Abraham Lincoln had his own problems with Congress in his attempt to pass the 13th Amendment outlawing slavery. Misrepresentation, payments made by lobbyists, and job offers well represented in the 2012 critically acclaimed film *Lincoln* leave the strong impression of a well-intentioned statesman forced to use less-than-pristine strategies to do what was right. Contemporary theater audiences cheered the outcome, but again were left with the message of a Congress easily bought and sold.

Congress on Television: Channeling Discontent

Members of Congress fail to fare much better on television entertainment programming than they do in the legitimate news or the movies. ABC soap opera *One Life to Live* offered a long-standing storyline of a senatorial candidate's machinations designed to cover up his daughter's role as a murderer.[10] Netflix's *House of Cards* expounds the manipulative and venal side of congressional politics where even murder is not beyond the strategies one might use to get ahead in politics.[11] In a world where the public often has great difficulty distinguishing between fact and fantasy, "Television certainly does not 'cause' negative perceptions of elected officials, but it certainly contributes to the perpetuation of stereotypes."[12]

Most films and television programs featuring Congress give a "relatively one-dimensional Hollywood view of the American congressional politician,"[13] identifying the good guys and the bad guys, with most screen time given to venal or incompetent legislators. Conflict not only triumphs

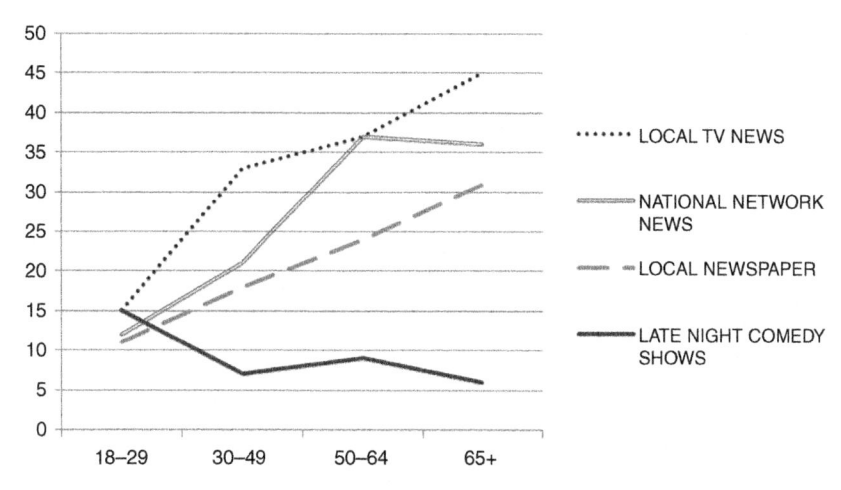

Figure 9.1 Political News Sources and Age in the 2012 Election (% Depending on Source)
Source: www.people-press.org/2012/02/07/section-1-campaign-interest-and-news-sources/

over cooperation, but is largely viewed as illegitimate. Citizens who eschew the negativity of traditional news reporting about Congress don't escape negative input when they opt out of traditional news for entertainment.

Late Night Comics

Starting with Johnny Carson and the *Tonight Show*, and progressing through a series of hosts such as Jay Leno, David Letterman, and Jimmy Fallon, late night television with political monologues have captured a solid audience base (see Figure 9.1). In the 2012 election period almost 10 percent of all voters relied on comedy shows for political news.[14] Among younger voters, comedy programs superseded the other major sources. This is particularly important since newsgathering was so limited by younger voters and the probability that patterns developed early would carry over into later life.

The criticisms are scathing and topical. Humor tends to give them more "punch" and fewer grounds for rebuttal (see Box 9.3). The jokes get another round of attention when repeated on Internet sites such as http://politicalhumor.about.com/. Members of Congress are not above using humor to take on their own institution. Humor often carries with it a significant kernel of truth, especially when accepted by those in line for its slings and arrows. As Congress' reputation began to fade, members picked up the cudgel of comedy themselves (see Box 9.4).

Box 9.3 You Can't Go to Bed Without Hearing This

1992 [On members of Congress pleading ignorance as a check-bouncing defense] That's not necessary. If there's one thing Congress doesn't have to plead, it's ignorance. (Jay Leno)[a]

1993 How is it that Congress can pass bills on ethics, which they know nothing about, but can't pass a bill on crime, on which they've had tremendous experience? (Jay Leno)[b]

2000 And Steve Forbes says he'll stay in the [presidential] race despite his poor showing in New Hampshire. This guy spent over $30 million and got nothing. Forget the presidency, he should be in Congress with a record like that. (Jay Leno)[c]

2005 Some scholars have argued [that] the Constitution clearly states only Congress can declare war, and they are not allowed to simply delegate that authority to the president. However, you can get around that with the legal technique of taking the word "constitution" and adding the word "schmonstitution" to the end of it. (Jon Stewart)[d]

2011 A new poll shows that disapproval of Congress is at an all-time high. Eighty-two percent of Americans disapprove of the job Congress is doing and the other 18 percent weren't home when the question was asked. (Jimmy Kimmel)[e]

2013 Today, members of the 113th Congress were sworn in at the Capitol. After which, they were like, "Well, that's enough work for the year." (Jimmy Fallon)[f]

Sources:
[a] *Tonight Show*, quoted in the *Washington Times*, March 29, 1992, p. 32.
[b] *Tonight Show*, April 8, 1993.
[c] "Laugh Lines," *Los Angeles Times*, February 8, 2000, p. E5.
[d] http://politicalhumor.about.com
[e] http://politicalirony.com/2011/08/14/late-night-political-humor-607/
[f] www.broadwayworld.com/bwwtv/article/Quotables-from-late-night-with-jimmy-fallon-week-of-12-20130107#.U3X5_vldUuc

Box 9.4 Members of Congress Doing Stand Up

One blue-collar worker elected to Congress got a laugh by portraying his service in Congress as a case of, "No job is beneath me."[a]

Pat Schroeder (D-CO) only half-jokingly explained, "Please don't tell my mother I'm a politician. She thinks I am a prostitute."[b]

Sources:
[a] Quoted in Mark J. Rozell, *In Contempt of Congress*, Westport, CT: Praeger, 1996, p. 3.
[b] Elaine Povich, *Partners and Adversaries*, Arlington, VA: The Freedom Forum, 1996, p. 20.

Pseudo News

It looks like an evening news set. A well-dressed "anchor" sits behind an impressive desk exuding authoritative tidbits of information. High quality graphics enhance stories. It is fun, irreverent, and entertaining, but is it news? The line between hard news, soft news, "infotainment," and entertainment has virtually disappeared. Jon Stewart's *The Daily Show* and its 2005 spinoff, Stephen Colbert's *Colbert Report*, eagerly took on pomposity and alleged stupidity of Congress and its members. Taking over the David Letterman show in 2015, he will undoubtedly use his monologues to skewer both Congress and other political institutions.

The most direct humorous attacks on Congress come in Stephen Colbert's "Better Know a District" (BKAD) segment. At first blush, it is hard to imagine why a member of Congress or congressional candidate would subject themselves to such abuse. Participation breaks many of the key rules for gaining good press coverage. The subject lacks control of the event, with Colbert and his staff retaining the right to edit the interview, often taking comments out of context. Colbert is known for asking off-the-wall inane questions outside the normal boundaries of respect and reveling in embarrassing his "guest." Party leaders have warned their followers to avoid subjecting themselves "to a comic edit."[15]

The profiled members (all of whom eventually won reelection) were likely to believe they were crazy like a fox. They saw the exposure provided by BKAD as a way for a relatively junior member to cut through the clutter of news and get some national attention. After the broadcast of their segment, members reveled at the positive reaction from their constituents who recognized them on the street. An appearance on BKAD also reverberated through the blogosphere, podcasting, and mainstream media giving the initial appearance another round of exposure. Additionally, the participants saw the value of revealing themselves as a good sport and being hip.[16] Despite Colbert's goal of embarrassing his guests, appearances on BKAD also allowed for "brief moments of advocacy, offering the kinds of short arguments in favor of positions that rank and file members are rarely afforded in other types of public affairs media."[17]

It probably should come as no surprise in the era of merging information dissemination and entertainment (infotainment) that hard-hitting comedy would be used to promote political goals. In the not so distant past, Richard Nixon did appear on *Laugh In* to utter their signature line, "Sock it to Me," Bill Clinton played his saxophone in the *Arsenio Hall Show*, and Senator John McCain has hosted *Saturday Night Live* numerous times.[18]

What? Me Worry?[19]

Concern with the impact of pop culture on politics in general and Congress in particular includes both discomfort with the message and the form of delivery.

The Message Is the Message

Representations of Congress in popular culture tend to portray a distorted view of politics. As previously discussed, politics is a process by which groups and individuals and/or groups seek to find compromises over issues over which reasonable people disagree and for which there is no socially "right" answer. Often basic principles must be tempered in order to come up with a solution a majority of decision-makers can live with. There is more drama in decision-makers selling out than facing reality and forging the best compromise possible. Television and film representations of Congress tend to err on the side of emphasizing connivance rather than reasonable compromise. There is no denying that trickery occurs on Capitol Hill, but film and television portrayals seem to exaggerate its predominance. Entertainment portrayals seem to see their value in giving a "behind the scenes" look at the dastardly underbelly of politics, rather than presenting a more balanced view.

Killing the Messenger?

While the distinction between hard news and entertainment persists, the bemoaning of the audience shift toward entertainment as bad for democracy by shutting out political learning may well be overstated. "Fake" news shows such as *The Daily Show* with Jon Stewart, or *The Colbert Report* regularly discuss events in Congress, although generally in a humorous *and* cynical way. Political leaders often have shown up on *Oprah, David Letterman, Jay Leno*, etc. While the choice to view those programs may lack political motivation, inadvertent exposure, especially when provided in an appealing package, has great potential to transmit information and affect political opinions.[20] There is a bit of an elitist and generational bias in the complaint that younger citizens fail to get their information in the time-tested way if the necessary information does get through. It may well be that this generation's great-grandparents chided their children about relying on this new-fangled thing called television. The proof is in the degree and content of relevant information transfer, not the particular medium used. We must remember that Plato expressed concern over the use of the written word to transmit information, arguing that it would undermine people's ability to remember.[21]

Comfort with a particular form of communication often translates into the false conclusion that it is both the best and the ultimate form. Emergent young citizens can't imagine the reality that twenty years from now (or even less) there will be no Internet as we know it today. It will be replaced by a new set of functionalities and they will look back at the communications options of their youth as archaic and backward as their parents look at CB radio, telegrams, and fax machines. The development of web pages, Facebook, and Twitter are well within the life span of current college students (see Chapter 11).

Notes

1 www.people-press.org/2012/02/07/section-1-campaign-interest-and-news-sources/
2 S. Robert Lichter, Joyce C. Baumgartner, and Jonathan S. Morris, *Politics Is a Joke*, Boulder, CO: Westview Press, 2015, p. 105. See also Media Monitor, press release, "Study: TV Comics Hit Democrats Hardest," August, 2013, available at: www.google.com/?gws_rd=ssl#q=media+monitor+TV+comics+hit+democrats
3 Terry Christianson, *Reel Politics: American Political Movies from Birth of a Nation to Platoon*, New York, NY: Basil Blackwell, 1987, p. 8.
4 Michael Canning, "The Hill on Film," paper presented at the 1997 meeting of the American Political Science Association, Washington, D.C., p. 3.
5 Ibid., p. 3.
6 Ibid., p. 6.
7 Ibid., p. 9.
8 Ibid., p. 14.
9 www.ew.com/ew/article/0,312631,00.html
10 Tracey L. Gladstone-Sovell, "Criminals and Buffoons: The Portrayal of Elected Officials on Entertainment Television," in David A. Schultz (ed.), *It's Show Time: Media, Politics, and Popular Culture*, New York, NY: Peter Lang, 2000, p. 117.
11 www.newyorker.com/arts/critics/television/2013/02/25/130225crte_television_nussbaum
12 Gladstone-Sovell, p. 129.
13 Canning, p. 16.
14 www.people-press.org/2012/02/07/section-1-campaign-interest-and-news-sources/
15 Geoffrey Baym, "Representation and the Politics of Play: Stephen Colbert's Better Know a District," *Political Communication*, vol. 24, no. 4, 2007, p. 364.
16 Ibid., pp. 364–365.
17 Ibid., p. 363.
18 www.saturday-night-live.com/qanda/guests.html
19 The classic line from *Mad Magazine's* Alfred E. Neuman, its comical portrayal of a befuddled citizen.
20 David R. Jones and Monika L. McDermott, *Americans, Congress, and Democratic Responsiveness*, Ann Arbor, MD: University of Michigan Press, 2009, p. 42.
21 www.fastcase.com/hate-twitter-plato-felt-the-same-way-about-the-written-word/

Chapter 10

C-SPAN

A Window on Congress

Most revolutions begin with a simple idea, a person who believes in it, and a lot of hard work. To a large degree, the more simple the idea the more revolutionary its consequences. America's founders believed in open government (although they did carry out their most creative task of writing the Constitution in secret). After a number of years on Capitol Hill as a senatorial aide and reporter, Brian Lamb had become tired of sound bites, journalists' "talking heads," and major stories failing to receive coverage. Even major political leaders found their well-reasoned ideas clipped and chopped. The average length of direct quotes for presidential candidates dropped from 43 seconds to a fifth of that twenty years later.[1] Members of Congress were afforded even less time to make their arguments. While the galleries of the House and Senate were open to the public, the distribution of the story had not kept up with new technology allowing the public to see what Congress was doing unedited and undiluted.

From his mid-1970s position as Washington reporter for *Cable Vision Magazine*, the professional communications vehicle for the fledgling cable industry, Lamb was in a unique position to observe the frustration of key players. Members of Congress felt the dominant media of the day (particularly television) passed them by in the battle for viewer "eyeballs" as measured by the rating system. Good ratings meant greater advertising revenue and Congress lost out to entertainment programming and the more easily covered president. Very few members received any national television time since the time it would take to describe them on a 90-second segment would leave little time for the rest of the story. A few well-known and often unrepresentative members dominated the airwaves. Congress became represented on television by short and exciting clips of atypical conflict between a few unique, but well-known members. Toiling away on Capitol Hill many members of Congress felt unappreciated and believed that "to know us is to love us." Lamb's "gut instinct ....was that if I'm interested enough to want to know more of what's going on behind the scenes, there's got to be more people who feel the same way."[2]

In the cable realm, shifting American public attitudes away from the "right" to free television to the imposition of cable delivery with a fee would require both legislation and the value-added benefit of cable programming not available on the free channels. Providing the public direct access to congressional activity would provide inexpensive and exclusive content, while perhaps making some friends on Capitol Hill in preparation for future policy battles.

Open House: The Marriage Broker

Discovering two sets of frustrated political players; Lamb set out to serve as a marriage broker between cable operators driven by the economic bottom line and members of Congress with political goals.

The Economic Driver

The cable industry in America emerged as a mechanism to provide television programming to mountainous areas with poor reception from broadcast signals. A legion of "mom and pop" entrepreneurs invested in satellite dishes to place on mountain tops and ran cables to customers for a modest fee. The business plan harbored a fatal flaw. Once reaching market penetration among locationally disadvantaged customers, how does one expand the market? The obvious answer lay in expanding programming. Since the future of the cable industry would also depend on the regulatory environment developed by Congress, emphasizing the demonstrably public service of informing citizens by giving voice to the regulators themselves seemed like good strategy. Lamb persuaded the cable operators to put up the money to get the network up and going and secured a promise that it would never become a commercial vehicle underwritten by advertising.

Political Pragmatism

Over a decade after television had become the primary news source of most Americans, Congress remained wary of its impact, but afraid to ignore its potency. While much of the rhetoric emphasized opening the "people's house" to the people, expanding public access carried with it an expected broader political benefit. In his early meetings with members of Congress, Lamb echoed the comments of Senator Lee Metcalf (D-MT) that:

A Congress unable to project its voice much beyond the banks of the Potomac ... can be neither representative nor responsive. A Congress only able to whisper, no matter how intelligently, cannot check and balance the power of the Executive or safeguard the liberty of individual citizens.[3]

The Legacy Media Take a Stand and Force a Choice

Still smarting from the opening of the galleries to radio and television reporters (see Chapter 2), print journalists showed little enthusiasm for cameras in the chamber. The traditional broadcast media indicated a willingness to bring their own cameras to the chambers, but only with complete editorial freedom of what to cover and when to cover it. The Public Broadcasting System (PBS) turned down the opportunity to serve as the distribution vehicle.[4]

The key issues revolved around control. Lamb negotiated a deal with Speaker Thomas P. "Tip" O'Neill that his cobbled-together C-SPAN (Cable Satellite Public Affairs Network) would take chamber feeds from cameras owned, operated, and controlled by the House leadership, and would distribute the signal gavel-to-gavel in unedited form.

Members feared being made fools of with uncontrolled cameramen scanning the chamber for sleeping members or visual "evidence" of back-room deals. The C-SPAN proposal of relinquishing camera control in exchange for access seemed like a reasonable compromise. The House explored the option first. Its members felt most undercovered by the media and in its perceived role as the chamber closer to the people, increased public access seemed most appropriate. The House first went on air in March of 1979. Any television outlet could use the feed from the House floor, but C-SPAN was committed to full coverage. One of the first reactions was an increased number of stories from the House floor on network news than in the pre-C-SPAN era where Senate coverage dominated the evening news. Lacking visuals of the Senate, House stories suddenly seemed much more appealing. With a free supply of visual news content, the network demand for House stories quickly followed.[5] The television journalists' twist on the old philosophical question, "If a tree falls in the forest and no one is there, is there any sound?" is the conclusion that if there is no camera to capture the tree falling, the event never really happened. Pictures from the House and Senate floor were so much more compelling than the still artistry of illustrators that they turned previously virtually ignored events into news.

The Reluctant Player

Accustomed to more adequate news coverage and concerned about upsetting its traditions and self-proclaimed status as the "greatest deliberative body," the Senate held back on allowing cameras into its chamber. Observing attention drifting to the House, Senate Minority Leader Howard Baker (R-TN) suggested, "If we don't open up the Senate to radio and television, I predict that in a few years ... in the public mind at least, the House will be the dominant branch."[6] Waxing more philosophical, Baker argued, "a democracy thrives on public support, and public support thrives on open government."[7] As an interesting commentary on use of the media, Baker took his argument to *TV Guide*, one of the most broadly distributed media outlets of the time to counter his colleagues' fear that the legislative process was just too complex and messy for the public to absorb. Using a humorous tack, Baker asserted, "Otto von Bismarck, the 'Iron Chancellor' of Germany, is supposed to have said, 'if you like laws and sausages, you should never watch either one being made.' I say 'Baloney'."[8]

Possible Derailment

With the trend among senators moving toward allowing televised proceedings, an event on the other side of the Hill almost killed off the initiative. Long fearful of public embarrassment, the House had attempted damage control by controlling the cameras and making it illegal for members or challengers to use floor footage in campaigns. The gavel-to-gavel agreement with C-SPAN and the House rule allowing any member to request time for a "special order" speech at the end of each day's session created an opening for the minority Republicans, who began a coordinated barrage of criticism of the ruling Democrats. Retaining control of the cameras, a frustrated Speaker Tip O'Neill (D-MA) decided to expose the foolishness of their efforts by ordering the camera operators to turn the cameras on the chamber to show that the Republicans were speaking to an empty House during the end-of-day session. The Republican spokesperson at the time, Robert Walker (R-PA), used the incident as "another example of the Democrat majority's arrogance of power." In the end, the brouhaha led to wider recognition of C-SPAN in the mainstream media, greater exposure of Republican leader Newt Gingrich (R-GA) and his colleagues, and eventually chastisement of the Speaker for intemperate words on the floor. The media dubbed the incident "Camscam" and probably whet the public's desire to see more of what goes on behind Congress' doors.

The Senate Joins the Television Era

In 1986, the Senate opened its doors to television, following the House's own approach of controlling their own cameras. The focus of House and Senate coverage is almost always on the official proceedings with no cutaway or reaction shots. The reaction of the television networks was to return the Senate to its dominant position in coverage, now that there was a supply of good visuals. The House's seven-year head start with television meant they had been "discovered" as a useful video source, and the coverage disadvantage relative to the Senate declined from earlier eras.[9]

Where is the Audience?

The media in America are big businesses with large audiences. C-SPAN is clearly a niche network with a relatively small and unique audience. Much of the C-SPAN audience is inadvertent. The timing of congressional proceedings is irregular. "Surfing" their options on cable channels, individuals land on one of the C-SPAN channels for a few seconds, assess their level of interest, and either tune in for a while or skip to another channel. C-SPAN's re-broadcasts of many segments potentially allow a broader audience, but do little to build program loyalty favored by other channels.

By the Numbers

Early in its development, C-SPAN was significantly constrained by the penetration of cable access and subscription. Today over 90 percent of households have access to C-SPAN programming via cable (83 percent) or the Internet (7 percent).[10] The issue in terms of audience today is one of demand, not supply. C-SPAN and all television programming are engaged in a largely zero-sum game, with a limited number of hours in each person's life to absorb media and growing types and venues to choose among. Only about 20–24 percent of the public report viewing C-SPAN at least sometimes and less than 3 percent report viewing on a regular basis.[11] Even with those numbers, weekly viewers account for an estimated 47 million adults.[12] As with most traditional media in an increasing crowded media environment, C-SPAN's audience has declined in recent years, but not as fast as other networks (see Figure 10.1). Before writing off C-SPAN as minuscule and irrelevant, it is important to consider who uses it and to what effect.

Evaluating the Messengers

Despite its over thirty years on the air, about one-third of the public are not familiar enough with C-SPAN to rate its credibility, the lowest percentage

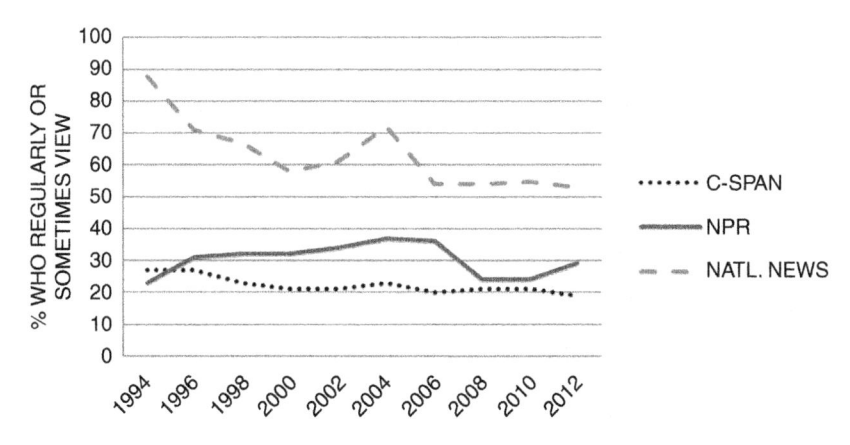

Figure 10.1 "Regular" and "Sometimes" Viewers of Selected Media
Source: www.people-press.org/files/legacy-pdf/2012%20News%20Consumption%20
Report.pdf

for the fourteen national news outlets rated by the Pew Center for the People and the Press.[13] For a network that presents entire events without commentary, it is surprising to find that it is in about the middle of the pack in terms of audience believability and has seen its believability drop considerably over the last fifteen years, especially among Republicans. It should be pointed out that C-SPAN is in "good company" in terms of decline since its over-time decline and partisan differential mirror that of most national media.[14]

Who Is the Audience and Why Should We Care?

C-SPAN viewers are far from a random sample of channel surfers. They tend to be somewhat older than other cable surfers, much better educated, and only slightly more Democrat and liberal.[15] It may well be that "C-SPAN offers the emerging group of information free-agents access to the raw uncut coverage of their political heroes, and sometimes perhaps their villains they can then share on blogs and social networks."[16]

Perhaps most important is the reported level of political behavior taken on by C-SPAN viewers. By and large, American politics is not a spectator sport. It responds to those who take initiative to see that their preferences get a fair hearing. Using self-reporting, a 2013 survey of weekly C-SPAN viewers reported the following Congress-related actions (see Box 10.1).

Box 10.1 Political Engagement and C-SPAN Viewership

	c-span viewers (2013)[a]	general public (2012)[b]
Voted in the last election	88%	80%
Watched their member of congress on c-span	43%	NA
Written or emailed a public official	35%	20%
Contributed to a political campaign	31%	1%
Used social media tool to express views	27%	NA
Talked to their member of congress in person	22%	NA
Campaigned for a congressional candidate	15%	4%

[a] www.mediabistro.com/tvnewser/c-span-47-million-watch-us-every-week_b171199

Note: Figures for self-reported data from the general public are inflated since the questions are much broader than specific actions related to Congress. For example, the campaigning question asks a respondent "Did you do any [other] work for one of the parties or candidates?" Additionally, American national election studies were done during the height of the election presumably increasing interest and involvement.

[b] 2012 National Election Study: www.electionstudies.org/studypages/anes_timeseries_2012/anes_timeseries_2012_userguidecodebook.pdf

---

Among the public, C-SPAN viewers tend to be political "movers and shakers," exceeding national averages in voting and contributing to political campaigns. Members of Congress report that town meeting questions are often sprinkled with prefaces such as "I saw on C-SPAN ..." C-SPAN viewers also tend to absorb a great deal of other media and reveal more basic knowledge about contemporary politics.[17]

C-SPAN's ability to directly inform the public is augmented by the fact that both policy-makers and members of the media rely on its coverage on a day-to-day basis. Journalists outside of Washington are "transported" to Washington-based congressional events. The development of a news story is an iterative process. Mentions of C-SPAN coverage often show up on talk radio or in the blogs. Some of those stories migrate to the traditional media, which then goes back to supplement their stories with C-SPAN video. Like a rock tossed into a pool, House and Senate television may well have a "multiplier effect," as the C-SPAN junkies transmit their newfound political knowledge using other media outlets. On the other hand, stories emerging from other realms find C-SPAN a useful megaphone for communicating to other media and the public.

Opening the Window

With two channels and twenty-four hours to fill, C-SPAN began looking for additional content. The committees became prime targets. Unlike the chamber rules, C-SPAN sends its own cameras to committee hearings. Unlike the networks, C-SPAN cameras take a "mouse in the corner" approach covering hearings in their entirety and avoiding reaction and other interpretive shots. In choosing hearings, C-SPAN editors put special emphasis on hearings that the networks choose not to cover. Independent of ratings, C-SPAN does not have to gravitate toward the most exciting or confrontational. In pursuing the journalistic paragon of objectivity, C-SPAN takes a different approach than most media. Rather than attempting to make each segment or program unbiased, they attempt to expose its audience *over time* to the widest range of relevant views and issues.

Washington is a town where active players are constantly using each other. Discussing politicians coming on C-SPAN to push their pet projects, C-SPAN founder Brian Lamb commented "I know they are using us to get air time, our job is to make sure that proponents of all relevant positions have an equal chance to use us."[18]

One-Stop Fact-Checking

For congressional "junkies," academic researchers, and interested citizens alike the C-SPAN website (www.c-span.org) provides a treasure trove of relevant information. C-SPAN's searchable video archives make available programming most of which was inaccessible in the past. Educational tutorials enhanced with video serve as new learning experiences or reviews of issues and procedures for both the public and the journalistic community. C-SPAN call-in programs confront journalists with questions from the public and provide the journalists with an additional venue to propagate their views. Journalists from other realms draw on C-SPAN video to verify their memories and to check against written records. Members of Congress can no longer legitimately say, "I never said that in the debate," even if they had used the "revise and extend" privilege to "correct" the *Congressional Record*.[19]

Impact of a Niche Medium

As is often the case in research, the easiest things to measure are the least important. While it is difficult to prove the exact implications of televised coverage most of the dire predictions of "grandstanding" members and disruption of procedures failed to materialize, although when it does emerge, the other media are quick to turn it into a story complete with video (see Box 10.2).

Box 10.2 Did I Just Say That?

Congressional rules make it inappropriate to call members by name, especially in a critical tone, and are especially harsh when questioning another's motives. The prescribed punishment is to have one's "words taken down" (struck from the *Congressional Record*). In an earlier age this was akin to sweeping it under the rug with only the people in the chamber the wiser. With a televised record, such punishment often becomes the occasion for a news story.

In 1995, when Robert Dornan (R-CA) questioned Bill Clinton's anti-war activity as "giving aid and comfort to the enemy," his words were taken down. When he repeated his charges, he was banned from the chamber for a day, thus leaving his constituency without a representative. The controversy was a major news story and helped lead to his defeat in the next election.[a]

During a 2010 debate on antitrust exemptions for insurance companies, Representative Anthony Weiner (D-NY) twice repeated the sentiment that "You gotta love these Republicans. I mean, you guys have chutzpah. The Republican party is a wholly owned subsidy of the insurance companies." His questioning of his colleagues' motives earned his words being taken down.[b]

In 2011 Representative Gene Taylor (D-MS) took exception to what he saw as hypocrisy and challenged Representative Tom Price (D-GA) saying,

> I wish you would have the decency, if you are going to do that to the people of south Mississippi, that maybe you ought to come visit south Mississippi before you hold them to a standard that you would never hold your own people to and that you failed to hold the Bush administration.

Taylor found his words taken down and the event covered in the media.[c]

The number of times members have had their words taken down is not at an all-time high despite the partisanship of the current era. The mid 1930s takes the record for the greatest punishment meted out on these grounds.[d] At that time, such punishment was largely an inside-the-beltway story, while perhaps contemporary members recognize the ability to the media to use video to legitimate the story and spread it far and wide.

Sources:
[a] http://pol411finalproject.blogspot.com/2010/04/blog-post.html
[b] Ibid.
[c] www.annenbergpublicpolicycenter.org/Downloads/Civility/ Civility_9-27-2011_Final.pdf and www.dailykos.com/story/2007/03/ 31/318083/-Gene-Taylor-D-Sticks-Up-for-Katrina-Victims-GOP-Crybabies-Whine-for-Apology
[d] Ibid.

On the other hand, optimistic hopes of creating a national dialogue of fully informed citizens on all issues have not been borne out. The "to know us is to love us" justification has faded into the resignation that "familiarity breeds contempt" among many members and staff. Polls show that regular C-SPAN viewers expressed more critical views about Congress than non-viewers.[20] Part of the problem lies in unrealistic public expectations. Careful deliberation becomes "delay and inaction" and reasonable policy differences are perceived as "partisan bickering."[21] While Congress is far from faultless when it comes to inefficiency and conflict, the Founders designed not for efficiency, but for the painful working out of conflicts over issues about which people have strongly held and reasonable differences of opinion. If a policy issue was easy, it would not end up on Congress' "plate," but rather be settled at a much lower level.

It is impossible to determine whether Congress' low levels of respect are related to the presence of cameras. Late in his career a former Speaker confided privately that allowing himself to be talked into having the cameras by Brian Lamb and others was the "worst damn fool mistake I ever made."[22]

More modest impacts of cameras in the chambers, such as an increase in the length of congressional sessions, are clear as members saw more value in speaking, even when the chamber audience was slim. Recognizing the visual nature of television, more members backed up their assertions with charts, graphs, and pictures. Some members and staff reported increased member efficiency due to the ability to monitor floor activity and the development of better-prepared floor speeches with the recognition of a wider audience. Television coverage does offer the expanded potential for some proceedings to enhance the national policy dialogue. To add legitimacy to their stories, journalists often cite C-SPAN as their source for congressional behavior.

On the individual member level, the impact may be more direct. One member who lived through the transition to televised coverage of Congress and the introduction of the Internet pointed out that with more information, more constituents would challenge his positions on issues.

"I would come back from a floor speech to face calls from constituents who had just seen me take a position. Not everyone watches C-SPAN, but enough of the most interested voters do and it makes a difference. They are the ones I need to take into account."[23]

Government in Sunshine

C-SPAN fits well with the general government movement toward government in sunshine. With initiatives such as the Freedom of Information Act and requirements for open meetings, less is done by stealth today. For better or worse, Congress is shown with both warts and beauty marks. Open government most often means open to the media first, with few members of the public availing themselves of the raw material. With their virtual seats in the chamber galleries and committee audiences, reporters physically far removed from actual events have the opportunity to cover them for their audiences.

C-SPAN is never going to rival the audiences of its cable or broadcast competitors. Much of what happens in Congress and distributed by C-SPAN is about as exciting as watching paint dry. The general public may not want to watch on a regular basis, but they want the *right* to watch. The symbolism of cameras in the chambers and the ability of other news media to spread certain messages imply that Congress has nothing to hide.

Notes

1 John Carmody, "The TV Column," *Washington Post*, November 18, 1992, p. 66.
2 Quoted in Marilyn Duff, "C-SPAN: The Way News Should Be," *Human Events*, November, 1994, p. 5.
3 Senator Lee Metcalf, Joint Committee on Congressional Operations, "Congress and Mass Communications," 93rd Congress, 2nd session, Hearings, p. 2.
4 Stephen Frantzich and John Sullivan, *The C-SPAN Revolution*, Norman, OK; University of Oklahoma Press, 1996, p. 34.
5 For data and expanded discussion, see ibid., p. 270.
6 Quoted in Tom Shale, "The Floor Show," *Washington Post*, December 1, 1981, p. b1.
7 US Congress, Senate, Committee on Rules and Administration, "Television and Radio Coverage of Proceedings in the Senate Chamber," 97th Congress, 1st Session, 1981, pp. 4–5.
8 Howard Baker, "We're Losing Political and Historical Treasures," *TV Guide*, July 21, 1984, p. 33.
9 Frantzich and Sullivan, p. 270.
10 www.cepro.com/article/cable_tv_penetration_continues_to_drop/ and http://advanced-television.com/2013/08/09/86-us-households-pay-tv-subscribers/

11 www.people-press.org/files/legacy-pdf/2012%20News%20Consumption%20Report.pdf

12 Based on a 2014 Hart Research Associates survey of adults. Summary available at: www.c-span.org/assets/documents/press/C-SPAN-at-34-A-Bi-Partisan-Politically-Active-Audience-Continues-to-Grow.pdf

13 www.people-press.org/2010/09/12/section-5-news-media-credibility/

14 Ibid.

15 www.ropercenterQuestionID1818891 and Hart, 2014.

16 www.people-press.org/files/legacy-pdf/2012%20News%20Consumption%20Report.pdf

17 Based on analysis of data in www.people-press.org/files/legacy-pdf/2012%20News%20Consumption%20Report.pdf

18 Author's interview.

19 The *Congressional Record* is supposed to be a verbatim record of congressional debate, but since the Courts continue to use it to determine legislative intent, both chambers allow its members to make corrections before it is printed. While the "revise and extend" privilege was designed to correct minor factual or grammatical errors, it can be used to make major changes or additions to what actually transpired.

20 Frantzich and Sullivan, pp. 249–251.

21 David Paletz, *The Media in American Politics*, New York, NY: Longman Publishers, 2002, p. 247.

22 Author's interview. See Stephen Frantzich, *Founding Father: How C-SPAN's Brian Lamb Changed Politics in America*, Lanham, MD: Rowman and Littlefield Publishers, 2008, p. 79.

23 Author's interview.

Chapter 11

Congress and the New Media

Challenges and Opportunities

New communication technologies tend to emerge on the scene like new babies whose arrival is heralded with excitement and grand expectations. The shortcomings of previous information delivery mechanisms are seen as evaporating in the face of the capabilities of the new technology. Radio and later television were heralded as overcoming the one-way elite nature of print journalism.[1] Each new technology was supposed to create a well-informed citizenry that would use the technology to connect, communicate, and deliberate with the result of higher satisfaction, better policy, and the fulfillment of democratic goals. After each new launch, a group of naysayers emerges to point out the failure of the most recent initiatives due to misuse or the appropriation of the technology by current power-holders to bolster their own positions. The debate between the "bright new future" and the "same old, same old" camps surround each new innovation. The truth usually resides somewhere in the middle, with new technologies seldom reaching their promised potential (and often not the one expected), but harboring identifiable consequences (both good and bad, intended and unintended).

Purported Advantages of New Media for Congress and its Members

Members of Congress have long grated under the frustration of being ignored by the media. They see the media as choosing to cover issues and behavior they would not have chosen themselves. Members grate at the traditional media's penchant for scandal and conflict and assert that in the process the public is shortchanged in acquiring information it needs to make realistic political choices. New media offer the potential of circumventing the traditional media and going directly to the public with the messages they prefer to the people who count.

The Expanded News Hole

The battle for media coverage faces the natural limitation of the available "news hole." There are only so many column inches in a newspaper or minutes on a television newscast. While it is true that some of the emerging media (24-hour newscasts, blogs, and tweets) conceptually have a larger news hole, they must confront the economic tasks of gathering more content and the willingness of an adequate audience to absorb more information. Many television viewers look to the 24-hour channels with a traditional mindset. Unless the goal is to catch up on a breaking story, viewers expect 24-hour news to give them a broad picture of what is going on in the world as did traditional newscasts, only repeated more often and at more convenient times.

Commenting on his thirty-five years in Congress, Thad Cochran (R-MS) quickly pointed out the media environment as the most important change he has seen on the Hill.

> There are simply so many more media venues. The press gallery is just the tip of the iceberg. No matter what you say or do someone is likely there to report it. Actions, whether wise or stupid, will be reported if the media sees it as news. It used to be we communicated with constituents via paper – regular newsletters spread the word. Now it is through press conferences and speeches; portions of which appear on blogs and websites.[2]

Congressional leaders and, even more so, individual members of Congress compete with a large number of newsmakers, each of which vie for the available news hole. While members of Congress can make speeches, grant interviews, and hold press conferences, "the final decision about coverage rests with journalists, and congressional leaders face extensive competition when trying to insert their issues and arguments."[3] New media promise more opportunities to have one's voice heard.

Social media offer the opportunity of a "multiplier effect" as traditional media pick up a story first distributed on blogs or tweets. Going viral on the Web often becomes a story in and of itself. In a similar multiplier vein, social media can push one's message to new and different audiences.[4] There is a temptation to look at each communications medium in isolation, but crossover interaction allows one medium to affect another. A tweet sent out by a congressional office may be picked up by the traditional print or electronic media as a lead for a story in their medium.[5] The member of Congress may react to a story with a tweet and the back-and-forth process expands the information disseminated.

Expanding the Members' Reach

The number of people a congressional office can reach through social media may well be less important than the perception that social media allow the office to communicate with people out of their reach using other media.[6] Since social media tend to reach younger potential voters, the value is increased by the fact that younger citizens are less partisan and/or individual-politician "brand loyal." With less of a personal voting pattern to defend, younger voters are more "up for grabs" by a charismatic politician or well-crafted message.

Finally, with election to Congress representing more of a career choice than in the past, existing members desire to solidify their electoral margin for the long run. With the influx of new younger voters and the departure of the members' original voting coalitions, it is important to follow the audience. By all accounts, incoming generations of voters increasingly ignore traditional print and television news sources. There is little evidence that this represents a life stage phenomenon, with those voters returning to traditional media later in life. Wise politicians bet on a generational explanation, suggesting that once lured away from traditional media into the clutching embrace of new technologies, new generations are unlikely to be enticed en masse back to printed newspapers or evening news programs.

Building an Image

Above and beyond increased control over the message, adoption of new media provides members with the symbolic bragging rights of appearing as forward-looking and "with it." In a twist on Marshall McLuhan's "the medium is the message," it is a case of "the *use* of the medium is the message." Members tout their Facebook pages and Twitter feeds with the implication that "If I can master the new technology, I can master the new problems of society."

Potential Public and Media Gains from New Media

New technology not only allows members of Congress new options for broadcasting their desired message, but also enhances the ability of the media and others to monitor the content and distribution of those messages.

Enhancing Public Access

The ability to track politicians has improved greatly as more and more actions have been captured and made searchable. The dedicated seeker of congressional information traditionally faced two challenges. In the first place one was faced with voluminous material lacking indexes or other finding guides. Determining the existence of a quote, newspaper article, set of data, or congressional report led to "content access." Even when one knew something existed, finding it in its entirety added the challenge of gaining "physical access." The digitization of print sources has greatly enhanced both types of access.

Prior to the late twentieth century, looking for inconsistencies in a member of Congress' statements meant either tapping the potentially faulty memory of others (see Box 11.1), or plowing through hundreds of pages in newspaper morgues. Only a few of the national newspapers offered printed indexes. By the 1970s online databases such as Lexis-Nexis provided full text access to thousands of print sources in an easily searchable form. The Library of Congress Thomas system (www.loc.thomas. gov) provided similar information free of charge a few years later. Radio and television raised a new historical access problem, with only a minuscule portion of their material recorded for posterity. A few of the radio and television sources began appearing in computer databases such as Lexis-Nexis. The arrival of the Vanderbilt Television News Archive (http://tvnews.vanderbilt.edu/) in 1968 provided extensive abstracts of both traditional news and news specials.

Box 11.1 Who Said So?

"It ain't so much the things we don't know that get us into trouble. It's the things we do know that just ain't so." – Artemus Ward[a]

Known for his pithy statements and gravelly voice, Senator Everett McKinley Dirksen (R-IL) found his words often quoted. Fellow members of the Senate and other political colleagues will swear they heard him bemoan the growing national budget saying "A billion here, a billion there, and pretty soon you're talking real money." After extensive research, the Dirksen Congressional Center admits that it can find no hard evidence that Dirksen ever used the quote. They even offered a reward for anyone who could find proof of the quote. The idea of a growing budget certainly fits his outlook, but he seemingly never expressed it in that way.[b] Today with full text searching of congressional documents, it would be easy to determine whether Dirksen uttered these words in the official records.

Sources:
[a] http://homepage.stat.uiowa.edu/~jcryer/artemusward.pdf
[b] www.dirksencenter.org/print_emd_billionhere.htm

Congress got into the game in the 1970s when it moved from the cumbersome and difficult-to-research hard-copy *Digest of General Bills and Resolutions*, allowing a number of commercial services to provide computer-based bill-tracking information. The full text and searchable *Congressional Record* followed soon after. C-SPAN (see Chapter 10) added the ability to view debates in their original form before editing and created a searchable archive of Congress and its committees in session (www.c-span.org/search/).

As new media entered the scene other monitoring sites joined the process of making Congress our most easily watched national institution. The Federal Elections Commission (FEC) put campaign spending records online (www.fec.gov), relieving members of the media from having to wait for paper copies or to crowd around a few "dumb" terminals in the FEC Washington office to develop their stories about who gave to congressional campaigns, who received it, and how the money was spent. Public interest sites such as Open Secrets (www.opensecrets.org/) repackaged FEC data providing more visual and interactive analysis options for both the media and the public. Legistorm (www.legistorm.com) allows free access to information on congressional staff salaries, official expenses by congressional offices, foreign gifts to legislators' earmarks (legislation designed to help a specific district), and a variety of other data used to paint a fuller picture of congressional life. With the advent of Twitter, Legistorm began capturing congressional tweets and presenting them in a searchable database.[7]

Facilitating Constituent Interactivity

New technologies hold potential for creating both the image and the reality of a more interactive relationship between members and their constituents so critical in representative government. Members worry about constituents who increasingly see them as detached from the public. In 2014 over three-quarters of the public felt that "public officials don't care about people like me," up from two-thirds a decade earlier.[8] The emergence of social media has encouraged some analysts to believe that it will change representative government by lowering the costs of information, providing tools for communication, and encouraging more people to participate in politics, but "no scholarly consensus has emerged on this issue."[9] Early studies do indicate that the Internet does increase the diversity and engagement *of those already politically involved*.[10] To the degree that some citizens acquire some information from new media, they may well pass it on to friends and neighbors in more traditional forms and stimulate public feedback.

Some denizens of Capitol Hill question the current utilization of new media as forces for interactivity. Congressional staff, probably representing the views of the members they serve, are at least three times more likely to rate each of the new social media as very important for "communicating members' views" as opposed to "understanding constituents' views."[11] Although new media offer the opportunity to enhance interaction with constituents and others, analyses of the content of messages belie congressional interest in enhancing two-way communication. Social media such as web pages, Facebook, and Twitter are largely used to *broadcast* favorable messages rather than to seek constituent opinion. Looking at the complexity of Internet options, Owen et al. point out that "members have embraced the new technologies ... not to facilitate interactivity with constituents, but primarily as an extension of their strategies of advertising themselves."[12]

Reducing Duplicity

Until relatively recently, members of Congress lived two lives, one in Washington and another in their districts. Constituents and journalists back in the district knew little about their member's Washington life and their colleagues and Washington-based journalists had little feel for what went on back home. To the degree that mutual understanding existed, the member served as the bridge. New technologies such as C-SPAN, blogging, and YouTube have breached the gap. "The days of saying one thing to the country club crowd and another to the workers at the Union hall are long gone, as well as the days of saying one thing at home and voting differently in Washington."[13] Inconsistencies can be recorded and distributed via social media, exposing that which in the past lay beyond the reach of the media and the public.

The Potential Dark Side of New Media

Both Congress and the legacy media (print, radio, television) are well advised to consider the impact of social media. Information processing is the "core technology" of politics, and changes in core technologies affect the personnel, process, and outcomes of politics.

The Challenge of Social Media to the Traditional Media

While beyond the focus of this book, the challenges of the new media are critical to existing media outlets as they compete for audiences and advertising dollars. Few of the new media platforms have developed viable business plans, especially if they have to create content on their own. Much of the congressional news is created by the legacy media and distributed by the new media without financial responsibility for its creation. These concerns keep newspaper publishers and television-station general managers up at night, but we will leave them to their own devices in our analysis. Our concern lies with some of the potential dangers of the new media for the Congress and the public.

The Challenges of Social Media for Congress and the Public

Members of Congress are accustomed to serving as senders of political messages, with the public largely in the receiver mode. Social media has the potential to change that relationship in ways some of the participants may find uncomfortable.

Loss of Control

The financial and staff effort costs of new technologies are relatively minimal for members of Congress. The dangers of misuse and/or embarrassment give more cause for pause. The immediacy expectation of the new technologies invites quick and potentially not well-thought-out responses. Mistaken postings can take on a life of their own. Once something is posted it is almost impossible to recall. The presence of cameras in the chamber and the ease of capturing videos at local events on cell phones for distribution on the Internet present a challenge, especially to members having less experience with the prying media. In one member's words, "Today there is less chance to have your mistakes overlooked and little opportunity for do-overs. You are judged on what you say, rehearsed and intended or off the cuff and unintended."[14] "Even the slightest miscues or controversial remarks can now be recorded by what, in today's parlance, are known as 'citizen journalists' "[15] but what we might have called in the past "snitches" or "spies."

Once out on the Internet, there is little chance to "un-ring the bell." Recognizing that speedy responses often lead to insightful but unintended messages from a Twitter account, Politwoops (http://politwoops. sunlightfoundation.com/) captures recently deleted tweets and allows one to search by a congressional member's name. While a dominant desire was once, "I wish I had said that," in the scramble to get one's words out, the new mantra is often more likely, "I wish I had not said that." A looming danger comes from legitimate inopportune comments or the potential of hackers to post inappropriate material.

New media often require new ways of thinking for optimal effect. The "broadcast mindset" which long dominated Capitol Hill provided members of Congress a comfort zone in which they controlled the timing and content of the messages they chose to share through floor speeches, press conferences, newsletters, and later web pages. Effective use of the new media (optimal web pages, Facebook, blogs, Twitter, and the like) requires a recalibrating of one's expectations and a revision of strategy. In order to get a recipient to attune to one's latest messages, it is important to keep one's content current. The goal of reaching the most people directly may well be replaced by the goal of reaching the right people effectively. Reaching a few people on Twitter or Facebook may dramatically amplify your voice if they take the time and effort to "like," "share," or pass on the intended message. The spread of one's message may well include people unavailable on the member's existing lists. While most tweets fail to go viral, "those that do are gold,"[16] assuming that the content is positive and intended. Losing control of distribution allows the potential for congressionally initiated messages to be changed or commented upon in ways that undermine the member's goals.

The importance of timeliness varies across the new media platforms. Twitter users have the highest expectation of immediacy. While the content of the other formats may have long-term shelf life, tweets are "in-the-moment" communications.[17] The danger of such speed emerges from the lack of time to carefully consider content. Off-the-cuff remarks, intended humor, or expressions of emotion may all result in misinterpretation.

The long-debated discussion as to whether members of Congress should act as "trustees" (looking out for the "interests" of their constituents more than their short-term "wishes") as opposed to "delegates" (expected to serve as direct conduits into the policy-making process without interjecting the representative's personal judgment) (see Box 1.2), receives a nudge toward the delegate position with the arrival of the new media. New media users expect increased interaction as much, or more than, increased information. Opening oneself up to a large volume of low effort communications makes it more difficult for a member to argue they had no idea as to what the interested members of their constituency think about an issue. In the past, to the degree that constituents did communicate with their members, much of it was after the fact and thus could have no effect on the member's policy choices. Users of the new media revel in its virtual real-time character, allowing messages to flow to their representative before key decisions are made. Faced with a segment of the public that communicates (albeit often an unrepresentative sample of constituents) and those who either seemingly do not care or lack the communication resources, it is much easier for the representative to fall back on the hard data of real communications. Members and their staffs face the danger of being overwhelmed with requests for attention from an audience of constituents accustomed to immediate response.[18]

New and Unpredictable Players

The emergence of new media outlets such as blogs, cable television, specialized print products, Twitter, and Facebook belie the old concept of a "mass" media populated by similarly trained journalists attempting to reach largely the same type of audience. Different rules of survival pertain to an environment where "narrowcasting" can attract an economically viable and often unique audience. Many of the old rules on who and what to cover go out the window. Additionally the pool of "reporters includes 'citizen news reporters' [having] the technological smarts to present more idiosyncratic information and interpretations about politics that are now added to the media mix."[19] The new players bring with them new definitions of news, new criteria for proof, and new potential for spreading their message broadly and quickly.

One of the powerful new tools for these "quasi" journalists is YouTube, which allows the recording of potentially relevant political behavior with inexpensive equipment and allows free uploads to the web. In a few cases (see Box 7.2) we saw the saga of former Congressman Weiner's "sexting" whose misunderstanding of the power of the new media led to his downfall. In other cases individuals with cell phone cameras have caught members of Congress acting inappropriately. In a world where we trust pictures more than textual explanations, photographs can create dramatic images (see Box 11.2).

Box 11.2 Smile – You're on Candid Camera

Freshman Representative Vance McAllister (R-LA), who ran as a principled conservative Christian, was caught in a video of a congressional staff member and himself in a romantic kiss. The local newspaper, the *Ouachita Citizen*, posted the video from a surveillance camera which interestingly came from within the congressman's office.[a] The video became a hot item both on YouTube and television news. The staff member quickly resigned. After apologizing to his family and constituents, MacAllister decided not to run for reelection.[b]

After the 2014 State of the Union Message, Congressman Michel Grimm (R-NY) took offense at a local reporter's question about an ongoing investigation of his campaign financing, threatening to throw the reporter over the balcony. The confrontation complete with cursing and aggressive action was a perfect vehicle for a viral video.[c] Grimm was forced to apologize, although as is usually the case, apologies garner much less media coverage. Grimm's problems did not stop there. A few weeks later he was indicted for tax evasion,[d] perhaps explaining his sensitivity to the reporter's questions.

Sources:
[a] www.politico.com/story/2014/04/vance-mcallister-video-kissing-staffer-105435.html
[b] www.bloomberg.com/news/2014-04-28/mcallister-to-retire-from-congress-after-kissing-scandal.html
[c] www.dailymail.co.uk/news/article-2547887/Rep-Michael-Grimm-caught-camera-threatening-TV-reporter-asking-campaign-finance-probe-State-Union.html
[d] www.cbsnews.com/news/can-indicted-michael-grimm-still-win-re-election/

With ease of creating and distributing videos, rumors, or "he said, she said" stories now have a solid a reputable platform on which to build. Removing the ability to say, "I never said that," or "I never did that," changes the level of congressional accountability.

The Complexity of Choice

As we all know from leaving the dessert table, there is such a thing as too much of a good thing. Expanded communication vehicles and content facilitated by new media are two-edged swords adding to the complexity of choices by both members of Congress and the constituents they seek.

Box 11.3 Pick Me, Pick Me: The Proliferation of Media Venues

Contemporary constituents live in a world of choices. In the not-so-distant past, a member of Congress could give an interview to the local television station, or write a column for the weeklies in his or her district and be assured that a large percentage of constituents would at least give a passing glance to the message as they got up to change channels or scanned the headlines for the stories they really wanted to read. A small, but politically involved and thereby important, segment of constituents would listen to the entire interview or read the full column and receive information largely within control of the member.

Today, the proliferation of media platforms and outlets challenge members of Congress as they attempt to determine where to focus their limited resources. Audiences are fragmented by platform (newspapers, radio, television, Internet, etc.) and by substantive interest (sports, entertainment, politics, etc.). Substantively specialized media (ESPN, MTV, the Home Shopping Channel) allow large segments of the possible recipients of a congressional message to drift away remaining totally unaware of the political realm as they indulge in their personal interest in sports, music, or some other non-political realm.

A further challenge arises from the fact that different segments of constituencies reveal different types of fragmentation. Wise politicians realize the danger of practicing a strategy of replacement. Discontinuing one's column in the local newspaper or diminishing one's pursuit of interviews with local television stations in order to free up resources for a top-notch website or an active Twitter presence may well increase the penetration of one's message among younger and higher income constituents, but in the process leave many of a congressman's long-term older voters with a void of member-generated information. The wise communication strategy is not one of "either or," but rather "this and," stretching congressional staff and the member's time and other resources.

> Constituents also face a growing set of choices. Waiting around for the weekly newspaper, or choosing among the three or four local television station's once-a-day television news programs has been replaced by choosing from a smorgasbord of choices laid out 24/7. Cable television brought with it the 24-hour news cycle as well as programming options with no legal or often economic stimulus to cover political events. The rise of the Internet led to an expectation of timeliness, and the ability of users to tailor information flow to their own interests presented a significant challenge to traditional print media. As audiences for traditional news programs and newspapers dropped, large segments of constituents gravitated toward cable television, the Internet, and social media to obtain the information they were interested in. The challenge for the citizen lay in choosing among the multitude of possible sources. Some of the most recent numbers are staggering.
>
> Over 2.4 billion Internet users producing over 15 billion e-mails each day, as of 2012[a]
>
> Over 640 million websites[b]
>
> Over 1 billion Facebook users[b]
>
> Over 175 million tweets per day[b]
>
> But by the time I type this sentence they will have increased again.
> The challenge for the member of Congress lies in getting their constituents to pick their message out of the panoply of options available.
>
> Sources:
> [a] http://royal.pingdom.com/2013/02/12/internet-users-time-zone/
> [b] http://royal.pingdom.com/2013/01/16/internet-2012-in-numbers/

The proliferation of websites, blogs, Twitter accounts, etc. provides an expanding number of outlets to talk *to*, but there is little guarantee that the intended messages will *get through*. We live in an era of "data smog."[20] Information *overload* has as much debilitating impact on becoming informed as data *underload*. The impact on members of Congress lies not in the traditional approach of prioritizing media to woo and conquer, but the pursual of a "shotgun" approach, giving a little attention to both the old and new media in the hope that some of it will get through. For the citizen, being "fire-hosed" with too much information may be just as incapacitating as lacking information.[21]

The Political Echo Chamber

Many observers of politics paint a picture of the ideal world where low-effort open access to wide bodies of objective information would lead to a more informed decision-making process in which areas of agreement could easily be found. Acceptable, if not universally approved, policy decisions would emerge. There is little question that new technologies have increased the ability to archive and locate a vastly increased body of knowledge. The ability of new media to better inform the public depends on the quantity, quality, and content of the information the public is willing to seek. Although ease of access could broaden one's perspective it could equally create an "echo chamber" in which the recipient gathers similar amounts of information, but digs deeper and deeper into purportedly supporting evidence for one political viewpoint. Previous research has shown that political activists, especially those with more extreme ideological perspectives, tend to seek more one-side information supporting the position they have already staked out.[22] Analyzing Twitter followers shows that conservatives were more likely to limit their exposure to conservative congressional tweets than liberal or left-wing. Since Republicans dominate the usage of Twitter and their supporters tend to insulate themselves from dissenting views, Twitter seems to potentially reinforce the political polarization of society.[23] Alternatively rather than "causing" polarization directly, the availability of more ideological cable and Internet outlets feeds the passions of the more politically interested, while the bulk of non-ideological Americans gravitate away from the news and in the process lose much of the inadvertent exposure to various outlooks included in traditional news programs.[24]

Congressional Adoption Patterns of New Media

Seemingly effortless facility with a new information technology not only marks a politician as being "with it," but also allows capitalizing on the media's novelty and characteristics. Franklin Roosevelt charmed and swayed the public on radio. John Kennedy used television in new and effective ways. Members of Congress have long been a little slow to adopt new technology.[25] Just as generals tend to fight the last war, members of Congress tend to arrive after relatively long careers in other realms and stay around for decades. Congress' bow to seniority tends to grant leadership positions to those surviving the longest. Their decreasing need to strengthen their political base and the fact that they made it in the political realm using traditional methods dampens interest in change. Echoing the Smith-Barney television ad, much of the congressional leadership believed "we made it in politics the old fashioned way, through speeches, handshaking and newspaper ads." Congress' discomfort with new technology can be seen in its late and initially tepid acceptance of television (see Chapter 10).

By the 1990s a new wave of politicians had moved up the leadership ladder in Congress. They saw the advantage of using television to their advantage. The poster boy for the new era was Newt Gingrich (R-GA), who asserted that "television is the dominant medium of our society ... the guys and gals in Congress who don't master it get killed."[26] A few years later, he would make similar statements about social media.

Most members of Congress exhibit strategic conservatism when it comes to their plans for gaining and maintaining political office, no matter what their political ideology looks like. Each new suggestion is run through a "worst case scenario," as to what might go wrong. With their careers on the line they find comfort in utilizing communication technologies and strategies proven effective for them in the past. When given the choice of new technologies, members consider applications likely to satisfy the most pressing problems rather than seek out innovation for innovation's sake. While computers could have been marshaled more heavily by congressional offices in the 1970s, much of the effort went toward managing the more mundane flow of mail, rather than building decision-making models, increasing the efficiency of scheduling, or a variety of other tasks that might have been accomplished.[27]

The decision to use a new media technology is often driven by the previous experience of the member, and often the staff. Research on communications strategies generally uses the individual member of Congress as the unit of analysis. The member serves as short-hand designation for the member and his or her staff which exists as a promotional enterprise with only one product to sell to the public, their member. While the member may encourage, or can usually veto staff initiatives, as long as the perceived benefits of a new technology seem to outweigh the perceived costs, most members give their staff considerable leeway in how they sell the "product." The decision to use television, create a website, initiate a Facebook page, or reveal a Twitter presence involves cost in terms of staff time.

The Adoption Process

Most politicians grant tried and true traditional technologies credit for electing them to office and accept worst-case scenarios as to how new technologies might backfire. The key question is seldom, "How can Twitter (or the Web or Facebook) improve the effectiveness of my communication," but rather "What if my account is hacked?" Members of Congress seldom lead the societal pack in terms of new adoptions, and when they adopt a new technology they stand out as laggards in terms of retaining redundant duplication of old approaches. Hard copy or faxed press releases are sent from congressional offices well after e-mail distribution is preferred on the receiving end. New technologies often become add-ons to more traditional methods. Promoters of new technologies complain that most congressional offices dedicate a great deal of their resources to traditional media, often to the detriment or exclusion of new media like websites and e-newsletters. That means offices are spending their time and money on media that reaches people who are less engaged.[28]

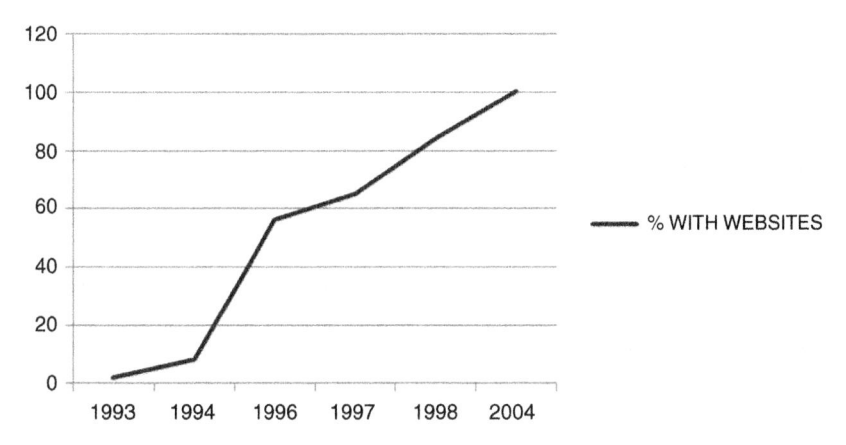

Figure 11.1 House Adoption of Websites
Sources: Scott Adler, Chariti E. Gent, and Cary B. Overmeyer, "The Home Style Home Page: Legislator Use of the World Wide Web for Constituency Contact," *Legislative Studies Quarterly*, vol. 23, no. 4, 1998, p. 586; "Daniel Lipinski and Gregory Neddenriep, "Using 'New' Media to Get 'Old' Media Coverage," *Press/Politics*, vol. 9, no. 1, 2004; Diana Owen, Richard Davis, and Vincent James Strickler, "Congress and the Internet," *Press/Politics*, vol. 4, no. 2, 1999, p. 10.

On the collective level, we have seen how both houses of Congress faced considerable internal opposition to opening their procedures to the television cameras (see Chapter 10). For years after television had proven itself in other realms as an effective communication tool, the naysayers held sway. It came as no surprise that the House with its greater influx of new members and its subservient position relevant to the Senate took the risk first.

On the individual level, research on previous adoption of new technologies reveals that risk takers came from those having recent experiences with the technology outside of Congress, younger members with less experience in traditional communications strategies, less electorally secure members, and those members disadvantaged in terms of power and/or position.[29]

Research on a wide variety of technologies indicates a similar pattern in aggregate adoption patterns that resembles an "S" curve: a few individuals step out early to try a new technology. As reports of the technology's success filter back to others, the rate of adoption increases. A few laggards hold out at the very end, but the technology becomes imbedded in the standard operating procedures of the entities using it and they cannot imagine what it might be like without it.[30] Once members of Congress began using the new technologies, the rate of adoption became steep and quick (see Figures 11.1 and 11.2).

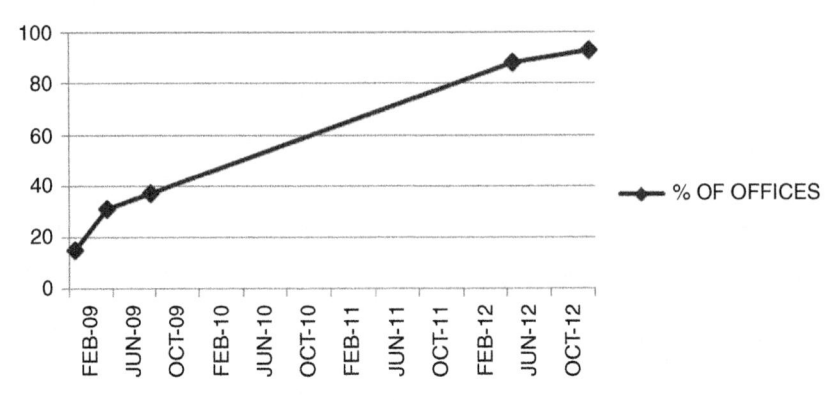

Figure 11.2 Congressional Offices with Twitter Accounts
Sources: Jennifer Golbeck, Justin M. Grimes, and Anthony Rogers, "Twitter Use by the U.S. Congress," *Journal of the American Society for Information Science and Technology*, vol. 61, no. 8, p. 614 and C. Williams and G. Gulati, "Communicating with Constituents in 140 Characters," paper presented at the 2010 meeting of the Midwest Political Science Association, http://opensiuc.lib.siu.edu/cgi/viewcontent.cgi?article=1042&context=pn_wp, p. 6.

The Pressure to Adopt

Traditionally most individual members of Congress dealt with relatively few media outlets and communication vehicles. Their individual actions were relevant to only a few newspapers and television stations. Other technologies lacked the critical mass of potential consumers to make them relevant. Using a "rifle" approach, members could pitch a few stories to a few outlets and have a relatively good chance of seeing them in print or on the air. Today with multiple outlets and little hard evidence as to where their target audiences are getting their messages, members tend to use a "shotgun" approach, distributing press releases, e-mails, tweets, and websites in the hopes that at least some of what they hope to communicate hits the intended target.[31]

The congressional leadership often plays a key role in determining chamber procedures and the use of resources. A change of leadership and influx of new members began pushing new technology in the 1980s and 1990s. The leadership began promoting technology both by encouragement and providing resources. Speaker Newt Gingrich (R-GA) helped usher in the Internet age in Congress, creating the "Cyber Congress" project expanding the House Information Resource Office.[32] As minority leader (and future Speaker) John Boehner (R-OH) urged Republican colleagues to be a "party of communication" and publicly held up junior members using tools such as Twitter for public praise.[33]

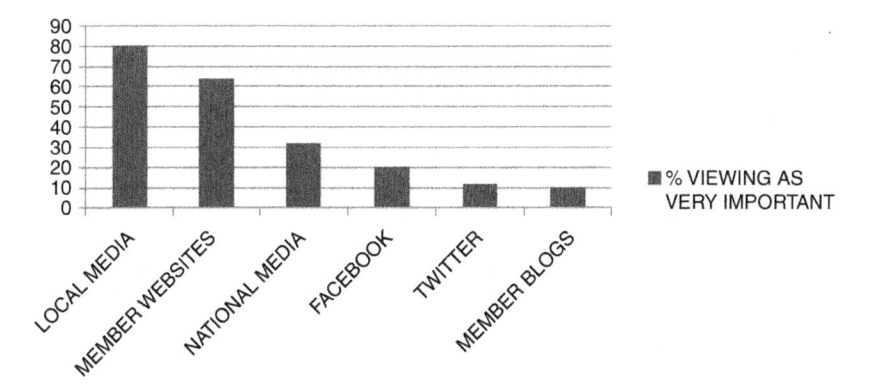

Figure 11.3 Relative Importance of Media Types for Congressional Staff
Source: Congressional Management Foundation, "#SocialCongress: Perceptions and Use of Social Media on Capitol Hill," 2010, www.congressfoundation.org/projects/communicating-with-congress/social-congress

In recent years, members of Congress have tended to "put their money where their mouth is" when it comes to new technology. Despite budget and staff cuts, the fastest growing staff position in the House of Representatives is communications director.[34] There is a keen recognition among members that communication with constituents is critical and that traditional strategies need revision.

Congressional offices see the value of new media, but still prefer local legacy media by a large margin. Websites emerge as a distant second for publicizing one's message, with other new media far behind (see Figure 11.3).

Congress and the Web

Adoption of a new technology involves an understanding of its potential, knowledge of its operation, the willingness to take risks, and the availability of human and material resources to purchase, personalize, and manage the technology. Although the member of Congress does not need to personally possess all these characteristics, he or she must find the skills and resources and approve their use.

It is no great surprise that younger members of the House gravitate toward the establishment of web pages more than older members.[35] Familiarity in school and the workplace reveals opportunities and reduces fears of risk.

Republicans showed significantly more interest in creating web pages during the early stage of adoption than did Democrats.[36] Newt Gingrich's rise to the speakership in 1995 and his encouragement undoubtedly had an impact on this partisan difference, as may well have the business background of many Republican members. The content of early Republican and Democratic web pages reveals an interesting difference. While Republicans emphasized policy and the member's background, Democrats used their websites more to emphasize what they could do to use government to help constituents through casework.[37]

The definition of a "good" website is to some degree a matter of taste. Experienced designers suggest the desirability of a site that is easy to navigate, uncluttered, and updated regularly. Focus groups on congressional websites revealed a preference for clear and understandable language on the content of bills and how their representative voted (see Box 11.4). They preferred

> solid content, without the hype and fanfare, and answers to simple questions: Where do I go when I have a problem with a federal agency? Who can I write to? Where will the senator or representative be during the next two weeks? What is the telephone number of the Washington or district office?[38]

Box 11.4 Using New Technology Appropriately

Each new medium requires an adjustment in terms of rhetoric and presentation. When working with the media Epolitics.com suggests the following for both websites and other new media:

- dial back the rhetoric and focus on the facts;
- include relevant content that is widely linked and likely to come up in a Google search;
- provide a special section on your website for journalists including:
  - press releases and statements easily indexed by topic;
  - issue fact sheets;
  - contact information for you and key staff;
  - an easy way to sign up for your press alert e-mail list.
- avoid lengthy e-mail attachments hard to access on mobile devices;
- present abstract ideas in visual ways that are easy to grasp.

To that list one might add:

- KISS (Keep it short, stupid).

Source: Colin Delany, "The Tools and Tactics of Digital Political Advocacy," January 2011, www.epolitics.com

---

The arrival of congressional websites reignited the debate over the potential for informing the public and enriching the policy dialogue. By 2004 all members of Congress had websites.[39] In order to be an effective tool for democratic participation, a technology needs an interested audience and a willing content provider. Congressional websites fall short on both sides of the equation. Unlike television or newspapers, consumers seldom stumble onto websites and absorb their content inadvertently. You have to want to go to a website.

Members attempt to increase the willingness to stay of users who happen to land on their website by providing an appealing design, gripping photographs, and often videos to personalize the member.

The importance of congressional websites emerges when one asks where a constituent would go to find a member's position on an issue. The 24 percent who would go directly to the member's websites dwarfs the 4–5 percent who would turn to print sources or television. Internet users prefer receiving congressional information from a website than from the traditional media. From a political strategy perspective, constituents contacting Congress about an issue come heavily from those who have visited their member's website, and website visitors are significantly more likely to vote.[40] Not only are increasing numbers of citizens turning to the Internet for the political information they need, but Internet users have also "become accustomed to digesting their information in bite-sized pieces that enable them to access further information if they choose. They are also increasingly accustomed to being able to comment on and share information at will."[41]

Despite the potential, many observers point out the shortcomings of existing congressional websites. Congressional websites also fail to encourage return visits by linking to timely news sites or providing updated content.[42] The "one stop visit" approach does not encourage much of a dialogue. Arrival at a website fails to result in visitor engagement. Only about one-third of congressional websites included search boxes, allowing users to quickly find what they were looking for.[43] True dialogue involves mutually interested partners who willingly share information and perspectives on a regular basis[44] and whose interaction ideally results in a mutually acceptable outcome. From the producer standpoint, the content and functionality members of Congress provide on their websites have little to do with dialogue. As Graeme Browning put it, "Congress is not interacting with the voters [using new technology] because they really don't want to. They liked it the way it was 20 years ago ... when they were kind of walled off and things were filtered."[45] While virtually all sites include contact information, members of Congress use their web pages more as bulletin boards to post biographies, press releases, and speeches.[46] Members prefer so-called "shovelware" that is "shoveled onto websites to fill them up" with little concern for its utility.[47] The information that members do provide is carefully stated so as not to offend anyone. Few members (under 10 percent) bared their soul to the degree that their website outlined their basic beliefs about the role of government or the basis of desirable policy.[48] Since politics involves tough decisions over hard issues, a key part of dialogue involves making those decisions. While most congressional websites (over 90 percent) allow visitors the generic opportunity to send a message to the member, less than 15 percent encourage them to express a specific choice on how the member should vote on an issue.[49] In short, congressional websites are much more of a monologue than a dialogue, with the member of Congress (through their staff) overwhelmingly dominating the stage.

Constituents are not the only target for websites. While we normally think of websites as open-access broadcast media, the party organizations have used them in other ways to facilitate coordinated media messages. The Republicans pioneered a party site with portions open only to Republican lawmakers providing them with talking points and information on upcoming legislation. Interest groups are allowed to post key bills on which they will "score" members in the annual ratings they send to the media to identify their "heroes" and "zeroes." While members often chafe at having their legislative record summarized in a single number, interest group scores appeal to the media. Such scores simplify the inherent conflicts within Congress by alerting the public to their political friends and enemies.

Relatively early in the adoption process, three-quarters of legislators reported using their websites to attract journalists from traditional media to get their message out.[50] By 2003, over 91 percent of newspaper and magazine editors reported that their staff used online sources in preparing stories, while all reporters covering Congress reported multiple uses of congressional websites. Early congressional websites included relatively traditional content (press releases 96 percent; speech texts 39 percent; and op-ed pieces 36 percent). In addition, 87 percent of senators maintained online newsrooms allowing journalists to sign up for automatic press releases and alerts, compared with 71 percent of House members).[51] For members of Congress, the Web has largely become another broadcast medium to get the member's face and accomplishments into the media and public consciousness.

Facebook: Creating Congressional Friends

Earlier studies of congressional adoption of computers for mail management[52] indicated the propensity for Republicans to stand out as early adopters. The partisan differential was explained by their minority status and personal experience in the business world with computers. The level of appreciation and use of Facebook thirty years later is less clear but definitely skewed toward Democrats.[53] This again may be the minority party in the chamber looking to technology to increase their power. There also may well be propensities in the Democrats' liberal penchant toward egalitarianism in participation and Facebook's model of interactive communication. Facebook users are constantly urged to expand their pool of "friends" and make comments about the posts of others. While Facebook allows "lurkers" who simply scroll through postings, those truly engaged post their own comments and reactions. Facebook has been described as more of a mobilization tool than one that simply informs in a one-way manner.[54]

YouTube: Visualizing Congress and its Members

YouTube allows members of Congress to upload videos promoting their careers and the issues in which they are interested. According to one member of Congress,

> When you go down on the House floor and make a speech to the C-SPAN audience you [reach] three to four million ... but take that video and put it on your YouTube site or put it on Twitter, put it on Facebook and then you're getting that multiplier effect.

The downside emerges from the ability of policy or political opponents to counter the members' messages.[55]

Tweeting from Capitol Hill

Tweeting provides members with a number of advantages. The startup costs are minimal; member offices control the content. Twitter allows direct communications with followers in ways unavailable through traditional media, the mail, or e-mail. There is the potential to create a two-way relationship with constituents while providing "an informed 'human' face to abstract ideas and principles."[56] The real-time nature of tweets adds to receiver interest, exemplifying the extreme application of Marshall McLuhan's assertion of over a half century ago that "instant information creates involvement."[57]

Twitter does present some potential risk. Staff time remains limited and managing a dynamic Twitter presence takes time away from other tasks. Inopportune tweets either due to member ignorance or lack of control over the account may lead to embarrassment as the original message is re-tweeted. An open question revolves around the spread of tweets. Chamber rules and court opinions make it illegal to use official resources to communicate with non-constituents. How those rules might apply to social media has yet to be determined.[58]

Twitter seemed to be the early adoption bailiwick of Republicans.[59] Numerous studies indicate congressional Republican proclivity to adopt Twitter earlier and at higher rates. In 2009, 50 percent of House Republicans as opposed to 31 percent of House Democrats had Twitter accounts. In the Senate, the difference was almost nonexistent with Twitter adopted by 10 percent of Republicans and 9 percent of Democrats. In terms of proportion of tweets, the Republican advantage was greater than adoption alone.[60]

In one of those difficult-to-explain correlations in social behavior, the originators of tweets from Congress and the recipients among the public fail to line up. Even though the early congressional adopters and heavy users of Twitter and those with a greater number of followers[61] are more likely to be Republican, those who tweet among the public tend more to be female and younger, characteristics associated with Democratic Party leanings.[62]

Based on a content analysis, the clear majority of congressional tweets (54 percent) contained information about an issue, often directing the recipient to a news article or webpage for further details. Twitter often emerges as an "entry portal" where the member announces congressional action or their position on an issue. Such tweets serve as mini press releases, attempting to tweak the recipient's interest and motivate them to seek more information. About a quarter of congressional tweets simply report on the member of Congress' current location or activity. Much smaller percentages dealt with descriptions of official business in Congress (ongoing votes or reports of meetings), personal messages, and requests for political action.[63] Noticeably absent from Twitter messages are calls to political action like contacting other political officials, signing a petition, or contributing money. Like other new media "Congress uses social media as a broadcast forum rather than as an engagement tool."[64] Congress tends to excise the "social" from social media.

Tweeting by members of Congress is more frequent when Congress is in session, particularly during the middle of the work week. When out of session, members informed followers about their current locations and events in the district. A significant number of tweets alerted followers to upcoming media events.[65]

Twitter serves as a prime example of the "law of unintended consequences," another case of where a technology's inventor failed to anticipate its use and implication. Originally designed to answer the questions, "Where are you?" and "What are you doing?" Twitter has morphed into a tool to build relationships, report news as to "what is happening," and collaborate on projects.[66]

The Twitter holdouts in Congress expressed frustration over the limited amount of information they could tweet. As Representative Wally Herger's (R-CA) office put it, "Twitter does not lend itself to thorough explanations."[67] Another member commented "I am not sure democracy gains much when members self-indulgently keep us appraised as to whether they are going to the gym or the john."[68]

Like websites, Twitter is largely a top-down communications utility for broadcasting a message rather than an interactive platform of relative equals sharing ideas and perspectives. The "friends" on Facebook are linguistically replaced with "followers" on Twitter. Given its basic format of short spurts of information (140 characters) it is hard to initiate and especially difficult to move toward a meaningful political dialogue.

Regulating the New Media

In developing the rules for new media usage, it is hard to draw the line between transparency and even the most self-serving outreach. Rules associated with traditional outreach tools (mail and newsletters) relied heavily on timing (i.e., typically no mass mailing within sixty days of the election) and content (no fund-raising pleas, use of official letterhead, or invitations to campaign events in official mailings). The volume of electronic messages makes it impossible for oversight committees to evaluate content. The tendency has been to relax the rules to allow unfettered use of social media by members of Congress.[69]

Proponents of unrestricted use of new media by Congress extol the virtues of open and transparent governmental action. Following the lead of Woodrow Wilson's mantra of "open covenants ..., openly arrived at"[70] supporters accept the assertion that the more the public can see, the more responsible legislators will be. That may well depend on the type of information provided. If members of Congress use technology to increase the efficiency of "outreach" (telling us what they want us to hear" rather than "transparency" (providing citizens the information they want and need to hear), more information may do little to improve representative government.[71] Since their reputation and livelihood is on the line, members of Congress tend to gravitate toward outreach, particularly those media over which they and their staffs have the most control.

House and Senate rules tend to discourage members from becoming a hub around which policy dialogue might take place. House and Senate rules make it illegal or inappropriate to use a member's website to solicit support, partake in grassroots lobbying, or instigate petitions to support their position on a policy issue. Senators also cannot link to another member's website without their permission, thus discouraging website visitors from exploring the other side of an issue.[72] Senators are not allowed to solicit constituents' input using their homepage or e-mail within sixty days of an election in which they are a candidate unless in response to a direct inquiry. This covers the very timeframe in which many voters begin to take an interest in policy.

House members may not use official funds to communicate unsolicited mass messages to constituents within ninety days of an election (sixty days for senators) in which they are a candidate. Originally designed to cover mass mailings, this rule now applies to tweets from the member's official account.[73] House members may also not link their official website to their campaign website, although they can have a link from their campaign website to their official website.[74] Neither type of link is allowed in the Senate.[75]

The Impact of the New Media

Despite the hype, it is important to remember that "......... [fill in the blank: Facebook, Twitter, Web Page presence, etc.]" is not a game changer, but an additional communications medium.[76]

Congressional staffs dismiss the promise that Internet communications would supersede the ability of traditional media to increase citizen understanding of congressional politics and improve the quality of interaction.[77] Surveys of staff indicate that "digital media is used as a 'thermometer' " to "check the pulse" of interest in key policy issues.[78] They argue that social media offer effective tools for "communicating a message quickly ... However, for pushing a message over the long term, traditional press strategies pay more dividends."[79]

While it is tempting to look at particular new media as having stand-alone importance, stories transmitted through websites, tweets, or Facebook pages have the potential for being picked up by the legacy media and spread even further.[80] A video on YouTube, especially if it challenges the morality or veracity of a member of Congress, has the potential for bursting into the news in a way congressional media managers only dream about. A standard storyline for print and television includes stories originating in the new media going viral and the presentation in the legacy media of the number of hits on the Web over a short period of time.

Notes

1 Sharon E. Jarvis and Kristen Wilkerson, "Congress on the Internet: Messages on the Homepages of the U.S. House of Representatives," 1996–2001, *Journal of Computer-Mediated Communication*, vol. 10, no. 2, 2005.
2 Author's interview.
3 Patrick Sellers, *Cycles of Spin: Strategic Communication in the United States Congress*, New York, NY: Cambridge University Press, 2010, p. 9.
4 www.emergingmediaresearchcouncil.com/wp-content/uploads/2011/04/Digital-Media-and-The-Hill_FMRC_April 2011.pdf
5 C. Williams and G. Gulati, "Communicating with Constituents in 140 Characters," paper presented at the 2010 meeting of the Midwest Political

Science Association, http://opensiuc.lib.siu.edu/cgi/viewcontent.cgi?article=1042&context=pn_wp, p. 11.

6 www.congressfoundation.org/projects/communicating-with-congress/social-congress

7 Kashmir Hill, "Congressional Staffers Upset that People Actually Want to Read Their Tweets," *Forbes*, April 5, 2013, p. 7.

8 Pew Research Center polls from iPoll databank.

9 Richard L. Fox and Jennifer M. Ramos, *iPolitics: Citizens, Elections and Governing in the New Media Era*, New York, NY: Cambridge University Press, 2011, p. 3.

10 Pippa Norris, *Digital Divide: Civic Engagement, Information Poverty and the Internet in Democratic Societies*, New York, NY: Cambridge University Press, 2001.

11 Congressional Management Foundation, "Communicating with Congress: Perceptions of Citizen Advocacy on Capitol Hill," 2011, p. 7.

12 Diana Owen, Richard Davis, and Vincent James Strickler, "Congress and the Internet," *Press/Politics*, vol. 4, no. 2, 1999, p. 10.

13 Craig Goodman and David C. W. Parker, "Who Franks: Explaining the Allocation of Official Resources," *Congress and the Presidency*, vol. 37, 2010, p. 237.

14 Author's interview.

15 Gary Lee Malecha and Daniel J. Reagan, *The Public Congress*, New York, NY: Routledge, 2012, p. 25.

16 www.epolitics.com/2012/12/26/socialmedia-cheat-sheet-10-rules-and-16-tips-for-success-on-twitter/

17 Ibid.

18 See The Congressional Management study available at: www.congressfoundation.org/projects/communicating-with-congress/social-congress

19 Timothy Cook, *Governing with the News: The News Media as a Political Institution*, Chicago, IL: University of Chicago Press, 2005, p. 165.

20 David Shenk, *Data Smog: Surviving the Data Glut*, San Francisco, CA: Harper Edge, 1997. See also Ross Baker, "Congress – Boom Box and Black Box," *Media Studies Journal*, vol. 10, no. 1, 1996, pp. 1–11.

21 J. Blumler and Dennis Kavanagh, "The Third Age of Political Communication: Influences and Features," *Political Communication*, vol. 16, no. 3, 1999.

22 See Andrei Boutyline and Robb Willer, "The Social Structure of Political Echo Chambers," Working paper, 2013, p. 8, available at: www.ocf.berkeley.edu/~andrei/EchoChambers.pdf

23 Ibid., p. 34.

24 Jane Mansbridge and Cathie Jo Martin (eds.), *Negotiating Agreement in Politics*, Washington, D.C.: The American Political Science Association, 2013, p. 32.

25 See Stephen Frantzich, *Computers in Congress: The Politics of Information*, Beverly Hills, CA: Sage, 1982.

26 Quoted in Julian Zelizer, *On Capitol Hill: The Struggle to Reform Congress and its Consequences, 1948–2000*, New York, NY: Cambridge University Press, 2004.

27 Frantzich, passim.

28 Brad Fitch and Kathy Goldschmidt, *Communicating with Congress: How Capitol Hill Is Coping with the Surge of Citizen Advocacy*, Washington, D.C.: Congressional Management Foundation, 2005, p. 45.

29 For computers, see Frantzich; for websites, see E. Scott Adler, Chariti E. Gent, and Casey B. Overmeyer, "The Home Style Homepage: Legislator Use of the

World Wide Web for Constituency Contact," *Legislative Studies Quarterly*, vol. 23, no. 4, 1998, p. 585; for Twitter, see David S. Lassen and Adam R. Brown, "Twitter: The Electoral Connection," *Social Science Computer Review*, vol. 29, no. 4, 2001, p. 419.

30 See Frantzich, pp. 75–81. See also www.innovation-point.com/Innovation_Lifecycles.pdf

31 See Blumler and Kavanagh, pp. 209–230.

32 Adler et al., p. 586.

33 Lassen and Brown, p. 42.

34 Lee Drutman, "How House Operating Budget Cuts Are Paving the Way for More Special Interest Influence," Sunlight Foundation Blog, January 17, 2012, http://sunlightfoundatioin.com/blog/1012/01/17/house-budget-cuts-special-interest-influence

35 Adler et al., p. 592.

36 Adler et al., p. 588.

37 Adler et al., p. 592.

38 C. Lawrence Evans and Walter Oleszek, "The Wired Congress," in James A. Thurber and Colton C. Campbell (eds.), *Congress and the Internet*, Upper Saddle River, NJ: Prentice Hall, 2003, p. 132.

39 Maureen Taylor and Michael L. Kent, "Congressional Web Sites and Their Potential for Public Dialogue," *Atlantic Journal of Communication*, vol. 12, no. 2, 2004, p. 60.

40 Kathy Goldschmidt and Leslie Ochreiter, "Communicating with Congress: How the Internet Has Changed Citizen Engagement," Washington, D.C.: Congressional Management Foundation, 2008, pp. 15–17, 25.

41 Ibid., p. 35.

42 Jarvis and Wilkerson.

43 Taylor and Kent, p. 71.

44 Ibid., p. 62.

45 Quoted in Jarvis and Wilkerson. See also P. Boczkowski, *Digitizing the News in Online Newspapers*, Cambridge, MA: MIT Press, 2004.

46 Taylor and Kent, p. 59.

47 Jarvis and Wilkerson.

48 Taylor and Kent, p. 71.

49 Jarvis and Taylor, p. 71.

50 Daniel Lipinski and Gregory Neddenriep, "Using 'New' Media to Get 'Old' Media Coverage," *Press/Politics*, vol. 9, no. 1, 2004, p. 4.

51 Ibid., pp. 11–15.

52 Frantzich.

53 www.congressfoundation.org/projects/communicating-with-congress/social-congress

54 Williams and Gulatti, p. 10.

55 www.congressfoundation.org/projects/communicating-with-congress/social-congress

56 F. Dianne Lux Wigand, "Twitter in Government: Building Relationships One Tweet at a Time," Seventh International Conference on Information Technology, 2010, p. 565.

57 Marshall McLuhan, *Understanding the Media*, Cambridge, MA: MA Press, 1964.

58 Jacob Strauss et al., "Communicating in 140 Characters or Less: Congressional Adoption of Twitter in the 11th Congress," *PS*, January 2013, p. 65.

59 See Feng Chi and Nathan Yang, "Twitter Adoption in Congress." Available at: ssrn.com/abstract=1620401, p. 9. See also Strauss et al., p. 61.
60 Matthew Eric Glassman, Jacob R. Strauss, and Colleen J. Shogan, "Social Networking and Constituent Communications: Member Use of Twitter During a Two-Month Period in the 11th Congress," CRS Report R42066, pp. 5–6.
61 Christopher Ingraham, "By the Numbers on Twitter, Republicans Look to Have the Edge," *Washington Post*, April 22, 2014, p. A12.
62 See Williams and Gulati, p. 8.
63 Jennifer Golbeck, Justin M. Grimes, and Anthony Rogers, "Twitter Use by the U.S. Congress," *Journal of the American Society for Information Science and Technology*, vol. 61, no. 8, 2010, p. 1616.
64 Libby Hemphill, Jahan Otterbacher, and Matthew A. Shapiro, "What's Congress Doing on Twitter?" Available at: http://repository.iit.edu/bitstream/handle/10560/2884/Hemphill%20et%20al%20Whats%20Congress%20Doing%20on%20Twitter.pdf?sequence=1
65 Glassman et al., pp. 1–9, 11.
66 Lux Wigand, p. 563.
67 Alicia M. Cohn, "More than 60 Members of Congress Just Say No to Twitter's 140 Characters," *The Hill*, September 25, 2013.
68 Author's interview.
69 Golbeck et al., p. 1619.
70 www.mtholyoke.edu/acad/intrel/doc31.htm
71 Golbeck et al., p. 1620.
72 http://cha.house.gov/handbooks/members-congressional-handbook#Members-Handbook-Comms-Advertisements-Internet and www.senate.gov/usage/internetpolicy.htm
73 http://ethics.house.gov/general-prohibition-against-using-official-resources-campaign-or-political-purposes#campaign_90_day_ban and www.ethics.senate.gov › Home › Ethics Rules.
74 http://thehill.com/blogs/hillicon-valley/technology/215687-ethics-committee-allows-law, see also Williams and Gulati.
75 www.ethics.senate.gov/downloads/pdffiles/campaign.pdf
76 Williams and Gulati.
77 Congressional Management Foundation, 2011, p. 2.
78 www.emergingmediaresearchcouncil.com/wp-content/uploads/2011/04/Digital-Media-and-The-Hill_EMRC_April-2011.pdf
79 House staff member quoted in www.emergingmediaresearchcouncil.com/wp-content/uploads/2011/04/Digital-Media-and-The-Hill_EMRC_April-2011.pdf
80 Lipinski and Neddenriep.

Chapter 12

Congress and the Media

The Continuing Odyssey

It is typical at this point in the analysis of a social phenomenon to reaffirm the ideal state of affairs, summarize the shortcomings, point fingers at the perpetrators whose actions thwart reaching the goals, and outline the necessary reforms. Alas, if it were only that easy in the complex relationship between the media and Congress. The numerous players and changing relationships lead the fingers of blame to point in many directions. On the other hand, some of the alleged shortcomings are not actually faults, but inherent characteristics of a vibrant system of representative government.

A Reminder of the Goals

Representative government requires an informed electorate able to legitimately reward or punish public officials. Public officials require vehicles for initiating and contributing to public policy decisions both among themselves and with the electorate. The media facilitate gathering and disseminating information necessary for those conversations to thrive. Both the shortcomings of Congress and its members and their accomplishments should be part of the mix of information in order to give a balanced view. At the same time media coverage needs to provide enough legitimacy for Congress to make the public feel it is worthwhile to turn its attention to Congress' efforts. This may mean giving short shrift to some of the minor human frailties and difficult-to-justify procedures of the legislative process.

The Congressional Management Foundation, a non-partisan think tank committed to enhancing Congress' relationship with an engaged and informed citizenry, defines ideal congressional communications as "trustworthy, authentic, effective and efficient."[1] The foundation sees new and emerging technologies as unique opportunities to help reach those goals to the benefit both of members of Congress and their constituents.

A Challenge to Researchers

The richness of the contemporary media environment poses a significant challenge for political communications researchers. Practical necessity usually results in parsing the influences and focusing on only one or two media. There is no guarantee that results based on print data apply to those of television, Twitter, or any other platform. In gathering data, two research problems arise. First the media receivers may well not know the origin of particular information. Directly asking, "Where did you get the impression that interest groups control most members of Congress?" may be met with a blank stare, unreliable guess, or generalization, "Well, everyone knows that." The second problem devolves from the first. Little pieces of information from a variety of sources repeat support for an assertion, giving the previous assertion more reliability and helping to build a web of supportive "evidence," whether true or not true. It is much more difficult to sort through the slow accumulation of facts, factoids, and misrepresentations in a series of layers developed by a stalactite approach, than to sort out the realities of a dramatic "shock and awe" event.

With technology lowering the entry cost for information it is reasonable to ask why the public is not more informed. One explanation asserts that researchers have begun at the wrong place in assessing the problem, by assuming a "digital divide" imposed by economic barriers limiting identifiable segments of the population's access to the cornucopia of new information. As the entry costs for using new technology have declined, no commensurate increase in knowledge has followed.

Simply correlating access to new forms of media and the level of political knowledge misses the potential for new media formats to allow individuals to choose *not* to be informed about particular realms. In the era of mass media with a few television networks dominating the landscape, television viewers receive a great deal of inadvertent information. In today's media-rich environment, one has the choice to opt out of particular types of information. A media consumer interested in sports or entertainment can effectively avoid "chance encounters ... with any political content."[2] Before asking whether individuals with access to particular media are politically informed or not, the initial question should be whether they *want* elucidation in a particular segment of knowledge. Technology "junkies" or particular generational groups (usually defined as "the young") are not empty airheads, but rather are informed on non-political things such as entertainment or popular culture. The challenge for democracy lies in the fact that given the choice and ease of access to numerous pools of knowledge, many potentially informed citizens opt out of the information they would need to make informed choices. Among those interested in politics, access to new media results in knowledge and political involvement. Those preferring entertainment eschew political information and are less politically informed.[3] In the earlier constrained media era, it was largely "politics by default" as media norms and government requirements for public service content dictated political coverage.[4] In the emerging era of broad options, absorption of political media becomes a matter of choice.

Some Characteristics of Contemporary Coverage

Many members of Congress might agree that if Congress gets any coverage at all, it is negative coverage. It can't be proven that negative media coverage *causes* negative views of Congress. Individuals more negative about Congress may simply be drawn to more media usage.[5] The barrage of negative images about Congress purveyed by a vast array of media platforms certainly does little to disabuse the public of those negative perceptions. The media emphasize conflict over compromise, generalize from single cases to the whole, and take specific interest in the personal foibles and shortcomings of relatively few members. Far from the cozy relationships of earlier eras which often obfuscated potentially questionable practices on Capitol Hill, the post-Watergate journalists arrived with a cynical chip on their shoulders, presuming guilt and expecting members of Congress to prove innocence. The Washington press corps accepted the collective mantra of "fool us once, your fault, fool us twice, our fault." Watching colleagues such as Bob Woodward and Carl Bernstein snatch Pulitzer Prizes for investigative journalism, the new generation sought out incompetence, inconsistency, and scandal with a passion. Stories from Capitol Hill moved away from transcriptions of events in favor of interpretive stories adding context, facts, and coherence between stories to reveal a pattern.[6] That pattern often failed to reflect positively on members of Congress.

Congress falls short of its educational role. Party leaders emphasize policy initiatives and party positions more than realistically explaining the congressional process. Individual members emphasize stories about how they used the political system to promote constituency interests. No one on the inside of Congress has much motivation to explain the rationale behind and the advantages of congressional workings. For most voters, Congress stands as an opaque box filled with a complex set of poorly meshed gears manipulated by self-interested party leaders unwilling to find a way to realign the gears in such a way that some reasonable product comes out the other end. From the outside, much congressional behavior looks like extreme members trying to throw sand into the gears.

While not all congressional procedures deserve public accolades, two hundred years of representative democracy with deep congressional involvement represent many successes – as long as one defines success as coming to a reasonable compromise over issues on which the partici-pants have deep disagreement. As former Senator Alan Simpson put it, "You can't hate politics and love democracy."[7] Clunky and inefficient as it is, the system generally works in the end. Decisions do get made. The Republic goes on.

In one sense, there is really no U.S. Congress. In reality it is a set of 535 independent actors who combine and reform into relatively permanent entities (political parties, committees, and caucuses), as well as a variety of short-term coalitions formed to take some action (passing or killing a bill). No one really speaks for the Congress as a whole, and explaining and justifying Congress as an institution legitimately falls on no one's shoulders. The media tend to gather snippets of information from policy proponents who denigrate the congressional processes if they lose or laud them if they win.

If concerns arise over the quality of congressional coverage, so does dissatisfaction with the quantity. The shortchanging of Congress' role as a co-equal branch of government (and as its supporters like to point out, the first branch as indicated by the Constitution), threatens the institu-tion's power among the branches.

Some Parting Words to the Players

Rather than outlining a series of structural changes, most of which are unlikely to be passed, or make much difference if they were, the following section suggests some self-reflection on the part of the various players in the Congress/media relationship.

The Media

Remember the power of words and pictures. The storylines pursued by the media become a part of, or at least reinforce, conventional wisdom. No one should ask the media to go back to a sycophantic era of cozy, but unrealistic reporting about Congress. On the other hand, to start every story with a cynical outlook assuming sleaze and illegality also fails to give a valid picture. It is enlightening to realize that long-time Washington correspondent David Broder felt it necessary to write a col-umn a few years ago entitled "Yes There Are Good People in Congress,"[8] a clear admission as to how far things had gone.

Journalists need to remember that the public fails to make clear dis-tinctions between its public institutions. In dragging down Congress, the media may well be hurting themselves. Counter-responses by members of Congress challenge journalists and their stories. The general growing distrust of all American public institutions may well lead to a "them" (the bad guys) versus "us" (the public) pattern of thinking. Increasingly, the public does not trust the media *or* the politicians. There is a perception that both groups are motivated solely by illegitimate self-interest.

Seeking the holy grail of objective journalism does not deny the importance of aggressive fact gathering and reporting. Objective journalists are skeptical, ask tough questions, and go beyond pre-packaged and self-serving answers in search of true illegality, inconsistency, and hypocrisy.

Observers and participants from a variety of perspectives develop similar goals for adequate coverage of Congress including goals such as:

1. Informing the public of their stake in upcoming legislation and the degree that stake should stimulate action on their part.
2. Alerting the public to emerging issues and assessing the likelihood of legislation and a timeline for getting involved.
3. Uncovering their representative's involvement in the legislative process (both in high and low visibility actions).
4. Providing alternative opinions and facts surrounding an issue.
5. Providing a mix of detailed coverage and broad generalizations.[9]

Members of Congress

Members of Congress have both the right and the responsibility to hold strong views on issues of personal interest to themselves and to their constituencies. Strong partisan and ideological points of view often "bring things into discourse that wouldn't otherwise be in the kind of very wishy-washy, moderate middle discourse."[10] On the other hand, treating Congress as nothing more than a sounding board for extreme opinions serves the public poorly. Pandering to narrow constituencies of supporters while condemning the attempts of others trying to make the decisions Congress is charged to make brings discredit on the institution as an ineffective debating society.

As spokespersons for Congress as an institution, members present the media with a great deal of raw material to use against the institution. In a classic case of "where you stand depends on where you sit," during the Democratic Party stewardship of the House during 1991 and 1994, 66 percent of the newsletter messages sent out by Democrats described positive initiatives about Congress, often praising its procedures, while Republican newsletters presented a positive slant only 19 percent of the time. With the Republican takeover of the majority in 1995, the figures reversed with 16 percent of the Democratic messages positive as opposed to 69 percent distributed by Republicans.[11] Amazingly Republicans took a more positive view about closed rules (not allowing amendments on the floor) a practice they had condemned in the past. Democrats were hardly less consistent.

One is tempted to cry out at Congress, "Clean up your act." By choosing to be in public office one must accept being a public commodity. Personal impropriety very quickly develops into a measure of public capability. With the numerous ways one's actions can be captured and transmitted, the old advice, that "If it itches, don't scratch," seems like good guidance in the intrusive media age. As with all public officials, members of Congress must precede their behavior with the thought, "How would this look in the *Washington Post* or if it went viral on the Internet?" It is a tough standard for fallible human beings. Some good members will fail, but it is the nature of the contemporary environment.

Those members of Congress who try to improve the institution's image take on a very difficult task. In the first place, unlike the White House, Congress fails to speak with one voice and is not organized to have "a press secretary to claim institutional credit for accomplishments."[12] Even the congressional leadership, who presumably have the greatest stake in upgrading the image of the institution they lead, express frustration. As former Speaker Jim Wright (D-TX) put it, "I might as well have been trying to teach cats to respect birds as getting the press to respect Congress."[13] Members of Congress buy into the negativism. While still in office, former representative Barney Frank (D-MA) mused:

> I am now enjoying the best press of my life. And it's because I'm attacking people and being negative. I get much more attention for three wisecracks and a point of order than I get for a full compromise to a difficult legislative solution.[14]

In a rare moment of modesty, members of Congress must recognize that legislators' messages form only a small part of a growing and potentially overwhelming body of information that the public receives.[15] The "big news" inside the beltway often fails to raise a bit of interest back home in one's constituency.

Members of Congress recognize the superior power of the media in getting a story out and try not to quarrel with the press. They follow the basic principle that one should "never argue with someone who buys ink by the barrel or newsprint by the ton." This often repeated quote, whose origin is lost to history, has an equivalent in the current era of "never pick a fight with someone who has 500,000 Twitter followers."[16] With the addition of new media opportunities, it seems that members of Congress (as all individuals trying to communicate with the public) must run faster just to stay in place. Each new medium has its own presentation rules, public expectations, and audiences. The concept of a "mass media" familiar to the bulk of members of Congress as they entered their era of political maturity (largely in the 1960s and 1970s) has given way to niche media and niche markets. Fragmented audiences making choices of what to attune to are more difficult to "chase" and "capture" than the inadvertent audiences unintentionally absorbing information they did not necessarily seek. As a common defense mechanism, congressional offices pursue a wide variety of media in order to assure that some of their messages reach the intended audience.

Creating a more open door was a painful but correct decision by both the House and Senate. Interested individuals with greater information are going to ask tougher questions. Members of Congress need to find better ways to explain what they do, and how they do it. Constituents will often respect a member willing to explain how he or she came to a tough decision more than one who simply makes the decision, writes off those offended, and moves on.

Congress is no place for the thin-skinned. Forced to deal with sensitive issues lacking widely accepted answers, criticism is inherently part of the job description. Members of Congress are easy targets to anyone with a strong political view. To some degree one can understand members of Congress who feel "damned if they do, and damned if they don't." As Mark Rozell put it in his analysis of media coverage from the early days of the Republic to the mid 1990s, "It seems that no matter what Congress does, people complain. Neither partisan nor policy change has improved the coverage of Congress and public views of its activities."[17]

The Public

Despite expressed preference for unbiased coverage, public evaluation of media coverage of Congress tends to follow personal partisanship. The public tends to see the media as "too easy" on leaders of the opposition party and "too tough" on leaders of its own party. The media can take solace in the fact that about half the public sees media coverage of Congress as either fair (about 40 percent) or something it does not follow.[18] Far from wanting to put Congress out of its mind, the public expresses the desire for more coverage of Congress. In terms of media influence on Congress the perceived impact of the media on congressional voting is dwarfed by the perceived influence of interest groups and campaign contributors, and matched by the influence of party leaders.[19]

Cartoonist Walt Kelly put the famous line in his star character Pogo's mouth that "We have met the enemy and he is us." Although the original sentiment referred to the responsibility for the environment, the idea of rightfully accepting blame applies to many realms. In terms of media coverage of Congress, despite all the public's "professed interest in policy decisions, it exhibits a vast appetite for personal stories."[20] As former Senator Warren Rudman (R-NH) opined, "the public has an excessive interest in things that titillate. Therefore, the press feels compelled to cover them."[21] That may refer to audience behavior, but poll figures turn some of the blame back on the media when it comes to opinions about coverage suggesting that the media panders to the public more than it needs to. While 60 percent of the public felt that the media devoted too much coverage to the personal lives of members of Congress, only 22 percent of journalists felt the same way.[22] In an environment where perceptions trump reality, journalists may be enthusiastically marching to the wrong beat.

Members of Congress fully realize the tendency of "echo chamber" information-gathering techniques in which individuals gravitate toward media sources reinforcing their existing biases and granting them more legitimacy. As one former member indicated, "If I ask a constituent what networks they listen to or what paper they read, I can tell you a great deal about them and their political views."[23] It is one thing for the member to understand this, and another to correct such defective information gathering.

In order for the public to ground their opinions on solid information and logic, they should be urged to seek a variety of opinions in the media. Journalists see different things in different ways. The identification of a new public policy problem and creative solutions depends on using a broad information-gathering net. The new media make it easier to only hear whatever makes one comfortable. If a news report, blog, or e-mail never makes you think about a congressional issue in a different way, maybe you are relying on the wrong sources. The fact that contemporary citizens live in the era of "data smog"[24] with such a glut of information, makes the task of picking and choosing even more difficult than in the past.

Assess the criteria against which you judge Congress. It is not all bad when Congress fails to make a decision. If there is gridlock among the public about a hot political issue, why should we not expect gridlock among our representatives? It is important to constantly evaluate your goals to determine whether you are using the correct standards of evaluation.

Future Cast

Analyzing Congress and the media is more than a pure academic exercise legitimated by its own findings. Congress is part of our form of government based on separation of powers, and the media are key players in allowing the other institutions to communicate with each other and with the public they are intended to serve. When one institution becomes the whipping boy in the system, all the other players face danger. A report by the American Political Science Association concludes that:

rarely these days does a news cycle pass without new stories of political dysfunction in Washington, D.C. News reports of stalemates, fiscal cliffs, and failed grand bargains have begun to erode the public confidence in the ability of our representative institutions to govern effectively.[25]

It is important to remember that the media tend to portray events as the "worst in history," or the "most important ever." The contemporary representation of congressional gridlock and dysfunction fails to point out that there have been many similar, or even worse, periods in history. Gridlock is not necessarily bad since it simply reflects that the political process has not led to the level of public support for a particular course of action that is necessary for consensus.

Congress and the media are unlikely to ever return to the cozy relationships of the past, and that serves the public well. The variety of media sources offers multiple opportunities for the media and the public to engage in the kind of democratic dialogue that breathes life into representative government. American political institutions, including the media, are unfinished products whose flaws and shortcomings are superseded by their accomplishments and opportunities.

Notes

1 Congressional Management Foundation, "Communicating with Congress: Recommendations for Improving the Democratic Dialogue," 2008, p. viii.
2 Markus Prior, "News vs. Entertainment: How Increasing Media Choice Widens Gaps in Political Knowledge and Turnout," *American Journal of Political Science*, vol. 49, no. 3, 2005, p. 578.
3 Ibid., p. 587.
4 Russell W. Neuman, "Political Communication Infrastructure," *Annals of the American Academy of Political and Social Science*, vol. 546, 1996, p. 19.
5 John R. Hibbing and Elizabeth Thiess-Morse, "The Media's Role in Public Negativity Toward Congress," *American Journal of Political Science*, vol. 42, no. 2, April 1998, pp. 475–498. See also Kevin Arceneaux and Martin Johnson, *Changing Minds or Changing Channels*, Chicago, IL: University of Chicago Press, 2013, p. 156.
6 Julian Zelizer, *On Capitol Hill: The Struggle to Reform Congress and its Consequences, 1948–2000*, New York, NY: Cambridge University Press, 2004, p. 222.
7 Alan Simpson, *Theodore H. White Lecture on Press and Politics*, Cambridge, MA: Harvard University Kennedy School, 2013.
8 David Broder, "Yes There Are Good People in Congress," *Washington Post*, November 6, 1991, p. 25.
9 See R. Douglas Arnold, *Congress, the Press, and Political Accountability*, New York, NY: Princeton University Press, 2004, p. 262 and Tom Allen, *Dangerous Convictions*, New York, NY: Oxford University Press, 2013, pp. 188–189.

10 William Kristol quoted in *The Theodore H. White Lecture with William Kristol*, Cambridge, MA: John F. Kennedy School of Government, 2004, p. 67.
11 Daniel Lipinski, *Congressional Communication*, Ann Arbor, MI: University of Michigan Press, 2004, p. 42.
12 Elaine Povich, *Partners and Adversaries*, Arlington, VA: The Freedom Forum, 1996, p. 25.
13 Ibid., p. 26.
14 Ibid., p. 57.
15 Patrick J. Sellers, "Manipulating the Message in the U.S. Congress," *Harvard International Journal of Press/Politics*, vol. 5, no. 22, 2000, available at: http://hj.sagepub.com/content//1/222
16 www.mediabistro.com/10000words/ink-by-the-barrel-on-the-internet_b11933
17 Mark Rozell, *In Contempt of Congress*, Westport, CT: Praeger, 1996, p. 115.
18 Pew Research Center for the People and the Press surveys of 999 US adults in 2010 and 2011, available at: webapps.ropercenter.ucon.edu
19 Democracy Corps/Public Campaign Action Fund Poll of 1012 registered voters, November 2012, available at: webapps.ropercenter.uconn.edu
20 Povich, p. 2.
21 Povich, p. 55.
22 Povich, p. 78.
23 Author's interview.
24 A term coined by David Shenk, *Data Smog: Surviving the Data Glut*, San Francisco, CA: Harper Edge, 1997.
25 Jane Mansbridge and Cathie Jo Martin (eds.), *Negotiating Agreement in Politics*, Washington, D.C.: The American Political Science Association, 2013, p. 19.

Index